NO LEFTOVERS

NO LEFTOVERS

Charles E. Nesbitt Jr.

To order additional copies of this book, contact:
Xlibris Corporation
1-888-795-4274
www.Xlibris.com
Orders@Xlibris.com
47170

Dedication

This Book is Dedicated to the memory of my father, Pastor Charles E. Nesbitt, Sr., my sister Marleen E. Kelly and my brother, Minister Wyndell W. Nesbitt, all of whom proceeded me to that "undiscovered country, from whose bourn no traveler returns".

Acknowledgments

Every journey involves people and places which determine position and progress. It is no different for me; there are many I'm indebted to, whose impact in my life is indelible and undeniable.

First, I'm grateful for my father, the late Charles E. Nesbitt, Sr. and my mother, Dorris Nesbitt, who laid a foundation of faith in me that engendered a love for God.

Secondly, Thank you to my wife Joanne, and our children Charles III, Alexandra and Jennifer who gave me both devotion and distance at the appropriate seasons, without which, I'd have no balance.

Finally, I'd like to thank the wonderful people of Providence Baptist Church for their support and encouragement, and to whom many of these devotions were originally shared in various forms.

An additional note of thanks to Pastors: Timothy Flemming, Joseph Johnson, Freddy Clark, Stephen Clay, Andy Lewter and Kevin Adams. Finally, thank you to my editor Anita Conley, Angela Genus, Carolyn Brown-Wilburn and Sharon Vicks, for their assistance in the preparation of this work.

JANUARY 1

Psalms 116: 12, 17—"What shall I render unto the Lord for all His benefits toward me? . . . I will offer to thee the sacrifice of thanksgiving, and will call upon the name of the Lord." (KJV)

When I was a child, my mother encouraged me at every meal, to eat all the food on my plate. She said if I did, I'd grow up to be big and strong. As I grew and matured, I realized whenever I ate 'all' my food, it was as much a tribute to my mother's cooking, as it was a contribution to my good health. My mother appreciated when I returned my plate to her with no leftovers. I think God appreciates worship without leftovers; when we give Him all the praise unreservedly, as a result of thinking about all He means to us.

The Psalmist says in Ps.116:17, that God deserves an offering of the "sacrifice of thanksgiving." He means like the sacrificial animals of the Old Testament, there should be no 'leftovers' of gratitude when we've completed our worship in His presence, because 'all' our thanks belong to God. Consequently, leftover praise is a sin, because it fails to give God all that's due Him. As much effort as most of us put into being fairly treated by our employers (getting our due), we must be even more diligent in giving God His due (glory). We are therefore called to give God our best each day, recognizing God alone is worthy of our best efforts and highest energy. No leftovers!

Prayer—"Lord, thank you for the blessing of another day and the opportunity it presents."

JANUARY 2

Psalms 116:12—"What shall I render unto the Lord for all His benefits toward me"? (KJV)

I remember reading some years ago, about a farmer noting family members eating without giving thanks. He said it reminded him of the hogs he fed, who ate the fallen chestnuts without looking up to see where they came from. Verse 12 of Ps. 116 commends gratitude to every believer as a response to God's blessings. Gratitude is a thoughtful emotion; much like a microscope which breaks down substances and identifies their components, gratitude breaks down our experiences to identify God as the source of our supply. The principle of divine gratitude is important, because it reminds us that the giver is always more important than the gift, and that relationships are more important than rewards. Thank God!

Prayer—"Lord, the gift of life is precious; Help me use this day to fulfill your will, and advance your Kingdom."

JANUARY 3

Psalms 116:12—"What shall I render unto the Lord for all His benefits toward me?" (KJV)

Let's continue with this verse, as we prepare for another day. The psalmist asks, "how can I repay God" for all His blessings? The question is really rhetorical, because the psalmist knows God's blessings are impossible to repay. The implication is we must express our gratitude to God, even if it doesn't 'repay' Him, because He's simply worthy. The word 'render' means to "turn back", or "return", which would imply anything we give to God originated with Him in the first place. Therefore, it's important to respond to God's blessings in some way because even though our response doesn't 'increase' Him, it does acknowledge Him as our benefactor, and that gives God glory.

Prayer—"Lord, help me see your hand in all my experiences and offer you thanks and praise in return."

JANUARY 4

Psalms 116: 12, 17—"What shall I render unto the Lord for all His benefits toward me . . . I will offer to thee the sacrifice of thanksgiving, and will call upon the name of the Lord." (KJV)

Let's return today to the sacrifice offered in vs. 17. Notice the psalmist does not offer a bull, goat, ram or turtledove, he offers himself, or a grateful heart. He offers himself because that's the best thing we can give God. When we give ourselves, it indicates a desire to seek and serve God obediently. Samuel reminded Saul in I Sam. 15:22, that "obedience is better than sacrifice", because it is the indicator of a heart which is after God's. Just as important though, is that the psalmist knows in giving himself, he's offering that which will make a difference in his personal growth, because his intent is to draw closer to God's image by virtue of a 'personal' offering. What are you offering God today? Is it a gift worthy of His blessings?

Prayer: "Draw me nearer, nearer blessed Lord to the cross where thou hast died . . . to thy precious bleeding side."

JANUARY 5

Matthew 6:33—"But seek ye first the Kingdom of God, and His righteousness; and all these things shall be added unto you." (KJV)

Not long ago, I invited my mother to visit myself and my family. My invitation to her included not only her, but everything she chose to bring with her, meaning her baggage or belongings. How could she feel welcome in my home, if she could not bring with her the things which define her comfort and character? The pursuit of God must always be understood as a desire to have a relationship with Him, but also as an acceptance of whatever baggage God brings with Him. Jesus said things like, "in this world ye shall have tribulation . . ." (John 16:33), and "men will hate you . . ." (Matthew 10:22); this is the baggage the Lord brings with Him, but just like my mother had a 'gift' for me in her bag when she came, so does the Lord have blessings with Him, even though some of His baggage's contents may not be our first choice. So take comfort in seeking both his kingdom 'and' His righteousness because God's got what you need "in the bag".

Prayer—"Lord, help me to accept your will for me in all things and trust your heart, even if I can't trace your hand."

JANUARY 6

Isaiah 55:6-7—"Seek the Lord while He may be found; call on Him while He is near. Let the wicked forsake his way and the evil man his thoughts. Let him turn to the Lord, and he will have mercy on him, and to our God, for He will freely pardon."(NIV)

When I was four years old, my father gave me a soccer-sized ball to play with. He sat down on the floor across from me to play a game of "roll the ball". My father rolled the ball to me, and then called for me to roll it back to him, but at first I refused. After several requests, I finally rolled the ball back to my father. My hesitation in rolling the ball back was because I wasn't sure if I rolled it to him, that he would roll it back to me. Not only did dad roll it back, but I felt a sense of joy and satisfaction when he did.

God says in this text, if we will commit (seek Him) our lives to Him, He will return the life we commit, better for having been in 'His' hands, because we'll experience the fullness of His influence and power in every facet of daily life. I recommend you roll your all to God.

Prayer—"Lord, I cast my cares and concerns on you, trusting your wisdom in all things."

JANUARY 7

John 13:6-8—"He came to Simon Peter, who said to Him, Lord, are you going to wash my feet? Jesus replied, you do not realize now what I am doing, but later you will understand. No, said Peter, you shall never wash my feet. Jesus answered, unless I wash you, you have no part with me."(NIV)

How hard it is sometimes to look beyond the moment. Peter protested the washing of his feet by Jesus. Jesus' response was, Peter would if patient, understand the method behind the master's madness at a future time, but to allow the act of foot washing in spite of it. Jesus' implication was that more than the act of foot washing was taking place; that a message was being conveyed by what was seemingly an inappropriate act of servitude. One of the great lessons all believers must learn, is to look beyond our experiences and the initial feelings they produce, to find the purpose or meaning which God is revealing. Jesus was able to do this in Gethsemane and endure the cross, which led to "a name above every other name" (Phil. 2:9). If you can look beyond the moment, God will elevate your spirit and give you a much needed 'eternal' outlook.

Prayer—"Lord, I choose to acknowledge your hand in all my affairs and see beyond my problems to the presence of your purpose and power in my life."

JANUARY 8

John 12:32—"And I, if I be lifted up from the earth, will draw all men unto me." (KJV)

One of the most important aspects of this verse for me, is that what believers are drawn to is not the cross, but Jesus. He said, "I'll draw all men unto me." This means we are drawn to Him for the purpose of relationship, because that relationship is presently and ultimately beneficial to us, and for us. Often in biological relationships, the relation is manifested through physical similarities. People often tell me I look like my mother; our physical appearance confirms our relationship. We are drawn to Christ to reflect His example and His manner, so others can see Him in us.

Additionally though, we are drawn to Him so He can provide us with access to Heaven's benefits. He did say no one comes to the Father "except by" Him (Jn.14:6). The greatest benefit of being drawn to Christ is the ongoing availability of resources, which could come no other way. Thank God for a Christ who is magnetic, mighty, and merciful!

Prayer—"Father, thank you not for the cross, but all its benefits and blessings; thank you for redemption."

JANUARY 9

Matthew 14:22—"Immediately Jesus made the disciples get into the boat and go on ahead of Him to the other side, while He dismissed the crowd." (NIV)

This lone verse is a picture of the church. The church is a collection of believers gathered as one, and headed somewhere. Additionally, we are headed to the same destination as we have been ordered by our Saviour, Jesus Christ. The success of the church is dependent on our acknowledgment of this truth, and our obedience to Him who is the head of the church. Jesus wants us to regard our movement not as a stroll or vacation, both of which are rather aimless, but as a journey which has as its ultimate goal, progress. It is the desire to be further along at sundown, than at sunrise. As a member of the body of Christ and your local church family, I pray you'll seek to join those who are spiritually related to you on this great journey of faith. Remember, "it does not yet appear what we shall be."

Prayer—"Lord, help me run this race with patience and perseverance, as I maintain progress as my goal."

JANUARY 10

Matthew 14:23, 24—"After He had dismissed them, He went up on a mountainside by himself to pray. When evening came, He was there alone, but the boat was already a considerable distance from land, buffeted by the waves because the wind was against it."(NIV)

When I was growing up, my parents disciplined me when I misbehaved. Sometimes it was just a rebuke and sometimes a spanking, but the message was always the same; that disobedience has consequences. This passage is interesting because the disciples experienced a storm, not as a result of disobedience, but as a consequence of obedience. That's a great lesson for believers; that you can do exactly what you are supposed to, and still have a storm. What's the meaning of such experiences? I believe we must learn that when storms are unmerited, they are obviously for the purpose of revealing some previously unknown aspect of God's glory to strengthen us and renew our faith (see Matt. 14:33). So when your storms arise and you can find no reason for them, pray for revelation and watch God bless you with development through discernment. God will not allow a storm and allow you to remain the same. Praise God!

Prayer—"Lord, help me not to waste time, when life becomes difficult. Help me find meaning in every experience, so I may grow as your child."

JANUARY 11

Matthew 14:22—"Immediately Jesus made the disciples get into the boat and go on ahead of Him to the other side, while He dismissed the crowd." (NIV)

Jesus sent His disciples off without Him, knowing they were heading into a serious challenge. The tone of vs. 22 seems to indicate reluctance on the part of the disciples to leave without the master, but they obeyed Him, in spite of their fears. Life is full of such challenges for believers. The issue is, do we know why, and what we should do when He does?

He sent them by themselves; because they already had what they needed (faith), if they'd just exercise it. It was a test. No teacher gives a test without first providing instruction. The many previous examples of Jesus were lessons enough for the disciples to confront and conquer this challenge without panic, but they were victimized by their fears anyway. How many lessons have you learned; how many times has God brought you through? Aren't those experiences enough to carry you through your next challenge? Well get up and get moving; you've got dragons to slay!

Prayer—"Lord, remind me what you've given me is more than enough for whatever today holds."

JANUARY 12

Matthew 14:23, 24—"After He had dismissed them, He went up on a mountainside by himself to pray, When evening came, He was there alone, but the boat was already a considerable distance from land, buffeted by the waves because the wind was against it." (NIV)

Again, Jesus sent the disciples into a challenge without His physical presence. Remember, God never sends us into difficulty unprepared. Verse 23 is key here; it says while the disciples were struggling, Jesus was praying. Jesus was in effect interceding for His disciples, while they wrestled with the waves. Heb. 7:25 says Christ "ever liveth to make intercession for us." (KJV) That's the impetus for me as I journey into the unknown of each day; the security of knowing that God through Christ has literally "prepared a table before me in the presence of my enemies." Why are you hesitating? Why are you anxious? Claim your victory through Christ and find your joy in His ongoing presence!

Prayer—"Lord, remind me each day that you've equipped me for victory through your presence and power."

JANUARY 13

Ecclesiastes 9:10—"Whatever your hand finds to do, do it with all your might . . ." (NIV)

Recently, I went to the supermarket to purchase a gallon of milk. I've learned though, not to necessarily grab the first milk I see. Most times, I bend down to see if there's a different freshness date between the milk in the front and the milk behind it. If there is, I take the time and effort to reach further for the milk that lasts longer. Isn't that a lesson for life? Doesn't it pay off ultimately, if we consciously stretch ourselves in the kingdom? Doesn't that lead to a blessing with an eternal freshness date on it?

Don't despise the labor you've been given as a servant of God. Give your best at every opportunity. Practice excellence in all your endeavors. Remember, "Success is being the best, but excellence is being your best." If excellence is your goal, your labor will not be in vain.

Prayer—"Lord, help me reach beyond my current boundaries and fulfill your desired destiny for me."

JANUARY 14

Isaiah 55:8—"For my thoughts are not your thoughts, neither are your ways my ways, declares the Lord." (NIV)

Isaiah says we do things differently than God; that ordinarily, God takes a different route than we do, to get to His destination. It refers us to how God processes and pursues His aims. I've noticed when I use an online mapping service; it always offers the options of "best route" and "shortest route". Obviously, sometimes the best route is longer than the shortest route. Similarly, in the kingdom, we often need to take a longer route to success than we would prefer, but the longer route is the road ordained by God and protected by His presence. There are no 'shortcuts' to an abiding blessing; no 'backdoor' solutions for the household of God. His thoughts are the recommended process for understanding our experiences, and His ways are the means by which those thoughts should be made manifested. If you want to know how to think and act like God, back up in Isaiah 55 to verse 6 and seek God, "while He may be found."

Prayer—"Lord, teach me to think like you and to respond to life's experiences as you direct."

JANUARY 15

Psalm 119:133—"Order my steps in thy word, and let not any iniquity have dominion over me." (KJV)

I have a Brita water pitcher at home; it's an interesting and useful creation. It allows me to drink ordinary tap water, without ingesting the many impurities found in it. The pitcher comes equipped with a charcoal filter, which is the secret to its usefulness. The charcoal in the filter traps more than 90% of the impurities in ordinary water as it passes through the filter. So the principle is, water begins one way, but after passing through the filter, it does so without the things that make it impure. What a lesson for believers! When we pass our experiences through the filter of our faith, faith traps the impurities produced by our feelings, so that what comes out of us is what God would have us do. If we can consistently learn to see things as God does, then we can respond as He does, with an eye on grace and righteousness, and a result we won't regret, or have to apologize for.

Prayer—"Dear God, elevate my thinking, so I may be an example of Godliness wherever I am."

JANUARY 16

Psalm 119:105—"Your word is a lamp to my feet and a light for my path."

Recently, I was returning to Atlanta from a preaching trip. As the plane began its final approach, I noticed how heavily fogged the Atlanta area was. No one on the plane seemed to mind though. The runway became only partially visible just seconds before we touched down, yet the passengers seemed unaffected by this lack of visibility. Our confidence rested in the pilot, and his confidence rested in the air traffic controller, whose job it is to sit in a tower, and using radar, guide 260 tons of metal, passengers, and cargo safely into the gate. Don't you see how unproductive worry is? We have a Father who sits above time, resting in eternity, and while we cannot always see clearly the road ahead, if we trust His skills (righteous radar), He'll always brings us to the port of His purpose.

Additionally, the air traffic controller successfully brings in multiple planes at the same time. Our God has the ability to guide you as well as me at the same time, without taxing Himself, because nothing's too hard for Him.

Prayer—"Dear Lord, guide my mind, tongue, and ears, so I might always fulfill your will for me."

JANUARY 17

John 15:26—"When the counselor comes, whom I will send to you from the Father, the Spirit of Truth, who goes out from the Father, He will testify about me." (NIV)

The National Basketball Association (NBA) has a six-day program designed to help first year players adjust to life as a professional basketball player. It's called the "NBA Transition Program". The players are given instruction in areas like sex, the media, finances, associations, and are led in these workshops by consultants with expertise in those areas. Those six days are intended to teach the players that while the game is the same, the level is different.

The same principle was apparent when Jesus was addressing His disciples in John 15. They were about to do the work of ministry, but at a different level; they were about to minister without the physical presence of Jesus. Jesus calmed their fears by bringing in a consultant to help them with the transition: the Holy Spirit. It is the Spirit's responsibility to help us with maintenance and memory as we make adjustments as believers, so never begin the transition of a new day without accessing the resources of the Spirit through prayer. He is our abiding presence.

Prayer—"Father, comfort and guide me by your Spirit, that all I say and do may be your will."

JANUARY 18

Luke 15:17a—"When he came to his senses . . ." (NIV)

The story of the Prodigal Son, which really focuses on the loving father, teaches us what and what not to do when you find yourself down. I'd like to, for the next several days examine this parable as a teaching tool for responding to a difficult situation. One option in a discouraging circumstance is to 'nurse' it. To nurse is to feed; to promote growth and development, for the purpose of making a thing a stronger presence in your life. It is to feed a person (breast-feeding) or situation your energy or resources, with the expectation of something valuable received in return. The Prodigal fed the far country his time and resources, but received little to nothing in return (Luke. 15:16); it's because he fed a circumstance which had no capacity to do anything for him except continue to drain him. There is a female character in the X-men movies named "Rogue". Rogue only has the capacity to take without giving, so any interaction with her leaves you worse at the end than you were at the beginning. Why not begin to examine your life, and see if you're nursing (feeding) something that's preventing your progress and possibilities. If it's so, begin to take steps to receive, even as you give.

Prayer—"Father, help me to locate those spaces and places that help me be the me you want me to be."

JANUARY 19

Luke 15:17a—"When he came to his senses . . ." (NIV)

Let's continue with our responses to challenging situations. Another option is to 'curse it'. To curse a thing is to utter a judgment against it; it is to denounce a thing not only as unacceptable, but as unholy as well. This is an emotional reaction; it vents or expresses feelings, but the reality is, when the feelings have been expressed the circumstance remains unchanged.

In 2 Kings 5:10-12, Naaman was instructed by Elisha to dip himself seven times in the Jordan River to heal his leprosy. Naaman's initial response was to curse the Jordan as unacceptable, but after he vented, he was still a leper. Only obedience could cure him. In Luke 23:39-43, a thief hanging next to Jesus cursed his circumstances by mocking Jesus. He insulted the only resource he had for deliverance, so his fate remained unchanged. The thief on the other side is instructive, because he recognized there was hope for him in the presence of this disrespected Galilean named Jesus, and his faith led to the promise of paradise. There obviously is a better response to your challenge than 'cursing it'. Why not allow the Spirit of God to direct your thoughts and responses today?

Prayer—"Lord, keep my mind, heart, and tongue, so I may be a godly example wherever I go."

JANUARY 20

Luke 15:17a—"When he came to his senses . . ." (NIV)

Here we are again trying to come to a conclusion on how to respond to a discouraging situation. We've discovered we shouldn't nurse it, and can't curse it. What's another option? We can 'rehearse' it. To rehearse is to practice over and over again, for the purpose of proficiency and competence. The result of rehearsal, is comfort with the thing that's been rehearsed, and therein is the problem with rehearsal; when it's done in the pigpen (Prodigal), it only makes you more comfortable with a lower standard of living. When you become comfortable in the low places, it hinders potential, obscures promise and blocks possibilities. The bleeding woman of Mark 5 bled for 12 years, but was never comfortable rehearsing that state (Mk. 5:26-27), so that when she heard of the coming presence of Jesus, she ran quickly to meet him, by pressing her way through the crowd. Obviously, we need an option other than 'rehearsing'. Let me encourage you today to avoid the responses that keep you down, by always seeking the pattern of Jesus Christ. Join me right back here tomorrow to conclude this section of our morning time together.

Prayer—"Father, help me to avoid repeating the same mistakes by guiding me with your Word and your Spirit."

JANUARY 21

Luke 15:17a— "When he came to his senses . . ." (NIV)

Obviously, nursing, cursing, and rehearsing are not viable options to our discouraging seasons. The only solution is to 'reverse' it. That's exactly what the Prodigal did in vs. 17 of Luke 15; he "came to himself". Coming to himself was manifested by adjusting his thinking, then his environment.

In his thinking, the Prodigal compared where he was (pigpen), with where he'd come from (father's house), and concluded he'd made a terrible error in judgment, because even his father's slaves were surpassingly better off than he was. Additionally, his clear thinking also helped him understand that his sin was first and foremost against God, because he'd not honored his father as God commanded (Ex. 20:12), and, he realized he was in the pigpen by choice, not compulsion.

The prodigal didn't end there though. He also adjusted his environment, because he realized it wasn't enough to see things clearly, but still be under the influence of negative surroundings. He understood how hard it is to maintain a good thing when you walk in the counsel of the ungodly, or stand in the way of sinners. Why not begin this day by reversing whatever's holding you down by asking God's Spirit to 'renew' your mind.

Prayer— "Dear God, take residence in my mind, and direct my thoughts, so I may fulfill your will for me."

JANUARY 22

Isaiah 26:3—*"You will keep him in perfect peace, whose mind is stayed on you, because he trusts in you." (NIV)*

The phrase, "You will keep him", is one word in the Hebrew, meaning 'garrison'. It's a military term, suggesting God will 'guard' your peace; God will not allow anyone or anything to take away the peace He gives you. Not long ago I saw the after affects of a terrible storm in Florida. Debris from houses, as well as cars and trucks were scattered everywhere. What caught my attention were the palm trees, still holding the positions they had before the driving winds and rain occurred. Apparently, the palm trees were blown over, but not blown down. That's exactly what God does for us; He does not prevent storms from coming, but through His abiding presence keeps us rooted in His redemptive power.

Let me add though, that this military reference also suggests that peace must be fought for; that peace is a precious commodity, because believers are involved in a spiritual warfare (Eph. 6:11), which requires the resources of God ("whole armor"), if this peace is to be maintained. So begin this day knowing challenges will come, but God is able to keep you in "perfect peace", as you exercise your faith.

Prayer—"Lord, guard my heart, as I confront my challenges, and give me victory in Your name."

JANUARY 23

Isaiah 26:3—"You will keep him in perfect peace, whose mind is stayed on You, because he trusts in You." (NIV)

Let's return to this verse today. In the Hebrew, the phrase, "perfect peace" is written "shalom, shalom". This literally means that God keeps His Children in "peace, peace". This means God's peace is not a pseudo peace, suggesting that every disturbing element is removed from your experience, because that's not realistic; storms came to everyone. The repetition of the word peace suggests the 'quality' of peace God offers. "Peace, peace is a superlative peace; it means God gives "peace to your peace."

I can remember lying in my parent's bed one night as a child, during a terrible storm. What a sense of security I felt. There I was with the sound of thunder in my ears, and the intermittent flashing of light through the window as the lightning criss-crossed the sky, yet I felt safe, surrounded by my parents and their love, in the midst of the storm. That's "peace, peace". That's what God gives those who truly trust Him. It can be yours today, if you keep your mind on Him.

Prayer—"Father, help me keep my mind on you, so I may have the peace which passes understanding."

JANUARY 24

Isaiah 26:3—"You will keep him in perfect peace, whose mind is stayed on You, because he trusts in You." (NIV)

This text suggests that the guarantee of peace is based on a contingency. It (peace) belongs to those who love and acknowledge God by keeping their minds on Him. The mind is important in our relationship with God, because it's an ocean of thoughts, emotions, and ideas, subject to our feelings. The mind is the birthplace of every action; you can change your mind, lose your mind, ease your mind, or make up your mind. The mind is so subject to variables, that we need a resource outside ourselves to help us keep it stable. That resource is Jesus Christ, because He gives 'peace' of mind.

As a young man, I never spent much on the mattresses I slept on. I never regarded it as an important investment. It took years to add up the backaches and sleepless nights, and attribute them to a bad mattress. I learned a good mattress is a worthwhile investment, though an expensive one. That's the lesson we must learn about Jesus Christ. There are other options for peace, but none are eternally sufficient. Every option other than Christ is just a temporary stop gap, with no real, lasting benefit. As you begin this day 'rest' your mind on the Lord and find real peace.

Prayer—"Lord, grant me your presence today, that my mind might have rest in you."

JANUARY 25

Isaiah 26:3—"You will keep him in perfect peace, whose mind is stayed on You, because he trusts in You." (NIV)

I thought I'd come back today to our minds 'staying' on Him (the Lord). This further means, that we must not lose our 'connection' with God, and that it is our minds or thought processes which facilitate that connection. Again, the mind is significant in my relationship with God. I must not allow God to be overshadowed or eclipsed in my mind, because the result of a lost connection is the denial of access to God's resources at critical times.

Recently, during a thunderstorm, I lost the television feed from my dish system. I was looking at a movie on an HBO network at the time. It occurred to me that although I'd lost my connection, HBO was still broadcasting the movie. The problem was not them, but the loss of 'my' connection. That's what happens between us and God when our minds aren't 'stayed' on Him. We lose our connection, but it doesn't diminish Him, because He's still waiting and ready to bless if we can refocus our thoughts. As you begin this new day, keep God close so you'll have what you need, when you need it.

Prayer—"Father, help me stay sensitive to your presence, so that today's challenges will not be more than I can bear."

JANUARY 26

Zechariah 14:17—"If any of the peoples of the earth do not go up to Jerusalem to worship the King, the Lord Almighty, they will have no rain." (NIV)

Obviously, God expects and desires worship from us. Worship is a precious commodity to God, because it's the one thing He did not create, yet it is the human expression which releases the blessings (rain) of God. Worship simply put, gives God His due; it is for us the 'main' key in our relationship with God, because everything else in our experience is contingent on consistent willing worship.

When I come to the office to work, I only have one key with me, and that's the main key to the building, which lets me in any exterior door. There are other rooms in the building which require a key, but that doesn't concern me. All I need is the 'main' key, and once I'm in the building, I can access any of the other rooms. That's what worship provides for us; when we truly worship, the other concerns of life like relationships, finances, and employment are subject to accessibility 'through' worship. Worship again, is the 'main' key. Let me encourage you today to give God His due (worship), through your words, attitude, and example then watch God shower you with His presence and power.

Prayer—"Even me Lord . . . let some drops now, fall on me."

JANUARY 27

Zechariah 14:17—"If any of the peoples of the earth do not go up to Jerusalem to worship the King, the Lord Almighty, they will have no rain." (NIV)

I cannot stress enough how important worship is to God. He did not 'create' worship, so He expects a spontaneous response from a grateful heart which recognizes and acknowledges Him as life's true and only source of blessings. God says that reaction (true worship) always receives rain (blessings).

It's interesting how rain takes place. When rain falls, it's because tiny particles of dust carried up in the atmosphere by updrafts of air, collide with droplets of water in clouds, forming a bond, and making the drops of water heavier. This happens over and over again until the water in the cloud becomes so heavy that the cloud can no longer hold the water and rain is released from above. Don't you see the principle? Something must go up before something comes down; praises must go up before blessings can come down. What are you looking for God to do in your life? Give God worship and see if God won't release His intentions in your life! He has a blessing with your name on it!

Prayer—"Lord, help me magnify you today, so I may benefit from true worship; rain on me today."

JANUARY 28

Psalm 29:2—"Ascribe to the Lord, the glory due His name; worship the Lord in the splendor of His holiness." (NIV)

Why is it important to give God His due (worship)? It's because God has in store for true worshippers, the requisite resources to meet their needs once they've departed from worship.

Not long ago, I was looking at the won/loss records of two professional basketball teams. I noted that while both teams had similar records, one team had a better record on the road than the other team, indicating their greater proficiency at winning in a 'hostile' environment. When we leave worship, we enter hostile territory; sometimes at the job, sometimes in the community, and sometimes even at home. What God does for us in worship, is provide the means to experience success outside the walls of the church building, by giving us a to-go plate in worship. What makes worship the blessing it is, is the carry-out nature of it; God's benefits are portable! So give God His due and take your blessings with you; there's no expiration date on God.

Prayer—"Father, I worship and praise you for all your benefits toward me. Walk with me as I seek to apply your presence in all things."

JANUARY 29

Proverbs 3:66—"... and he shall direct thy paths." (KJV)

Most mornings I head to the office, I take a minute to watch the traffic report on television. Atlanta's traffic is pretty congested and I'm generally impatient in stop and go traffic, so I'll either look for an alternate route or wait until there's less congestion. I've become dependent on that report; the gentleman who pilots the helicopter is called the "eye in the sky". I trust him because he's up and out before I am, and he takes a look at where I'm going before I get there, so when he speaks, I value his words because "he's been where I'm going".

Isn't that what God does for us? Isn't He the real "eye in the sky?" Doesn't He check things out before we get there? Solomon commends trusting God to us, because God knows more than we do and He alone has the capacity to "direct our paths". But don't stop there, because another difference between God and the 'copter pilot is, God has the capacity to affect your route and your result before you even begin. The traffic reporter can tell you where the problems are, but he's limited to revelation without redemption. God is able to inform and transform, so why not trust Him with all your heart?

Prayer—"Dear Lord, direct my path today, by your precious spirit, so I may fulfill today's destiny."

JANUARY 30

Matthew 5:38, 39—"You have heard that it was said, 'eye for eye, and tooth for tooth'. But I tell you, do not resist an evil person. If someone strikes you on the right check, turn to him the other also." (NIV)

Jesus' basic thought here is to resist the inclination and tendency to repay evil with evil; the instinct in us to always give as good as we get. It is of course our nature to feel emotionally unfulfilled when we are wronged without a chance to respond in some form, which reveals our dissatisfaction. The key principle in these verses is that there is no chance for society to improve itself, if Christians are not setting a higher standard. We are called upon to do more than the law expects or demands; we are called upon to give the world a set of responses to strive to reach.

You may wonder whether it's even possible to meet this standard. I believe it is. When I was a student in high school, my parents often reprimanded me for low grades. I thought their complaints were unreasonable, because I had "passing grades". My parents complained because they knew I could do better; that it was "in me" to excel. God knows the same of us; being in His image, it's "in us" to do better and not settle for the first response motivated by our feelings. I encourage you today to allow your responses to be informed by God's Spirit; show the world a "more excellent way".

Prayer—"Lord, help me to love my neighbor and to show that love as an example for others."

JANUARY 31

Matthew 5:40—"And if someone wants to sue you and take your tunic, let him have your cloak as well." (NIV)

Again, let's look at how we should respond to others in terms of the example Jesus sets. What it comes down to is holding your personal rights 'loosely', or with an unselfish attitude. We need to be reminded that in reality, we own nothing; that we belong to God through creation and crucifixion and are therefore debtors to God. With that in mind, my personal rights are not so crucial, that they become more important than God's kingdom and cause. God is asking me to accept vulnerability as a way of life, believing that it is ultimately beneficial to do so.

Vulnerability is not a problem for me, or for most believers I think, as long as we know God has us covered. I believe God gives us that guarantee in His word. In Psalms 23:4, David willingly accepted the vulnerability of the valley of the shadow of death, because he knew his commitment to the shepherd guaranteed him the shepherd's protection and provision. In Philippians 2:5-11, Jesus' willingness to accept the vulnerability of the cross led Him to "a name above every other name." This is God's promise to us; when we go beyond the world's expectation and set a godly example, "God's got our back."

Prayer—"Father, I pray for strength today to meet my challenges in the spirit of patience and perseverance."

FEBRUARY 1

Galatians 6:9—"Let us not become weary in doing good, for at the proper time we will reap a harvest if we do not give up." (NIV)

Success for Christians comes to those who persevere; who do not quit, or give up easily, knowing God's will is to our advantage. My car is equipped with a fuel gauge that lets me know when I'm running low on gas. At the point that happens, a light comes on with a message that says, "distance 45 miles". This means under normal highway conditions, I have approximately 45 miles of gasoline left in my tank. For me, that means I don't have to panic; that I can go a little further before stopping. Isn't that instructive for every believer? Isn't it good to know that with faith, you can run on and not fear being broke down and disabled in life's emergency lane?

The harvest mentioned in our verse for the day, does not come to those who plant and walk away, but to those who understand nature and nurture; to those who plant and cultivate, knowing that everything has it's "due season". Let me encourage you to keep giving your all knowing God will supply your needs and guarantee that your labor's not in vain.

Prayer—"Father, prop me up when I lean, and remind me that in due time, 'I shall come forth as pure gold'."

FEBRUARY 2

Matthew 8:3a—"Jesus reached out his hand and touched the man."

Matthew 8 has the account of a leper healed by Jesus. Leprosy made its victims outcasts, physically and socially, and was generally considered to be incurable. Here was a man unable to enjoy his family, friends, and faith. Anyone who touched him was regarded as unclean, because the leper was pronounced unclean, yet Jesus touched him before He healed him. I think that is significant.

Jesus wants us to know that relationships are more important than regulations and people are more important than programs. Jesus touched him before He healed him, because the demands of love are always greater than the demands of the law. What good is it to be healed and healthy, and still be an outcast? Jesus teaches us that 'touch' means acceptance, love, and fellowship; that's what people crave most and what Christians are called upon to do. Remember, Jesus didn't have to touch to heal, but in this case it was necessary to touch his heart before healing his body. Is there anyone you've overlooked recently? Someone who could use a touch, an embrace? Why not extend the grace that God extended to you by 'touching' a soul in need today?

Prayer—"Dear Lord, use me as an instrument of your love today to touch someone's life."

FEBRUARY 3

Luke 2:49b— *"Wist ye not that I must be about my Father's business?" (NIV)*

Some people are more serious than others about fulfilling their purpose, or "takin' care of business". Jesus had no such problem. He identified early on who He was, and what He had come to do. One of the ingredients Jesus found important in fulfilling His purpose was a respect for tradition. Verse 42 of Lk. 2, says Jesus and His family made it a custom to go to the Passover Feast each year. This meant they honored consistently the God who brought Israel out of Egypt and into the Promised Land. Jehovah is a God of covenant and confirmation.

Jesus obviously, even at twelve understood the importance of identifying what, or who, brought Him to where He was at the moment; that we are all the products of people and experiences that shape and mold us, and those contributors must not be overlooked or diminished. My life is the result of multiple fingerprints: parents, siblings, teachers, friends, fellow believers, and strangers. I honor them, because they are the ingredients in the recipe of my life's results. It is therefore, impossible to navigate my present and chart my future without remembering respectfully my past. I encourage you to begin this day with an acknowledgment of God, and the godly people who've made you a product of divine purpose.

Prayer— *"Dear God, I honor the blessings of my past and use them today, as the inspiration for all my today's and tomorrows."*

FEBRUARY 4

Luke 2:42—"And when He was twelve years old, they went up to Jerusalem after the custom of the feast." (KJV)

Back to this notion of "respecting tradition". Respecting it requires that we know the difference between tradition and traditionalism, because one is healthy, while the other is both distracting and destructive.

Tradition is the "living faith of the dead; traditionalism is the dead faith of the living" (Jaroslav Pelikan). This means that traditionalism worships the tradition itself, making a god out of long standing practices, while tradition honors the power behind the practices, who adds His intangible presence to make our practices bear fruit. It's one thing to worship the God who brings us across the bridge, and another thing altogether to worship the bridge itself. The latter attitude is what keeps people stuck in the mire of mediocrity with no chance for success or satisfaction.

Every believer must learn to respect tradition by living in dialogue with the past, yet recognizing the present age, and making the necessary adjustments. We must not 'live' in the past; only use it as a tool of information and inspiration. This is the balanced and proper approach to connecting with our past.

Prayer—"Father, help me honor my past without ignoring your presence in my life."

FEBRUARY 5

Luke 2:46—"And it came to pass, that after three days they found Him in the temple, sitting in the midst of the doctors, both hearing them, and asking them questions." (KJV)

We discovered two days ago, that Jesus had identified His purpose by the time He was twelve years old. He was, "takin' care of business". Another of the principles Jesus exposes in this text is the need for preparation/training before the fulfillment of purpose can take place. The reality is, it does no good to show up anywhere, without the requisite tools to do the job; to arrive without any idea of what to do after the arrival. Many are guilty of this fatal flaw in their relationships, whether related to marriage or ministry. Jesus knew if He was to teach in the temple later, He'd have to spend time there early on 'steeping' Himself in His faith.

This verse teaches us to value process and performance. If you've ever enjoyed a sporting event, concert, play or movie, please consider how much practice went into the performance. Long tedious hours are required to make the performance memorable. Think of a touchdown play in a football game; it doesn't take place until after the 'huddle'. Believers must spend time 'huddling' with God before they can execute life well. I'm sure you expect a great result for your life today, but every great result requires a recipe. Don't forget your ingredients!

Prayer—"God, help me not disparage the little things that add up to big results!"

FEBRUARY 6

Luke 2:46—"And it came to pass, that after three days they found Him in the temple, sitting in the midst of the doctors, both hearing them, and asking them questions." (KJV)

Here we are again this morning, trying to follow Jesus' example of "takin' care of business". In this verse the master suggests that one of the ingredients of your success is to surround yourself with people who challenge and raise the level of your thinking. This means that our social interaction and conversations are important in our development. We must not take these experiences lightly; otherwise, we will live our entire lives without fulfilling God's purpose. Think of the importance of resistance in the development of muscles. What resistance (exercise) does, is increases the 'capacity' of the muscle, enabling it to carry or endure more. This is what the resistance of thought-provoking engagement of the mind does; it increases the believer's capacity to grasp and apply the things of God.

I have a peace lily plant in my office, and every few weeks or so, I turn it around because it invariably leans in the direction of the sun. I turn it to straighten the leaves by giving it a 'fresh' perspective. That's what every Christian needs to maintain growth; the fresh perspective of challenging experiences.

Prayer—"God, help me seek out people who will help me draw closer to you, and your purpose for me."

FEBRUARY 7

Matthew 9:14-15—"Then John's disciples came and asked Him, how is it that we and the Pharisees fast, but your disciples do not fast?" Jesus answered, "how can the guests of the bridegroom mourn while he is with them? The time will come when the bridegroom will be taken from them; then they will fast."

One of the things I believe Jesus is addressing here is the demeanor of Christians. Jesus claims that the church is in a period of feasting, rather than fasting; that this is a time of joy rather than sorrow. It's based on the premise that the groom (Jesus Christ) has already provided everything the bride (church) needs, so why behave as if we've yet to receive our blessing?

This is important because many believers need a mood adjustment; a clear understanding of what it is God's already done. Jesus said things like, "I've overcome the world", and "I'm with you always . . .", to remind us of His complete abiding presence as the source of our comfort and security. With that in mind, it's important that we believers display a demeanor that expresses our confidence and joy in facing our daily challenges. Others need to know we sing "because we're happy . . .", and they need to see that joy 'applied' so they know our God is able and willing to meet the believer's 'every' need.

Prayer—"Father, help me advertise your presence and power in my life, so I may lead others to you."

FEBRUARY 8

Luke 2:49c—"... I must be about my Father's business." (KJV)

Jesus is always "takin' care of business". He encourages us to do the same. Another necessary principle for this kind of success is to be found in the 'places' which most benefit the fulfillment of our life's purpose. Luke 2:46 says Jesus' parents found Him "in the temple". The temple, or church, is the house of God; it's where God and His people intersect, so exchange can take place. That exchange involves our reverence and God's revelation. There are a great many places believers can go which are not sinful, but the best 'place' for believers, if we are to fulfill our purpose, is the church. The church is both a refuge and resource, because it's the only place God promised the gates of Hell would not prevail against (Matt. 16:18).

We need the church, because it provides an atmosphere conducive for our growth and development; it helps us focus our minds on where our resources really come from, and helps us hear from God, as to what His purpose for us is. I read a story years ago, about a boy disappointed with his visit to the circus, because he spent his money on the sideshow, rather than the activity in the big top. He saw the 'freaks' of nature rather than the exciting performances. That's why the church is important. Everything else is just a 'sideshow'.

Prayer—"Dear God, help me to seek out the places which will produce your purpose for me."

FEBRUARY 9

Luke 2:49c—"... I must be about my Father's business." (KJV)

This passage is so inexhaustible! It continues to define and deliver what it means to "take care of business". Another principle found in this passage, is the necessity of developing the ability to identify priorities. Jesus said, "I must be about . . ." identifying the work of God as His sole priority. Whether you're looking at the Ten Commandments or The Lord's Prayer each of those directives for believers begins with an acknowledgment of who God is, for the purpose of giving God the glory.

In the parable of the pearls (Matt. 13:4-46), the merchant was looking for 'fine' pearls, but suspended his search when he found a pearl beyond compare. The merchant knew he'd found a pearl which would set him up for life, and that he need search no more. He had fine pearls as a priority and when he found the best there was, his goal was more than fulfilled. This is the responsibility of every believer; to find the best there is and employ it.

To do that, spiritual sensitivity is a requirement. The reason I prefer FM radio to AM radio is because the FM signal is stronger and clearer, and FM radio is a 24-hour operation. God is trying to develop an FM spirit in us; a spirit that listens for Him all the time and clearly identifies His voice.

Prayer—"Lord, fine tune my spirit, so I can hear your voice and heed your call."

FEBRUARY 10

Luke 2:49c—". . . I must be about my Father's business." (KJV)

"Takin' care of business" requires that we follow certain necessary principles to achieve success. We've discovered already what some of them are, but we have not yet exhausted this scripture in our search for direction.

Another principle to remember in this passage is to know 'who' you are. Jesus referred in this verse to being about "His Father's" business. This of course means He knew by the time He was twelve, that He had a unique relationship with God and a special calling on His life. Knowing His identity led Him to know what His purpose and path was. Identity awareness is important, because it 'frees' you to be all you can. At twelve, our Savior knew both that He was the Jesus of time and the Christ of eternity. This knowledge freed Him to fulfill His purpose of pleasing God and redeeming humankind. Not long ago, I read the story of an eagle that grew up with chickens, and consequently, thought of itself as a chicken. Later, in the eagle's life he discovered he could do things the chickens couldn't do, but only when he discovered his true nature (identity), was he able to leave the barnyard and soar to new heights. That's exactly what you'll discover when you identify who and whose you are!

Prayer—"Father, show me who I am in Christ, so I may achieve new levels of success in your name."

FEBRUARY 11

Luke 2:49c—"... I must be about my Father's business." (KJV)

"Takin' care of business" is our current morning theme and we've been looking at the example of a twelve year old Jesus for principles to give us direction and insight.

I thought it interesting that Jesus returned home with His parents in Lk. 2:51. It seems Jesus had also, a sense of timing. He knew who He was, but He also knew it wasn't time to "go public". Jesus understood the seasonal nature of life; that there is a "time for everything . . . under Heaven" (Eccl. 3:1 NIV), and that this truth is fundamental to the Bible as well as believers. Our recognition of 'timing' presupposes that although men and women make judgments in the political, social and religious arenas that seem to shape history, that it is really God, through grace and judgment that directs history toward an ultimate goal, in spite of the works of men. Joseph said it best in Gen. 50:20, when he told his brothers, "you meant evil against me, but God meant it for good" (NKJV).

'Timing' reminds me to follow God's direction. I once was detoured as I traveled home, but as long as I followed the signs, I arrived at my intended destination without a problem. That's what God expects from us; to follow His signs in His own time.

Prayer—"God, help me hear your voice, so I may be sensitive to your timing for me."

FEBRUARY 12

Romans 8:28—"... all things work together for good to them that love God..." (KJV)

I can remember being given a paper in kindergarten, with a series of dots on it. The dots were numbered, and the teacher told the class that there was an image hidden on the paper, which would be revealed if we connected the dots. I didn't know it then, but that experience is a great lesson for life; it teaches us that success does not come to believers without 'connecting' every circumstance, whether good or bad. The fact is, it's impossible to get a 'true' picture of life, without including everything you experience, because everything has some kind of individual impact, as well as contributing to the overall effect.

The other part of that experience I remember is the need to connect the dots 'sequentially' to come up with the true image from the paper. It meant that nothing could be left out or overlooked, if the real picture was to be seen. How true for us as well. We are often tempted to subtract one day from a week's experiences, because that day was unpleasant, but God suggests we include that day because without it we'd forget how God brought us through. So as you begin this day, however it turns out, God has the resources to redeem it for your good.

Prayer—"Father, help me connect the dots of each day so I may see clearly your will for me."

FEBRUARY 13

John 7:66—"... my time is not yet come ..." (KJV)

In this verse, Jesus speaks of the need to do things according to the will of God, recognizing how important timing is for us. At the time, Jesus was preparing to attend the Feast of Tabernacles, but only at the time His Father directed Him to go. Jesus refused to allow His brothers to dictate His itinerary. Hearing and heeding God insures the receipt of all things God purposes for His children.

One of the most interesting plays I've ever seen in a football game is the 'timing' play, involving the quarterback and wide receiver. It requires a mental count between the quarterback and wide receiver, for the purpose of a successful pass between them. The key moment is when the wide receiver makes a turn or 'cut' in his running route, because when he cuts, the ball is already in the air, requiring him to be precise in the 'pattern' he runs. If he is precise, he will have turned at just the right time, and be prepared to receive what has already been sent. That's a spiritual lesson for us. God is directing blessings to His children, but we also require spiritual sensitivity to be "in step" with God's count so we can receive it at the time God ordains. Only daily prayer and meditation can keeps us in step with God and positions us to receive the bounty of God's intention. What time is it for you?

Prayer—"Dear Lord, tell me what time it is; it's my desire to live this day completely in your will."

FEBRUARY 14

John 12:32—"And I, if I be lifted up from the earth, will draw all men unto me." (KJV)

Crucifixion was an excruciatingly painful, public, and sometimes agonizingly slow death. The victims of such deaths were generally individuals convicted of the most heinous, horrific crimes, but not so with Jesus. There was "no fault in Him", yet He was crucified anyway. Still, He did say there was some benefit to the experience; He said, it was and would be magnetic.

What we are drawn to though is not the cross, but the Christ. Jesus said, "I'll draw all men unto me". That's important; what we are drawn to is not religion, but a relationship, and Jesus is attractive to us because of His willingness to be "lifted up", so we wouldn't be let down. God has always been intent on establishing a relationship with His creation. His interaction with Adam, Abraham, Moses, and David, as well as Jesus' training of the disciples and story of the Prodigal Son, all reveal the heart of a God who wants nothing more than to be our Heavenly Father and relate to us from that basis. What makes life what it is, is relationships; that's why God said it wasn't good for man "to be alone". I encourage you today to take advantage of what God has provided through Christ; walk in the fullness of a relationship which has no end.

Prayer—"Heavenly Father, stay close to me today; your presence gives me power and reminds me of your love."

FEBRUARY 15

Hebrews 4:15b—"... but we have one who has been tempted in every way, just as we are, yet was without sin." (KJV)

My brother is a minister of the Gospel, but I've never called on him for preaching or pastoring advice, because his experience is much more limited than mine. I always call on individuals who've already "been there and done that." That's what makes Jesus Christ such a blessing to every believer. When we end our prayers with, "in Jesus name", we can be confident in our supplications, because of the 'level' of Jesus' experience as one of us. Our Savior is more than equal to the challenges our prayers present.

This verse suggests that you and I can be comfortable with the commitment we've made as Christians, because God understands us from our perspective, since He became one of us through Jesus. Our prayers are therefore meaningful to God because every experience is familiar to God. Isn't it a joy to know that when we pray, God nods knowingly because He understands? Isn't it discouraging to engage someone ignorant of our experiences in dialogue? That's why our Christ is so great; He knows and He understands, so pray with confidence! Hebrews 2:17-3:1 says Christ is greater than Moses, because He's greater than the law, and greater than Joshua, because He gives a greater rest than Joshua, who led Israel to the Promised Land. Pray on!

Prayer—"God, I thank you that you know and understand all my thoughts and ways. I trust your guidance today."

FEBRUARY 16

Hebrews 4:14—"Therefore, since we have a great high priest who has gone through the heavens, Jesus the Son of God, . . ." (NIV)

The author of Hebrews says that the greatness of Jesus Christ is in His priesthood. Our confidence in Jesus is in His ability to represent us with no restrictions, unlike the Old Testament priests, who in spite of their roles, were subject to human fallibility. Jesus' priesthood was greater for a number of reasons. First, Old Testament priests could offer sacrifices for sin, but had no power to remove sin. Jesus died as the ultimate and final sacrifice for sin. His priesthood is greater. Secondly, the Old Testament priest could enter the "holy of holies" once a year to atone for the nation's sins. Jesus has ongoing and unrestricted access (Heb. 7:25) to God, in the highest sanctuary (Heaven), to insure our daily need is met. His priesthood is greater.

Then, the Old Testament priest interceded between God and the people, but the priest was sinful himself. Jesus intercedes as the 'sinless' Son of God, assuring us of God's forgiveness. His priesthood is greater. Finally, the high priest was the highest religious authority of his day, but Jesus is a higher authority, because He is God and man; He joins humanity and divinity in a unique and ultimately beneficial way. We have a High Priest who now provides us unfettered access to God. The door is open; what are you waiting for?

Prayer—"Father, thank you for your unlimited grace and mercy and thank you for your Son, Jesus Christ"

FEBRUARY 17

Hebrews 4:15b—"... but we have one who has been tempted in every way, just as we are—yet was without sin." (NIV)

The greatness of Jesus Christ as a savior is also related to Him as a 'partner'. Heb. 4:15b implies that Jesus can relate to our struggles while assuring us of the power to overcome them. This means that although Jesus was the Son of God, he was not disqualified from sharing the problems of the human experience, because He was as much man as He was God. So because He experienced all a human can, He has an unequaled capacity to sympathize and save.

This is an important truth. It keeps us from assuming that temptation was 'easy' for Jesus. The fact is He 'earned' His sinlessness because He faced temptation at the highest level, because of 'who' He was. For most of us, certain temptations don't take long for us to give in to, and that's because the enemy knows where to attack us, but for Jesus, because the stakes were greater and His identity divine, His challenge was greater than ours.

I appreciate Jesus' ability to identify with my struggles. I could have no confidence in Him as Savior, if unlike Jacob, He didn't have to struggle for the blessing, and just as Jacob left with a limp, Jesus left with nail scarred hands and feet. He is my partner!

Prayer—"God, thank you for partnering in my salvation; your presence is my confidence."

FEBRUARY 18

Hebrews 4:16—"Let us then approach the throne of grace with confidence, so that we may receive mercy and find grace to help us in our time of need." (NIV)

We've already seen from this passage that Jesus is our priest and partner, but our author also suggests that Jesus is our 'pathway' as well. It's based on Heb. 4:14 referring to Jesus going "through the heavens", after satisfying God's demand for justice for our sins (Rom. 6:23). Because Christ has accomplished this, every believer now has direct and open access to God as a result.

What is it access to? The "throne of grace." Grace is the unmerited favor of God; therefore, getting to God is not an earned privilege, but a right to every believer who rests his/her faith on Christ as the ultimate answer to God's requirements.

Yet, even more than Christ as our pathway to God, is the confidence we can go with as we approach God. We don't have to cower in the presence of God like Adam and Eve did (Gen.3:8); our God is also our Father, who like a loving parent, understands our faults and failures, and has made provisions for us through His Son, Jesus Christ. You are a child of the King, and like the Prodigal Son, your place is not among the "hired servants", but at the table with the King. As an 'heir' of the Father, claim your blessing today!

Prayer—"Dear Lord, thank you for an open road to your throne; thank you for your Son, Jesus Christ."

FEBRUARY 19

John 8:12—"... Jesus ... said, 'I am the light of the world' ...."
(NIV)

This is one of the "I am" statements of Jesus in John's gospel (true vine, bread of life, good shepherd, resurrection and the life). All these "I am" declarations of Jesus refer to Him embodying or fulfilling aspects of the kingdom of God. This means that in Christ, we find fullness of revelation (truth) about the work of God in our world.

Light is of course, a great part of our daily experience as well as a symbol of Jesus' meaning to every Christian believer. According to Genesis, light was God's first creation and God is referred to as a light in Ps. 27:1, as well as His word in Ps. 119:105. John the Evangelist, called Jesus a light in Jn. 1:4-5, to show Jesus as the embodiment of all that can be humanly known about God. John's point was that truth was not what Jesus said or did, but who He was.

When you come to know Jesus as the light of the world, then you will find the resource to help you distinguish between truth and error and know unequivocally that your ability to make that distinction rests solely on an intimate, committed relationship with Him. If you are searching for truth (light), His example is the answer. Walk in the light.

Prayer—"Dear God, illumine my path with your presence; show me the ways of your Son that I may follow Him."

FEBRUARY 20

Psalms 119:133—"Direct my steps by your Word, and let no iniquity have dominion over me." (NIV)

I've always thought it interesting that people who have had addictions in the past do not refer to themselves as ex-addicts, but as 'recovering' addicts, even if they've been 'clean' for ten years. It obviously is because addicts recognize the need to 'maintain' the recovery by practicing certain habits on a daily basis, because of the very real possibility of relapse. This means that recovery is only established by maintaining a consistent pattern or approach.

Psalm 119:133 says it is extremely important for every believer to be directed by the Word of God, for the purpose of maintaining daily victory over challenging circumstances. The word 'direct' in this verse literally means 'establish', implying the need to consistently seek God's direction, so no relapses (backsliding) take place in our walk with God. Earlier, I mentioned the word 'pattern'. Think of each day as a recipe and how your result always depends on following the recipe to the letter, so your result is the same. That's what this verse challenges us to do; to allow God's word to be our recipe for success each day, insuring that God's will is done in us, as it is in Heaven.

Prayer—"Father, direct my steps in your purpose for me and lead me in a 'plain' path."

FEBRUARY 21

Psalms 119:133—"Direct my steps by your Word, and let no iniquity have dominion over me." (NIV)

How about another look at this verse? The Psalmist here links obedience with victory, meaning when God's word is observed and obeyed, the inevitable result is victory. In Matt. 7:24-27, Jesus relates the parable of two men, who through diligence or the lack of it, experience defeat or victory. He then likened the man whose house remained standing through the conflict, to a man who esteems or values the Word of God. Jesus' own life was a testament to that principle and because He was obedient to the Father's will throughout His earthly life, He experienced the victory of the resurrection and a "name above every other name" (Phil.2:9). Obviously, the obedient life and the victorious life go hand in hand.

Obedience inevitably leads to victory because obedience creates an environment conducive to God manifesting His power. What happens when you pepper spray a room full of people? Everyone is affected by the environmental change; they begin to choke and cough without exception. That's what obedience does for every believer; it creates an environment that cannot help but 'choke' your challenges and provides ultimate victory. Why not obey the Lord today by doing His will for you?

Prayer—"Dear God, help me be obedient to your will and show others the blessings that follow."

FEBRUARY 22

Psalms 119:133—"Direct my steps by your Word, and let no iniquity have dominion over me." (NIV)

This verse is as much about power, as it is about pattern. The word 'by' in this verse implies not only that the word offers us a pattern for living and victory, but that the word also has an inherent power to help us apply that pattern. That then means that obedience to the word generates power from the word. I'm sure you'd agree with me it's better to have not just a guidepost, but a guide as well. God's word will not only show you where to go, but take you there as well on the strength of God's authority. God promised us an unfailing word (Matt. 24:35).

How can God's word be so reliable? I believe it's because Genesis 1 reveals no difference between God's words and His works; that His words are deeds and vice-versa. Remember, in Genesis, God said "Let there be . . .", and everything He declared came to pass, just because He "said so". God's word shows me the path and gives me power to stay in it, if I obey that word. Where Matthew 24:35 says, "Heaven and Earth will pass away, but my words . . ." is our "money-back guarantee" on the reliability of God's word. Let this word for today be your guide and goal, and watch God work in your life.

Prayer—"Father, open your power for living to me as I obey your Word."

FEBRUARY 23

Ephesians 3:20—"Now to Him who is able to do immeasurably more than all we ask or imagine . . ." (NIV)

Several years ago, I was waiting at the airport to fly to Ohio. While at the gate, I ran into an old college friend who happened to work for the airline I was flying on. We talked for almost half an hour reminiscing and catching up on the years since we'd lost touch. After exchanging phone numbers, we said goodbye and I prepared to board my flight, but I discovered a change in my seat assignment. My college friend had moved me from coach to first class! It was his way of saying how glad he was to see me again, and a blessing I had done nothing to earn or merit.

I can't tell you how many times my relationship with God has produced more than I expected, and more than I deserved. My life, as with all believers, is an ongoing experience of grace. God keeps moving me from coach to "first class" not because I'm deserving, but because I've embraced His Son as my Savior and seek to stay focused on His example. What a God we serve; who blesses us with favor and forgives us freely through His Son! I'm riding in "first class", because I'm a child of the King!

Prayer—"Lord, thank you for grace, and thank you for the gift of your Son as my Savior."

FEBRUARY 24

I Samuel 16:7—" . . . Man looks at the outward appearance, but the Lord looks at the heart." (NIV)

A mother once told her son repeatedly to sit down. Steadfastly, the boy refused her command. Finally, the mother physically forced her son into a chair and told the boy not to move. The son looked at his mother and replied, "Mother, I may be sittin' down on the outside, but I'm standin' up on the inside!" How like all of us this boy is; to do the things we do, but with the desire to do the opposite. God is not always impressed with what we do, because He knows sometimes our actions are not consistent with our attitude.

Perhaps it is easy to do what is right or politically correct, even when we are insincere, because we feel no one knows, but this verse reminds us that God does, even if He's invisible to us. This verse is not only a description of how God chooses a King, but also a warning to those who believe they can take advantage of life. I don't believe God wants to scare us into righteousness, but I do think God expects respect for who He is and a heart that wants to do the right thing based on His grace and mercy. I'm glad He's both judge and father.

Prayer—"Dear God, remind me of your intimate knowledge of me, and help me live a life which pleases you."

FEBRUARY 25

Luke 8:8—"... He, who has ears to hear, let him hear." (NIV)

Luke 8:14-21 contains the parable of the sower and its explanation. The parable does not focus on the sower (preacher) or seed (word of God), but on the soil (hearers). This is important because in the parable, Jesus uses the word 'hear' nine times to indicate the importance of hearing in the process of successful living. Why is hearing important? It's important, because by it we 'receive' God's word.

There are several live plants in my office. I can always tell when they are in need of water because their leaves droop. After I've watered them, some two or three hours later, the leaves reflect the evidence of the moisture they've received by standing up or out. This means that what was given (water) has been received and absorbed. That's exactly what God desires and expects from us when He speaks, whether it's through His word or our experiences; God expects us to receive His word through attentiveness and to show the evidence of its absorption through practical application. Further, the application of God's word in our example is a manifestation of the life of God in us for the benefit of others, who are searching for answers. This is an expression of faith, which reminds us that "faith comes by 'hearing' and 'hearing' by the word of God." (Rom. 10:17) Open your ears!

Prayer—"Dear God, speak to me, but help me also to tune you in and do your will."

FEBRUARY 26

Luke 8:11—". . . the seed is the Word of God." (NIV)

Again in this chapter, Jesus tells the parable of the sower, seed, and soils with the emphasis on the soils, which represents those who hear God's word. Jesus places major emphasis on hearing in this passage, because of the importance of the seed (word of God). Because the word is seed, it implies that God's word contains life in it which goes untapped until that word is planted. Once the word of God is planted in someone's spirit and is heard, understood and received, that word produces 'fruit' (clear evidence), which manifests itself in relationships and reactions. Just as a seed cannot release its life until it's buried in the soil and is surrounded by the properties which activate that life, so is the word, which must be planted (heard) in our spirits and surrounded by circumstances, which activate/release its benefits.

This is the reason it's so important to listen today. God speaks in varied ways, which requires that we fine tune our spirits by prayer and meditation. Prayer, because it's our two-way exchange with God and meditation because it produces a conducive atmosphere for processing (thinking) God's answers when we pray. Begin this day with a heart open to hear and receive God and watch Him produce fruit unto righteousness in you.

Prayer—"Father, I open my heart to receive you; plant your desires for me in my spirit now."

FEBRUARY 27

Luke 8:5-8—"A farmer went out to sow seed... some fell along the path... some fell on rock... other seed fell among thorns... still other seed fell on good soil."(NIV)

I hope you're not tired of this passage yet. It's so rich with truth. It's interesting that Jesus implies that only 25% of hearers actually bear fruit. Obviously, God expects more from churchgoers than regular attendance at worship celebrations; He expects some manifestation of growth in believers. Since we've already concluded from this chapter that God's word is seed, it's obvious that seed does not produce fruit if it's not 'cultivated' after it's buried in the soil.

The plants in my office require regular attention (cultivation) to maintain their life and appearance. The same is true of my relationship to the word of God; its fruit in me depends on regular attention to what God has said, and what God meant when He said it. That's why the psalmist referred to meditating on what God has said "day and night" (Ps. 1:2). It is the constant attention to God's desires for me that creates a "new person" who no longer walks, stands, or sits in the wrong places (Ps.1:1), but takes residence in God's word. It's that person committed to God's word, who finds the fruit of faithfulness, and the joy of living which the world cannot diminish.

Prayer—"Dear God, I seek to cultivate your word in me that my life might be a harvest of holiness."

FEBRUARY 28

Luke 8:19—"... consider carefully how you listen ..." (NIV)

Christ calls upon us not just to hear, but to take care 'how' we hear. Why? Because how we receive anything determines our ability to use it successfully later. The fact is, God's word is a light and lamp (Ps. 119:105), and anything which illuminates is meant to be shared with others, but if we are careless in how we handle (receive) God's word, sharing it effectively will be impossible.

The five foolish virgins in Matt. 25:1-13 were careless in their handling of preparations for a marriage celebration, and as a result they were barred from the festivities. They had the appropriate capacity (lamp), without an adequate condition (oil). That's a dangerous state to be in if you intend to do anything worthwhile for God's kingdom.

'How' we hear is important because God gives for the purpose of empowering us to give. God is by nature giving, because Jn. 3:16 says so; "... so loved, that He gave ..."; so if God gives so that we can, then how we hear will determine whether we fulfill God's aspirations for us and His word. What's the best answer to the 'how' of hearing? Be prayerful and open at all times, so we may be effective channels of God's grace and His gospel.

Prayer—"Dear Lord, be in my mind and my hearing; direct my thoughts and sanctify my ears."

MARCH 1

Luke 8:8—"... he who has ears to hear, let him hear."(NIV)

The 'how' and the 'what' of hearing are important, but so is the 'why'. Christ calls us to hear Him, because He wants to draw us into a relationship with Him. It's not just about hearing and doing what He says, but valuing Him and His words so much that we follow Him out of love and reverence.

In coveting a relationship with God, when we hear Him, the result is the reproduction of His nature internally and the manifestation of that nature externally. As a child, I discovered my relationship with my parents to be at its best when I heard and obeyed them for no other reason than my love for them and trust in their guidance. When the Prodigal (Lk. 15:11-24) returned home and had a party thrown in his honor, it was because he was ready to love, honor, and obey his father. When God expressed His good pleasure with His son, Jesus Christ (Matt. 3:17; 17:5), it was the result of Jesus loving, honoring, and obeying His Father.

How valuable is your relationship with God? Enough to make Him and His will a priority? Remember, if you truly love God, hearing and doing His will is sometimes a challenge, but it's never a chore.

Prayer—"Father, I love you and your word, and your will is my highest priority."

MARCH 2

Romans 12:1—"... offer your bodies as living sacrifices."(NIV)

One of the truths I try to never forget, is when giving or offering anything to God, I must always keep in mind the principle which suggests that the object of our gifts really determines and defines the nature of our gifts. That is to say, when giving anything to God I must bear in mind the gift God would appreciate most.

This verse suggests that what God appreciates most as a gift is not our substance, but we ourselves, and that the thought behind the gift is what God most pays attention to. Obviously then, God wants worship rather than gestures because worship is most often internal at its root while gestures have the potential of being purely external. God wants acts from us which are not ritualistic, but an outgrowth of our consciousness of who He is and what He's done; acts which aren't done for recognition, but like rain clouds, so full, that we cannot contain ourselves in response to Him.

God deserves and expects the best I have, which is me, and I've determined based on His many mercies and blessings to give Him unreserved praise today. How about you?

Prayer—"Dear Lord, I offer myself to you today; knowing your purpose for me is my highest achievement."

MARCH 3

Romans 12:1—" . . . offer your bodies as living sacrifices . . ." (NIV)

In 1998, the congregation I lead moved into a new facility. Since it was a pre-existing church building some modifications were necessary to accommodate our needs. One of those modifications was the location of my office space. I chose an area which had formerly been used for teaching nursery age children. The space is large, but of course needed major changes to facilitate my needs. I outlined my desires and our fellowship proceeded to fulfill my requests, so I'd be comfortable doing my day to day office work. The point is, the area I chose, formerly used for something else was set apart for my use and desires.

That's what Paul refers to in Rom. 12:1, as he commends the offering of our bodies to God. It implies a complete renovation of the person who now is set apart for God's use and desires. As a "set apart" person in God's kingdom, the context of your body's involvement has changed, because you now belong to God through the redemption of the blood of Christ. So from the point you acknowledge Jesus Christ as Lord, the way you use your body must reflect your knowledge of God as your owner and everything you do with your body must be pleasing to Him. So what will you do with your body today?

Prayer—"Dear God, help me dedicate my body to your service and keep me in the path of righteousness."

MARCH 4

Romans 12:1—". . . present your bodies a living sacrifice, holy, acceptable unto God . . ." (KJV)

God's desire is that we present ourselves to Him. Paul here says if we present ourselves as living sacrifices to Him, it is a holy and 'acceptable' offering. Let's concentrate on the word 'acceptable' today.

Not long ago there was a vacant house in my neighborhood. The length of its vacancy produced a number of problems, both internally and externally. Outside the house, the grass and shrubbery was overgrown, the roof shingles needed replacing, the window trim needed painting, and some of the siding needed replacing. Of course, all these problems presented aesthetic problems and affected property values in the community. After some time though, I passed by the house and noticed the grass, shrubs, roof, trim, and siding had all been taken care of. It was all the result of someone taking ownership of the house and when they moved in the external problems were eliminated; the house had become 'acceptable'.

That's why Paul says a living sacrifice is acceptable to God; it's because when God takes possession of someone internally, their external presentation (offering) to God pleases God, because it originates with a mind and heart under God's control. With my status of acceptability to God (because of Christ), I'm free to fulfill my potential in the security of God's satisfaction. Today is going to be a great day!

Prayer—"Father, thank you for your acceptance of me, and thank you for your Son, who makes it possible."

MARCH 5

Romans 12:1—"... present your bodies a living sacrifice, holy, acceptable ... which is your reasonable service." (KJV)

The church, at which I serve, Providence Baptist Church, had as its focus for 2004 'excellence'. We adopted that as our goal because we believe God expects and accepts nothing more, nothing less, and nothing else. The same is true of most of us in our earthly relationships, whether family or business related; there are some things we find simply unacceptable and we have no problem expressing our displeasure and expecting more.

Paul says in Rom. 12:1 that God deserves an acceptable sacrifice and he characterizes it as a presentation of our 'bodies' to God. The root of our acceptability to God is in fact, Jesus Christ. Why? Because God looks at believers 'through' His Son and when He does that God sees a cross and an empty grave and knows that we are acquitted of charges that we're really guilty of. This means that God sees us in the light of what Jesus Christ has accomplished for us. Therefore, we are acceptable to the Father, because He's well-pleased with His Son. So every time I kneel to pray and feel the confidence of God's presence and listening ear, I can thank God for Jesus, who died for my sins, rose for my eternal benefit, and provides me with unrestricted access to God. I'm acceptable because Christ Jesus is!

Prayer—"Dear God, I thank you for accepting me and for making it possible through your only begotten Son."

MARCH 6

Romans 12:1—"... present your bodies a living sacrifice ... which is your reasonable service." (KJV)

I've always looked with bemusement at young boys who wear their pants well below their waists. For me, it's not a moral or fashion issue, it's practical. I don't understand how it's possible to do anything hurriedly and be effective if you have to use one hand to hold your pants up. To me, that's impractical and irrational; it's not a 'reasoned' approach to a common experience.

Paul says in Rom. 12:1, that the offering of ourselves to God is "reasonable worship". He means this sacrifice of the self to God is a reasoned or reasonable act; that it's done as the result of thought and consideration. What should I consider? God's love for me, expressed in His daily provision and protection, as well as the giving of His Son for my redemption. That's not all though. I'm also the beneficiary of the Spirit of God, who helps me maintain my walk with God by enlightening my mind and activating my memory (Jn. 14:26). All these factors when considered, make me want to give God my best, because He's so worthy of it. A songwriter wrote, "When I think of the goodness of Jesus and all He's done for me, my soul cries out Hallelujah, thank God for saving me!" It just makes sense to give God your best.

Prayer—"Father, remind me of your goodness, so I may give you my all, in joy and gratitude."

MARCH 7

Romans 12:2—"Do not conform any longer to the pattern of this world, but be transformed by the renewing of your mind." (NIV)

A tune-up is defined as, "a regular maintenance, usually associated with the replacement and adjustment of parts and components in the electrical and fuel systems of a vehicle for the purpose of attaining optimum performance." Romans 12:1 suggests that we offer our bodies to God as living sacrifices; Paul calls for a decisive commitment on our part in vs.1, but it's vs. 2 that tells us how to 'maintain' that commitment, or keep ourselves 'tuned-up' to insure we offer ourselves to God consistently at the optimum level.

The key is, understanding we live in a challenging environment; one that wears and tears on us spiritually, requiring that we have a process which can restore us to our best, so God receives the best we have to offer. Romans 12:1 is the vehicle by which we offer (our bodies) and vs. 2 is the tune-up (renewed mind) that keeps the vehicle at its optimum performance. Paul calls upon our minds, renewed by God, to direct our acts of giving, so that God's kingdom is advanced, His will done, and His Son magnified. It all begins with the mind. Why not begin to 'think' on these things as you begin your day?

Prayer—"Dear God, be in my mind and direct my thoughts anew. Use me as your instrument."

MARCH 8

Romans 12:2—"Do not confirm any longer to the pattern of this world, but be transformed by the renewing of your mind." (NIV)

Let's go back today to 'maintaining' our self offering to God. Paul in Rom. 12:2 says it begins with observing the pattern of the world we're living in. Relaxed standards, the absence of genuine love, and the disregard for other's lives and property are part of the current state of affairs. We must be not only sensitive to the presence of that standard, but sensitive to its influence as well and not fall prey to its appeal. The word 'conform' in this verse is written in a tense which implies a continuous action, obviously recognizing the rising influence of a declining standard of living.

If we are to avoid conforming to the 'pattern' of the world, or current age, it is important to see the natural world through spiritual eyes. In Jn. 4, Jesus was able to minister to a Samaritan woman of questionable lifestyle, because He saw her through spiritual eyes; He looked beyond what she was, to what she could be. Jesus knew she had multiple marriages and a less than desirable domestic condition, but He saw what she could be if influenced by the Spirit. We must do the same to maintain a spiritual standard; we must look beyond the current state of things and remind ourselves we are citizens of a greater kingdom and not give in or become discouraged by what seems to be an endless cycle. Our inheritance is spiritual and God's promise of it is guaranteed. So hang in there and trust God's plan for you today.

Prayer—"Heavenly Father, I need to walk the path which pleases you and I need your constant presence to do it."

MARCH 9

Romans 12:2—"And be not conformed to this world, but be ye transformed by the renewing of your mind . . ." (NIV)

To be 'conformed' is to be boxed in by a standard that never allows your fulfillment; it is to never reach beyond the boundaries of your human nature and never experience the untapped possibilities of your deeper consciousness. It's somewhat like beginning a job at entry level with no possibility of advancement. I've met few people who are content with entry level; most folks I know at least have the desire to move up. That's what 'transformed' means in this verse. It is to be born anew through Jesus Christ, break out of the entry level nature received at birth and experience a whole new world of possibilities. This new birth produces the 'inherited' nature of the one who gives us life, namely, Jesus Christ.

I learned recently that the difference between a newspaper cartoon and television cartoon is animation. The 'animator' takes what you see in the newspaper and gives it life by drawing the character in various positions of incremental movement. When those positions are run rapidly, they give the image of unbroken movement. The spiritual point I'm making is the 'funnies' is not the best you can do; that's being conformed. To be transformed is to be animated by the Spirit of God, through Jesus Christ and experience fullness of life through His presence and power. Walk in His life today.

Prayer—"Dear Lord, make me alive through your presence, and use my example as a blessing to others."

MARCH 10

John 17:16, 18—"They are not of the world, even as I am not of it . . . . I have sent them into the world." (NIV)

Recently, I was online at my computer and happened to notice a website which offered wetsuits to individuals who participate in rescue missions involving icy waters. The company guaranteed their suits against seepage and chill, which would allow a diver to be submerged for extended periods of time without fear of hypothermia. Think of that principle; to endure an unnatural environment successfully because you're protected by something which covers you.

Our text for the day suggests that disciples of Christ are in the world, but not of it. The problem with believers is so often they concentrate on the "not of", while paying no attention to the 'in' of our discipleship. It is possible for Christians to be so heavenly minded they are no earthly good. When Jesus says we are not of the world, it's not a call to neglect or ignore where we are, but to apply the benefits of the spirit world to the conditions of the natural world. Jesus did just that. He fully invested Himself in the human experience and was successful, because He maintained His focus on His purpose and identity. That was His 'wetsuit'. You and I have the same protection, so there's no need to fear being active in our world. Because of Christ and the Spirit, we are the salt of the earth and the light of the world.

Prayer—"Father, remind me of your protection and provision as I face today's challenges."

MARCH 11

Mark 2:14—"And as He passed by . . ." (KJV)

I learned recently that the word "opportunity" is rooted in the Latin phrase, 'ob portu', which refers to ships relying on the flood tide to bring them into harbor before the days of modern ports. Spiritually speaking, it means that our opportunities as Christians are where the flood tide of God's favor and grace seek to bring us into the port of God's purpose.

Mark 2:14 was an opportunity for Matthew to become a disciple for Christ. It happened as Jesus "passed by". The truth about opportunity is it must be joined to wisdom so its potential can be maximized, otherwise it becomes an unpleasant memory and a wasted chance. Too many people play roulette with life, accepting what life gives without engaging God, who has placed blessings along the path of life to provide us with certain guarantees. This means that there is a recipe for life and every recipe, when followed, has a guaranteed result. Remember that Matt. 6:33 reminds us to seek God's kingdom as a priority and that God in response will supply our needs. This means that every opportunity for the Christian is a call to trust God unreservedly and watch God do the rest.

Prayer—"Dear God, help me take advantage of my opportunities with faith and wisdom."

MARCH 12

Mark 10:47—"When he heard that it was Jesus of Nazareth, he began to shout, Jesus, Son of David, have mercy on me!" (NIV)

This verse refers to a blind man, named Bartimaeus, who responded to Jesus' presence because he 'heard' Jesus was passing by. He could not 'see', but he did respond to something he 'heard'. That's important, because it means that we mustn't shut the whole program down just because a perceived important component is missing. Bartimaeus did not allow his lack of sight to keep him from hearing that his opportunity for healing was near. The absence of one ingredient does not mean you can't fulfill your potential, or do God's will for you.

For believers, just like show business, "the show must go on". Why? Because opportunities and possibilities are not lost to us just because a person or product is missing; our God, who spoke the created order into existence, is still willing to, and capable of, speaking our harvest, even if we thought we lacked the seed! Remember what happened in Jn. 6? The people had spent all day with Jesus and at the end of the day, when the disciples questioned their ability to feed the crowd, Jesus said, "the show must go on". So Jesus took a lad's lunch and fed the multitude and still had leftovers when He was done! Wherever you are today at this moment in your life, don't shut down the program, because God's got your plan in place!

Prayer—"Father, make me sensitive to all the ways you speak, so I may fulfill each day's purpose."

MARCH 13

Mark 10:47—"When he heard that it was Jesus of Nazareth, he began to shout, Jesus, Son of David, have mercy on me!"(NIV)

In Mark 10 a blind man named Bartimaeus had an encounter with Jesus. After hearing in vs. 47 that Jesus of Nazareth was passing by, Bartimaeus referred to Jesus as the "Son of David". By doing so, Bartimaeus was attributing to Jesus more than had been referred to when he heard Jesus was passing by. That means Bartimaeus' reference to Jesus was an 'upgrade'. Bartimaeus saw in Jesus the fulfillment of God's promise to Israel and David concerning the "anointed one" or 'messiah'; the one who would bring to pass the purpose of God for His people.

Most people would love to upgrade when they travel, because the benefits are greater. When you upgrade from coach to first class on a flight, certain benefits are part of that upgrade. First, you sit closer to the pilot; secondly, you get more individual attention; then, service items are of greater quality, and finally, before September 11, 2001 there was a curtain that divided you from the coach passengers. Those same principles apply to us when we upgrade Jesus Christ from prophet to savior; we gain proximity, personal attention, greater provision, and divine protection. Bartimaeus' simple reference of faith positioned him for a great blessing. What do you give God, simple respect or reverence?

Prayer—"God, remind me of who you are and whose I am, so I may walk where you lead."

MARCH 14

Mark 10:47—"When he heard that it was Jesus of Nazareth, he began to shout, Jesus, Son of David, have mercy on me!"(NIV)

We discovered yesterday that Bartimaeus upgraded Jesus when he called him, "Son of David", but vs. 48 of Mark 10, says that the blessing from your upgrade does not come easy. Many in the crowd that day tried to stifle Bartimaeus' plea. The principle is, you never meet stiff opposition in life until you try to turn your life around and upgrade your circumstance. Even sadder is the reality that sometimes Christians get in the way of seekers for Christ, because Mk. 9:38-41 and Mk. 10:13-16 both contain episodes where Jesus' own disciples sought to hinder other's blessings.

So then, we who love God, and seek His path must constantly remind ourselves of the potential of opposition both from without and within the church. No real blessing is ever easy to come by; the leper in Mk. 1, Jairus and the bleeding woman in Mk. 5, all testify to the burden which precedes our blessing. They also remind us though, of the need to persevere like the Sockeye salmon of Ontario, Canada. The Sockeye swims upstream to the Sauble River each year to spawn and lay eggs, in spite of the odds against it. Why is that upstream swim so important? Because the spawning ground is where new life takes begins! Perhaps you're going against the flow today for your blessing, but hang in there, because there's life on the other side.

Prayer—"Heavenly Father, give me your strength as I meet the challenge of achieving your purpose."

MARCH 15

Luke 4:1, 2—"And Jesus being full of the Holy Ghost returned from Jordan, and was led by the Spirit into the wilderness, being forty days tempted of the devil . . ." (KJV)

Tests are neither bad nor unique, especially as it relates to Christians. Actually, tests are beneficial to believers because they reveal things about us we would not know otherwise; they are the means by which we assess ourselves and determine whether life and God have taught us needed lessons.

There are several universal principles applicable to the testing experience. The first is that we generally are not given a test without having first been prepared or trained for it. Secondly, tests never include questions that we are unfamiliar with. Then, none of us are ever tested at a level beyond our experience. Additionally, we can be sure that whoever administers the test, knows all the answers. Finally, we are never tested until it's time to move on.

In Luke 4, Jesus was tested by the adversary for forty days and nights, but the issue was not the tests, but His response to them that was important. What God wants us to do when our tests come is to avoid the frustration that causes us to take matters into our own hands and rest our faith in Him, while looking for His providence and His purpose.

Prayer—"Dear God, I know tests are a part of the fabric of life; give me strength and direct my thoughts."

MARCH 16

Luke 4:1—"And Jesus being full of the Holy Ghost . . ." (KJV)

Let's continue with this examination of tests in the life of a Christian. Lk. 4 contains the testing of Jesus in the wilderness. Verse 1 says that Jesus entered that experience 'full' of the Holy Spirit. The implication is that He was fully 'equipped' for whatever confronted Him in the wilderness, because He was 'totally' under the Spirit's control. 'Full' is the operative word here. I've always enjoyed the 'Batman' movies because Batman carries a utility belt which equips him for any of his enemy's tricks. Batman is an ordinary human, but able to confront his enemies because he never goes out unprepared. What a lesson for us today. We are just human beings, but we don't have to go out unprepared; we can face each day in the power of God's Spirit, feeling fully confident in His presence and power.

When Jesus went into the wilderness, it was after the baptism at Jordan, when God affirmed Jesus as His beloved Son. So Jesus left the place of refreshment, going immediately into the place of barrenness, but doing so equipped by the Spirit. When we have the Spirit's anointing, we should never be intimated by any circumstance. Recently, I was driving in a heavy thunderstorm. I felt a sense of confidence though, because although I had to go through the storm, I was in a protected environment. That's what the Spirit promises and will do for you today.

Prayer—"Heavenly Father, fill me with your Spirit and direct the choices I make today."

MARCH 17

Luke 4:1, 2—"Jesus, full of the Holy Spirit, returned from the Jordan and was led by the Spirit in the desert, where for forty days He was tempted by the devil . . ." (NIV)

Let's stay with this text a few more days. It is significant that Jesus was full of the Spirit, and therefore, led by the Spirit. It suggests that Jesus' conflict in the wilderness was initiated by the Spirit and not by the adversary. Jesus was not dragged into this experience kicking and screaming, but confident in the anointing of the Holy Spirit to 'confront' Satan in the place of testing. That's what the Spirit's presence does; He emboldens us as we confront our challenges. I remember seeing a friend quench a lit match with his fingers. The key was, he wet his fingers beforehand so the moisture would absorb the heat and act as a buffer between his fingers and the fire. That's what the Holy Spirit does for us; He gives us confidence through His capacity to absorb the heat of our fiery trials.

The boldness which comes from the Spirit is a 'mind' thing. It is the result of a 'renewed' mind (Rom. 12:2). This means God's Spirit helps us see things as they really are, so nothing ever appears bigger to us than God. It requires that we both know scripture and apply scripture to see its benefits manifested. We must consistently repeat scriptural truths to ourselves to see their benefit. As you begin your day, why not say to yourself, "I can do all things through Christ which strengtheneth me" (KJV).

Prayer—"Dear God, make me bold through your presence, and ready me for today's challenges."

MARCH 18

Luke 4:2—"... forty days tempted of the devil. And in those days He did eat nothing; and when they were ended, He afterward hungered." (KJV)

This passage, as with all scriptures, is a treasure trove of inspiration. Today, note that in the direst of settings, Jesus deprived Himself physically while being tested by the adversary. This was a test of the physical and spiritual natures of Jesus, but the most important aspect of the test was spiritual. Why? Because the Spirit has the capacity to sustain the body. Jesus was able to deprive His body, because spiritually, He trusted His father to provide.

Our only question then is, is that enough? To answer that question, think of the very first words of the bible. They read, "In the beginning God . . .", which suggests that at some point, all there was, was God. From that point though, things began to happen, because if all there is, is God, you have the foundation for 'creative' answers to all your questions. So Jesus faced physical deprivation and Satan's tests in the power of the Spirit and it was enough! I'm a fan of the 90's television show, 'MacGyver'. The reason I'm a fan is because MacGyver can handle any conflict using what appears to be unusable: he can use milk chocolate to stop an acid leak, or a paper clip to disarm a missile. He's creative in a conflict. That's what God's Spirit does for us; He provides resources in seemingly hopeless circumstances, because with God, all things are possible!

Prayer—"Father, show me your sufficiency in all things and increase my faith."

MARCH 19

Luke 4:1—"Jesus, full of the Holy Spirit . . ." (NIV)

I guess it's a little repetitive to come back to the word 'full', but I can't help it. I find in that one word the solution to our daily battles and this is a daily devotional isn't it? I cannot stress enough the importance of equipping ourselves for this ongoing warfare in which we are engaged. I find it extremely helpful to have a toolbox in my garage for those minor home repairs that come up occasionally. That toolbox equips me for responsibilities in my home without having to step beyond my own resources. Yet, there are times when what I need is beyond my capabilities and someone must be called in to do that job. It's like that in my relationship with God; some things He's equipped me to do, but sometimes I must reach outside myself and be full of His Spirit if I am to succeed.

I drive with a different mindset when my gas tank is full compared to when it's almost empty. The difference is a full tank allows you to focus your thoughts where they should be; you're not worried about having enough gas to get to the next station. That's why it's important to be full of the Spirit. Consciousness of His presence will not allow you to worry about problems which are already solved. So as you begin your day, don't forget to ask God to fill 'er up!

Prayer—"Dear God, fill my life with your Spirit and my thoughts with your guidance; empower me for today's journey."

MARCH 20

Luke 4:2—"Being forty days tempted of the devil." (KJV)

Jesus spent forty days in the desert being tested before He began His public ministry. On the surface, the individual temptations Jesus experienced appear to be appeals to His pride and physical hunger, but they were in reality much deeper. These tests Jesus experienced were actually temptations to make choices without referencing the will of God. That's why Jesus referenced scripture in His response to each test.

The reality is every test a Christian faces is a temptation to make a choice without consulting and committing to God. Our adversary is aware of the battle between flesh and spirit and seeks to exploit that warfare to entice us to choose our own path without seeking God's guidance. The key is to understand that every offer Satan made to Jesus was hollow, because there are no shortcuts to the kind of success and security we seek. Every worthy goal has a difficult road attached to it, and the supreme example of that truth lies between the boundaries of Friday night and Sunday morning of Easter weekend. What are your desires, your aspirations? Whatever they are, there are tests along the way and your passing grade depends upon how closely you walk with God and follow His example.

Prayer—"Dear God, remind me of your incomparable resources as I begin another day."

MARCH 21

Luke 4:9, 10—"The devil led Him to Jerusalem . . . , he said, throw yourself down . . . for it is written . . ." (NIV)

It's not surprising that Satan used scripture to test Jesus is it? After all, Jesus had responded with scripture the two previous tests hadn't He? The reality is the adversary is as acquainted with scriptures as we are; probably more so. Obviously, it's not enough to 'know' scripture; it is more important that we can interpret correctly, so application can be made to our advantage. Sadly, too many people receive information, whether secular or sacred, without the skill or desire to interpret and apply it. Why was Jesus successful in this battle against Satan? Because He was acquainted with the words of scripture as well as their meaning.

How can you and I reach that level of maturity with God's word? By using the Psalmist's words in Ps. 1:2, delighting in God's word and meditating on it day and night. When study is coupled with the ministry of the Spirit, whose job it is to bless our minds and memories (Jn. 14:26), information leads to inspiration, inspiration produces interpretation, and interpretation leads to correct application. Before you begin your day, read Lk. 4: 1-13 again and ask God for understanding. God will not allow you to leave home without a blessing!

Prayer—"God, grant me understanding and the wisdom to apply it today."

MARCH 22

Psalm 90:1—"Lord, you have been our dwelling place throughout all generations." (NIV)

What is a home? It's an earthly picture of a heavenly reality. It's the place where we rest, refresh, reflect, and relate. This is in reality, what God means to us; He is our 'home', our dwelling place.

Psalm 90 is attributed to Moses, who in this verse is apparently not confused about the real source of his comfort and confidence. Moses knew his sense of security was not in a place, but a person; that relationships, not neighborhoods are the true basis of our fulfillment. This then means that God alone has the capacity to be all things to all people. What's interesting, yet profound, is that when Moses penned these words, Israel was in the wilderness, 40 years from settling in the Promised Land. What Moses was declaring then was, "Lord, although we haven't arrived yet in the land of promise, we acknowledge, that you have been our home, our dwelling place from the beginning." What does this mean for us? It means no matter where you are right now, or what you're doing, or how far you are from your goal, you can find rest and refreshment in the presence of God, who is our 'real' home.

Prayer—"Dear God, I find my rest in you; comfort me with your presence."

MARCH 23

Psalms 90:1—"Lord, you have been our dwelling place throughout all generations." (NIV)

Let's revisit this verse today. Moses says God has been our 'home' throughout 'all' generations. This verse additionally references God as a consistent provider for His people. Between Abraham and Moses there were six generations: Abraham, Isaac, Jacob, Levi, Kohath, Amram, and Moses. The one constant through all those generations was God. Why? Because between Abraham and Moses, so many mistakes and missteps were made and so many lies were told, but God, who maintains His covenant with His people, was steadfast and faithful. The implication of this verse is, while things change, God does not. In our lifetimes we experience death, loss, love, marriage, divorce, unemployment, and transition. These things are inherent in life, but what 'keeps' us through all these things is the knowledge that God is 'with' us.

Moses makes reference to all 'generations' in this verse. A generation is a revolution of time; a cycle made up of your birth, to the birth of your child. This means God is not seasonal, but same. That's the kind of consistency you and I need in a world of constant upheaval. As you begin your day, remember whatever life presents, God is your constant!

Prayer—"Father, thank you for your abiding presence; I find my peace in you."

MARCH 24

Matthew 16:17—"Jesus replied, blessed are you Simon, son of Jonah, for this was not revealed to you by man, but by my Father in Heaven." (NIV)

Jesus said in Jn. 10:4 that His sheep know His voice. Obviously, that means Christians are sensitive to the voice of their Savior; our spirits are fine-tuned to God's leading. This is important because even in Christian circles, there is a diversity of doctrine and believers must develop the requisite capacity to separate truth from error. That's why Christian education in the local church is of paramount importance and every believer should commit to receiving truth in that corporate setting.

In our devotional text for the day, Jesus commended Peter for having a spirit tuned into God. Jesus congratulated Peter for separating compliment from clarity. Peter knew that Jesus was more than a prophet; that He was in fact the Christ. Peter was tuned in! I have a piano in my living room, which I have 'tuned' on a regular basis. I do that because an untuned piano can play music, but the 'pitch' is off, which means it's not quite up to par. Every believer needs the tuning of consistent prayer, study, and meditation otherwise we're just a little off pitch as God's representatives, even though our intentions may be good. So stay tuned! God has a signal for you.

Prayer—"Heavenly Father, tune me into your word and will; help me be sensitive to your direction."

MARCH 25

Matthew 16:13—"When Jesus came to the region of Caesarea Philippi, He asked His disciples, who do people say the son of man is?" (NIV)

The setting of Jesus' question to His disciples is very interesting. Caesarea Philippi was a region heavily influenced by several ancient religions. Jesus posed His question to the disciples to determine if they could express spiritual clarity in the midst of religious competition. The fact is, none of us ever commits to God through Christ, without the voices of competing systems of belief calling out to us. That's why Jesus commended Peter in Matt. 16:17. Peter, while speaking for himself as well as the other disciples, expressed a clarity of discernment which led to identifying Jesus correctly.

Discernment is a needed strength for every Christian. In Lk. 8:45, when the bleeding woman touched Jesus' clothes, His response was "who touched me?" This reflected Jesus' ability to differentiate a voluntary touch from an involuntary one. Jesus needed discernment, and all of us do too, if we are to shut out the voices of unreliable philosophies and systems of thought. Today is a good day to pray for discernment.

Prayer—"God, open my mind, my thoughts; help me hear your voice and do your will."

MARCH 26

Matthew 16:19—"I will give you the keys of the kingdom of Heaven; whatever you bind on earth will be bound in Heaven . . ." (NIV)

I remember giving my son a set of keys to the house for the first time. Those keys were a symbol of authority, but also of trust. It was the result of feeling my son had grown enough to be trusted with that responsibility.

When Peter referred to Jesus as the Christ in Matt. 16:16, Jesus knew Peter was ready for more responsibility; that Peter could be trusted with a certain level of authority for God's kingdom. So Jesus gave Peter 'keys' to the kingdom. Jesus knew Peter was ready to use those keys, open doors and practice leadership and discipline. Jesus was saying in effect to Peter, "You've handled your previous responsibilities well enough to move to another level in this ministry." That's what every Christian should aspire to hear from God in his/her walk with God.

"Keys" are a part of a process, like going to the store alone for the first time, or driving alone for the first time. It's a matter of maturity and the trust which results from it, and drawing from another's guidance to carry out the assignment as if that person was with you. So how much is God willing to trust you with?

Prayer—"Heavenly Father, train me for service and grant me opportunities to fulfill your desires."

MARCH 27

Matthew 16:17—"Jesus replied, 'Blessed are you Simon, son of Jonah, for this was not revealed to you by man, but by my father in Heaven.'"(NIV)

I've learned many things in my lifetime, but the most important thing I've learned is that life's ultimate truths are always revelations from God; they are never lessons we learn on our own. That's why God must always be glorified. He positions us to receive truth and gives it to us through the vehicle of His Spirit. Peter, in Matt. 16, was commended for observing Jesus, trusting Him, and arriving at the spiritually sound conclusion that Jesus was the Christ. The process is unchanging. If truth is to be known, God must be acknowledged as its primary source.

The good thing is, God has organized life so that everything we need is already in place. God said as much in Gen. 1:28-29, when He told Adam and Eve they had everything they needed for their fulfillment. Since that is so, our only obligation is to take advantage of God's framework of life. God has made truth accessible, so we must be spiritually minded to discern it. Ultimately, this means life is a "set-up"; that God has already placed every needed resource for His creation in reachable locations. That's why I praise Him. God has set me up for victory and I'm walking in it each day!

Prayer—"Dear Lord, thank you for the availability of your resources; help me to access and use them wisely."

MARCH 28

Psalms 24:1—"The earth is the Lord's and the fullness thereof; the world and they that dwell therein."

Psalms 24:1 is important because it speaks directly to our stewardship of the planet by relating it to God's ownership of it. The implication is, we must treat the earth well, because she belongs to God. It's interesting that the Psalmist here does not refer to the sun, moon, and stars as belonging to God. I'm sure it's because the earth is the only mass in the universe where God's ownership must be asserted and reasserted. Obviously, our regular worship of God is a testimony to our need to be reminded of who our lives depend on. Without that reminder, we are prone to lose our spiritual focus and turn inward for help, rather than outward to God in prayer.

This verse declares that God created and sustains the world. Note that God did not just create the world and withdraw, but that the world and everything in it continues to depend on God for support and sustenance. That's important, because it means we have an ongoing resource for our daily experiences. Most major appliance purchases have a maintenance agreement. It means the manufacturer stands behind its product by maintaining an ongoing relationship with the product, even after the sale. Thank God, He loves us enough to provide a maintenance agreement on creation. Therein is my daily security.

Prayer—"God, owner of all things, help me use your resources according to your will."

MARCH 29

Psalms 24:1—"The earth is the Lord's and the fullness thereof; the world, and they that dwell therein." (KJV)

The Psalmist's claim of God's ownership in this verse has important implications for us. Sometimes, ownership is the result of conquest or domination; taking what formerly belonged to someone else. That's what kings and dictators have done, but this verse declares that God's ownership of the earth is based on creation, not conquest. The world and all that's in it belongs to God because they find their origination in the creative power of God.

This obviously means that everything in the created order not only owes its existence to God, but also, continues to rely on Him for its ongoing life and vitality. John 1:3 says it best; "Through Him all things were made; without Him nothing was made that has been made" (NIV). This means unequivocally that there is no existence for us apart from God, because there is no alternative to God. In Lk. 15, the Prodigal Son went home, because he realized what he needed could only be found in his father's house. That's why so many lives are filled with sporadic success; some have yet to settle the issue of an 'absolute' need for God. I can choose one from among a host of gas, electric, and phone service providers, when it comes to the house I live in, but when it comes to my life, there is no option for me, but God (Josh 24:15). I hope you carry that sense of need with you as you begin your day.

Prayer—"God, I need your abiding presence for my ongoing problems; stay by my side and comfort my heart."

MARCH 30

Psalms 24:1—"The earth is the Lord's and the fullness thereof; the world, and they that dwell therein." (KJV)

The word 'fullness' and the expression "they that dwell therein", are expansions on the words 'earth' and 'world' in this verse. They indicate that God is not just concerned about humans and their salvation, but also about 'everything' in the created order. Obviously then, the world is not fertile and fruitful for exploitation, which would imply our ownership, but for God's glory and honor, which implies our stewardship. God wants all things to be treated according to His word. In Ex. 23:12 and Lev. 25:4-5, God commanded that even the beasts of the field and the land also should have periods of rest. God is so concerned for all of His creation, that even in Gen. 7, when He flooded the earth, it was as much about cleansing the earth, as it was about punishing sin.

God cares for our planet and wants us to as well. What good does it do to consistently wash and wax a car without ever maintaining the engine? It is the most essential part of the vehicle. It is important to God that individuals and institutions not give priority to economics over ecology. We are all responsible for spiritual stewardship for a material world; it is the engine which drives our daily experiences.

Prayer—"Dear Lord, help me to see this world as yours and treat her with respect."

MARCH 31

Phil. 3:14—"I press toward the mark for the prize of the high calling of God in Christ Jesus." (NIV)

Life is a pilgrimage; a journey. There is a definite goal or end in mind, which means life is not a meaningless stroll, or vacation in which you return to your starting point; it's always seeking new levels of accomplishment. This is true in all aspects of living for the Christian and the Bible witnesses the same. When Jesus said He was about His "Father's business" (Lk. 2:49), and Abraham "looked for a city whose builder and maker is God" (Heb. 11:10), their examples were reminding us of how important it is to locate our marks and 'press' in that direction.

More importantly, once we realize life is a journey, we must identify the proper source of direction, otherwise it would be better just to leave the car parked. Today's verse identifies the value of the spiritual goal, as well as the source of direction for that goal. Paul says the value of the goal is significant because it's prized, due to its relationship to God; it's worth having because God has ordained and anointed His will for us as our highest aspiration. Secondly, our source of direction for that goal is Jesus Christ, who because of His sinless walk and matchless wisdom, is the best pattern for fulfilling God's purpose. All you need to follow Christ's example is contained within the Bible, so read it to be wise and apply it to be successful.

Prayer—"Heavenly Father, give me strength as I seek to reach my goals and fulfill your will."

APRIL 1

Genesis 50:20—". . . you meant evil against me; but God meant it for good . . ." (NKJ)

Joseph spoke these words to his brothers after the death of Jacob, in response to their fears of his retaliation following their cruelty to him decades earlier. Joseph's response to his brothers is interesting because it gives us a perspective on malicious actions against us. First, by malicious, I do not mean mistaken or unintentional harm, but intentional actions which target our reputations and relationships. In many of Jesus' encounters with the religious leaders of His day, His opponents were misguided, but still intentionally malicious toward Him after a certain point in His ministry. This is the attitude Joseph addresses in Gen. 50:20, and the spirit we need, to face similar conflicts.

What Joseph implies is the actions which are intended to harm God's children can ultimately help them. Obviously, God has the capacity to re-channel actions taken against us with evil intent; God doesn't have to dismiss or eliminate the act, just redirect the energy. Jesus used that principle of power in discipling Peter. He didn't change Peter's energy, just his focus and that made Peter a better disciple and successful apostle. I want to continue with this verse tomorrow, but in the meantime, take joy in God's presence and praise Him for His ability to take the worst and make it the best!

Prayer—"Dear God, thank you for your intercession in my life; you alone are my sword and shield."

APRIL 2

Genesis 50:20—"... you meant evil against me; but God meant it for good..." (NKJ)

Let's take another look at Joseph's words today. Yesterday, we discovered that God can take the negative energy exercised against you and redirect it for your benefit. The point was and is, that malicious actions are just energy on the wrong track, and our God is a master at converting the worst into the best.

What this means is, behind all events and human plans, lies the unchanging plan of God; that God truly works "all things together for good", for those who seek His will and acknowledge His call. With that in mind, I can approach each day with confidence knowing nothing's bigger than God, and He operates behind the scenes to insure an ultimate benefit for every one of my circumstances. This is an important truth because we can become discouraged by making the mistake of placing too much trust in friends and loved ones; that's a lateral confidence. We need a vertical faith if we expect an irreversible victory and only our "Father in Heaven" can insure that result. Remember, the Wizard of Oz was revealed to be only a man behind a curtain with no real power, but our God, who is from everlasting to everlasting has the resources to supply your every need.

Prayer—"Dear Lord, keep using my experiences to teach me about your sovereign power."

APRIL 3

John 16:33—"... in the world ye shall have tribulation: but be of good cheer; I have overcome the world."(KJV)

One of the things God wants us to understand as Christians is the ongoing availability of His power to assist us in every circumstance. Our failure then is never about God's unwillingness, unavailability or inability, but about our application of God's readily available resources. Isaiah 59:1 says God's arms are not too short to save and His ears not too dull to hear. Not long ago, my car wouldn't start and I began to suspect my battery was dead, or I had a bad alternator. When I lifted the hood I discovered my problem was corrosion on my battery terminals. That meant the power was available, but the 'connection' was hindered. Isn't that our problem so often? Jesus says He's already overcome the world, so the power's there, but our doubts or fears hinder our connection to His sufficiency.

The promise of Jn. 16:33, is that we can overcome problems and people because they've already been 'subdued' by Christ. All we need do is make application of His eternal victory. During my high school years, a number of teachers told me that I was a good student, but I didn't 'apply' myself; I didn't take advantage of inherent abilities. I've resolved as a Christian to never allow that to happen in my walk with God; He's got too much for me, to waste His blessings.

Prayer—"Dear God, help me take advantage of your presence in my life; remind me of your victory at the cross."

APRIL 4

Psalms 119:11—"Thy word have I hid in mine heart, that I might not sin against thee." (KJV)

This verse, and in fact the entire 119th Psalm, is a testimony to the value of God's word. In the mind of the Psalmist, God's word includes everything God has said, done and revealed in human history. Verse 11 implies the value of God's word is related to both the nature of the word itself and where the word is deposited. We will continue with this thought for a few days, but for today, let's concentrate on why God's word is so valuable.

First, the Psalmist here restricts this principle of 'hiding' to God's word alone. That means no one else's words deserve this kind of response. Why is that? Because only what God says has the capacity to unfailingly bless those who hear and heed God's word. The word 'hide' in this verse means 'reserve'. Note that reserving anything means to store for later use. Most people grocery shop with at least a week in mind. This means they buy food with the intent of reserving some of it for several days ahead. That's exactly the principle the Psalmist references here; he knows the word is valuable enough to reserve and employ at anytime in the future, because everything God's said is both timely and timeless. If God's word is 'reserved' in your heart, you have everything you need for the remainder of your day and remainder of your life.

Prayer—"Dear God, reserve your word in my heart, and order my steps accordingly."

APRIL 5

Psalms 119:11—"Thy word have I hid in mine heart, that I might not sin against thee." (KJV)

The Psalmist recommends we hide God's word in our hearts. That's important because this word 'heart' represents the center of our being; the seat of our emotions and will. Anything at the center is preeminent in its position, because everything else revolves around it. If the Word has such a place in your life, then wherever you are in your daily experience, because God's word is at your center, will keep you from straying what God says and what God wants. So the blessing of this verse is the constant proximity to God's word.

Our planet is the third in a row of nine planets which revolve around then sun. Because the sun is at the center of our solar system, it provides us with climate, seasons, warmth, energy and fertility. All this while keeping the earth in her place by its gravitational pull. Likewise, when God's word is at the center of one's spirit, it provides a multitude of benefits, whether it's employment, relationships, finance, wisdom or health. God's word provides all these blessings while keeping us spiritually gravitated toward God, so that our minds are "stayed on Him" (Isa. 26:3). As you begin your day treat His word like a credit card, "don't leave home without it."

Prayer—"Heavenly Father, help me center your word in my spirit, that my choices might revolve around your will."

APRIL 6

Psalms 119:11—"Thy word have I hid in mine heart, that I might not sin against thee." (KJV)

For the Christian, God's word is of supreme importance, because it's the believer's manual for life. That's why the Psalmist says he hides it in his heart. God's word is of inestimable value to him as it is to us today. In Ex. 25:10-16, God told Moses to have the Israelites construct a container for His word. That container made of premium wood and overlaid with gold, was called the Ark of the Covenant. The Ark, made of invaluable materials, represented its invaluable contents. That again is why the Psalmist hides the word in his heart; both the word and the heart are of supreme value to the individual.

The word of God is also of great value to us, because it's the only weapon God has placed in the hands of the Christian with both offense and defense in mind (Eph. 6:17). That's why Jesus' response to Satan's tests in Lk. 4:1-12, was always, "it is written". Jesus knew God's word was His only means of defeating the enemy. Without a doubt, the Ark of the Covenant finds a greater fulfillment in Jesus Christ. The wood represents Jesus' humanity and the gold His divinity. Jesus shows us what life is like when God's word truly lives within. Open your heart today to God's word.

Prayer—"Dear God, remind me of the 'value' of all you've said and done, that I might treasure your word."

APRIL 7

Psalms 119:11—"Thy word have I hid in mine heart, that I might not sin against thee." (KJV)

Let's finish our look at this verse today by looking at the 'purpose' for hiding the word in your heart. The Psalmist expresses it as, "that I might not sin against thee." The implication is, you reserve God's word within, to maintain your walk in the path of righteousness, or within the will of God. What the Psalmist suggests here is that there's no way to guarantee his actions and reactions as productive, if he does not base them on the principles of God's word.

In the state of Georgia, many of our major highways have reflectors on either side of the lanes for the purpose of giving greater definition to each lane. These reflectors are especially helpful at night, because they show drivers where they are with respect to other drivers. In addition, if you drift out of your lane, the reflectors provide a little bump, to remind you to move back into place. That's what God's word hidden in the heart does for the believer; it shows us God's path of righteousness as we live and interact with others and gives us a gentle nudge when we begin to drift from God's will. If you have reserved His word in your heart, God will direct your steps today.

Prayer—"Heavenly Father, your will is my desire and your word is my guide; focus my thoughts today."

APRIL 8

Ecclesiastes 9:10—"Whatsoever thy hand findeth to do, do it with thy might . . ." (KJV)

God is not only a God of power, but of purpose as well. He made us for a reason and we are not at our best, until we discover and deliver on that purpose. The writer of Ecclesiastes says in this verse that God creates us with ability and with opportunities to implement those abilities. In Eccl. 9:10, the word 'hand' represents ability and the phrase "findeth to do" represents opportunity. This means that God gives us feet and then doors to walk through; He gives us eyes and then windows for revelation; He gives us minds and then circumstances which require thinking through. God gives us this balance, so that ability will not be wasted. I learned recently that the African Impala can leap as high as 10 feet in the air but will not jump if it can't see where its feet are going to land. That's giftedness without faith. What a shame to have ability and neglect opportunity.

God placed us in a 'balanced' world. God's intent was to insure that every area and aspect of creation has every opportunity to fulfill its purpose. You are probably already aware of your skills and gifts. Don't let today's opportunities pass without giving your very best.

Prayer—"Dear God, help me do my best and anoint my efforts for your glory and honor."

APRIL 9

Ecclesiastes 9:10—"Whatsoever thy hand findeth to do, do it with thy might . . ." (KJV)

God desires that we meet every opportunity and challenge with our very best effort. Eccl. 9:10 is a call to discipline and excellence; to do our best, but to do it at 'all' times. Discipline is no doubt the hardest achievement for most people. It's not difficult to feel a rush of adrenaline in certain situations and as a result, give a great performance; the questions is, can you do it when seemingly nothing is on the line, or when no one is there to praise you? The reality is, it's nice to "rise to the occasion", but God expects more than occasional excellence from us; He expects the discipline that inspires us to "shoot for the moon" every time we get a shot.

I was inspired by the Olympic excellence of Michael Johnson in 1996, when he won the 200 and 400 meter events, but I couldn't help but think of all those lonely mornings when he trained diligently without the crowds there to applaud him. That's discipline, and that's what produced his excellence in Atlanta in 1996. Discipline is the root of excellence, and while it is a challenging task, it is rewarding. God wants us to be aware that no piano plays beautiful music when the strings aren't tightened. Discipline is tightening the strings to be in 'harmony' with God's will.

Prayer—"God show me the way of discipline; my desire is for spiritual and physical excellence."

APRIL 10

Habakkuk 2:20—"... But the Lord is in His holy temple; let all the earth be silent before Him." (NIV)

Remember the old phone booths that sat on just about every corner in any metropolitan business area? One of the universal characteristics of those phone booths was you had to shut the door for the light to come on. That's a great principle for believers, even now. Revelation cannot take place until we shut everything else out, so God can speak. That's the principle Habakkuk gives in this devotional text for the day.

The fact is, we sometimes fail, because instead of saying nothing, we say too much, or the wrong thing; we do not wait for God to speak, because we are impatient or too self confident. As a Christian, I've discovered silence is an ally. The problem today is, so many are 'addicted' to noise and they've become addicted to it because they're afraid of the challenge of silence; they're afraid of being left alone with their thoughts. I pray in the next few days, you will discover that silence allows for a real encounter with God, whose voice can only be heard when every other voice is shut out for His sake. He deserves that kind of attention, because His words alone have the capacity to move us from where we are to where we should be.

Prayer—"Dear God, help me silence myself and others, so I may hear clearly your voice."

APRIL 11

Hab. 2:20—"... But the Lord is in His holy temple; let all the earth be silent before Him." (NIV)

Sometimes in worship we mistake activity and noise for worship, because we haven't discovered that you can praise without worshipping; that you can make 'noise' without really honoring God, or declaring His 'worth' (that's what worship is). Praise is an external exercise, while worship is an internal adoration of God. Therefore, you can praise without worshipping (sounding brass), but you cannot worship God without praising Him, because worship is the root of 'true' praise.

When I reflexively respond to physical pain, it doesn't happen until a message has been received in the brain that there's pain somewhere in the body. This means I don't physically react to the pain, until my mind has told me to do so. The same principle applies with worship and praise. It's not until my mind has considered all the blessings of God and what He means to me (adoration), that my hands, feet, and mouth respond reflexively (praise); but it all begins with silence (thought). This means that the true order of worship is you have to "shut-up before you shout". I'm sure if you take a moment this morning to think of God's goodness, it won't be long before you give Him praise!

Prayer—Heavenly Father, help me be still and know that you are God; give purpose to my praise."

APRIL 12

Hab. 2:20—". . . But the Lord is in His holy temple; let all the earth be silent before Him." (NIV)

In the kingdom of God noise is often a trick of the enemy. The word of God reminds us of the value of meditation (Ps. 1:2), but meditation is difficult when we are distracted by the voices and noises of God's competition. It's important to live a focused life, so that our thoughts are concentrated on life's most important realities.

In I Kings 18-19, Elijah won a great victory for God, but then was intimidated by Jezebel's threat against him. As a result, Elijah ran for his life (I Kings 19:3-9), driven by his thoughts and the 'commotion' of his fears. God could not speak to Elijah at the time, because Elijah was too distracted by the noise of his own anxiety. Elijah's assumption was that he alone was committed to God.

Before God ministered to Elijah, he fed and rested the prophet, because God knew Elijah was too weary and worried to hear His voice clearly. It's the same with us as well. We must learn to value stillness and silence as preparation for worship and revelation; otherwise, our progress will be mitigated by the things we allow to eclipse the presence of God. Take a moment now to do and say nothing and let God fill your mind and heart.

Prayer—"God, I will be quiet while you speak; I will wait patiently for a word from you."

APRIL 13

Hab. 2:20—" . . . But the Lord is in His holy temple; let all the earth be silent before Him." (NIV)

If God should be approached in silence, it must mean that God has something to say, and if He does, we must proceed under the assumption that His words are infinitely better than ours. Therefore, this verse is a call to come before God with respect for who He is, dependency on His grace, and submission to His will; it's a reminder to reject the frenzy of our fears and trust the sufficiency of His resources. Why should we do it? Because Hab. 2:20 says God is right where He should be with respect to our needs; He's in His holy temple.

Silencing ourselves and listening to God requires a conscious and committed choice, because it's not the easiest thing to do. It's difficult to shut things out and give God's voice priority, when you have a strong level of self confidence, or when you feel God is moving too slowly, but that's the only option for avoiding failure and its frustration. In Ex. 32, Aaron listened to the voices of the Israelites and made a golden calf; it satisfied the people, but it adversely affected the worship of God. If we seek success in hearing God, we must do as Mary did in Lk. 10:42 and choose the "good part", which involves sitting at Jesus' feet and giving His words our undivided attention.

Prayer—"Heavenly Father, your voice is my source of direction; help me hear you amid the many voices which seek to crowd you out."

APRIL 14

Joshua 24:15—"... choose you this day whom ye will serve ..." (KJV)

Joshua's declaration to Israel in this verse expresses the need for wise decisions in the life of a Christian. Joshua's implication was that Israel could not access her destiny in God without accepting God's will dutifully. In the Bible, God shows us the importance of choice by presenting repeatedly the doctrine of "two ways". It's God's way of simplifying the path to success for believers. God began with the option of two ways for Adam and Eve in Gen. 2:16-17, continued with Elijah in I Kings 18:21 and brought it to a climax with Jesus Christ in Matt. 7:13-27, when He spoke of two gates, two roads, two trees, and two foundations.

Obviously, successful living is about making wise choices and ultimately, a wise choice is tied to a relationship with God 'through' Christ. Why? Let me illustrate. Suppose you were walking down a road and suddenly it forked in two directions and you didn't know which way to go. If at the fork there were two men and one was alive while the other was dead, who would you ask for directions? That's why wise living is based on knowing Christ; He's alive forevermore!

Prayer—"Dear God, help me make wise choices and thank you for a living Lord!"

APRIL 15

John 1:1—"In the beginning was the Word, and the Word was with God, and the Word was God." (NIV)

John the Evangelist, in his reference to Jesus as the 'Word' makes clear that there never was a time when the Word (Christ) did not exist. This is fundamental to the credibility of Jesus Christ, because it means that our awareness of Jesus' identity makes us aware of who God is. More importantly though, Jesus is the 'timeless' Christ, and is therefore greater than time and as changeless as eternity. Now that's credibility!

What John 1:1 helps us avoid is miscategorizing Jesus like other religions do. Whenever someone, or some thing is miscategorized, there exists no opportunity to enjoy the full benefit of that which is misplaced. I remember several years ago a young quarterback being drafted out of college by the NFL, but the team which drafted him wanted him to play another position. His complaint was that his football skills could not be fully utilized if he was playing out of his 'natural' position. That is precisely why some fail to receive full spiritual benefits; they've placed Jesus in a category which doesn't fully take advantage of who He is. If you need direction today, begin by recognizing that Jesus is God. He's a credible presence!

Prayer—"Dear God, thank you for Jesus and all you've done through Him for me."

APRIL 16

John 1:1—"In the beginning was the Word, and the Word was with God, and the Word was God." (NIV)

John seeks in this verse to expand our understanding of the reality of God, when he refers to Jesus Christ (the Word) as 'with' God. John literally says the 'word' has an identity of its own, although it has the same essence as God. Additionally, the implication is that this separate identity issue poses no problem because of the nature of God's relationship to His word.

'With' God implies that the word (Christ) was and is always "face to face" with God. This means that there is nothing that hinders the fellowship and conversation between God the Father and God the Son; the level of communication between them provides for absolute understanding and direction. Why is that important? Because in following the example of Jesus you can be sure God is pleased, because there is never disagreement between the Father and the Son. So if it is your desire to please God in all you do, you need look no further than the life of Jesus, who was with God, and is God. His pattern should be your priority and if it is, God will in some way express His pleasure with you as He did His only begotten son at the Jordan River (Matt. 3:17).

Prayer—"Dear Lord, thank you for the example of Jesus Christ; help me walk obediently in His footsteps."

APRIL 17

John 1:1—"In the beginning was the Word, and the Word was with God, and the Word was God." (NIV)

Let's continue with this verse today. John says that the word is more than a message; it's a man. That means the word is personal because it has an identity; a personality. So, although 'words' refer to information or knowledge, this word is more about 'who' than 'what'. The reality is, information is always more about whom, than it is about what. If a man is an expert in nuclear physics, it's the 'who' in his life that determines the application of that knowledge. If he is self-determined, he might very well use that knowledge to create a destructive nuclear force, but if Christ is the main 'who' in his life, he'll apply that knowledge in a more service-oriented manner.

In the Garden of Eden, Adam and Eve overestimated the information they received from the tree of the knowledge of good and evil. They thought they could rival God with it, but instead they discovered information without the correct inspiration can only lead to frustration and failure. As a result, they forfeited their place in paradise, because they valued knowledge more than their relationship with God. The point is, revelation has an identity and it is Jesus Christ, so I can only 'harvest' knowledge when I acknowledge Him as its source and substance. Remember, facts need faith if life is to be fruitful.

Prayer—"Heavenly Father, help me combine what you say and who you are, and to see no difference between the two."

APRIL 18

John 1:1—"In the beginning was the Word, and the Word was with God, and the Word was God." (NIV)

Let's conclude on this word today. John says that the word 'was' God. This means you can differentiate between the person, but not the purpose. The main point is, whatever can be said of God the Father, can be said of God the Son (Christ); they are alike in thought and purpose, because they are alike in essence. Notice that John does not say that "God was the word", but that "the word was God', because the former statement would cancel the separate identity of the 'word' and leave us an inadequate understanding of God and His nature.

The key here is, understanding that although God is unseen (He is spirit), there is one who has manifested for us all we need to know about God, because He was and is God himself. I really can't explain how it is so; I just know when I follow Jesus, I'm following God. Jesus Christ is the main ingredient in my search for truth and a relationship with God. How is that possible? When Dorothy and her friends finally met the Wizard of Oz, they discovered he was approachable, because he was just like them. Initially, a lack of knowledge of him made him seem unapproachable. The same principle applies to Jesus; now that I 'know' Him, I can approach God with the confidence that God cares and understands. Praise God!

Prayer—"God, thank you for availability and accessibility; you are everything I need."

APRIL 19

John 1:14—"The Word became flesh and made His dwelling among us . . ." (NIV)

It is important to see that John used the word 'flesh' here rather than 'man' or 'body' to indicate the true humanity of Jesus. That is important because it means Jesus became one of us. He literally took upon Himself the thing that produces our weakness and failures. In doing so, Jesus accepted our limitations, but also revealed our great potential.

Look at it again. Jesus "put on" that which introduced sin in the garden (flesh), which caused Moses and David's missteps; that which makes us stumble at the very worst times. The Bible says the flesh is weak (Matt. 26:41), sinful (Rom. 8:3), and lusteth against the Spirit (Gal. 5:17). This is the thing Christ wrapped Himself in leaving behind His eternal substance (Phil. 2:7), not just to redeem our sins, but also to show the human possibilities and potential to those who truly trust God and seek to obey Him. The flesh may be weak, but when that flesh is given to God's dominion and authority, great things become possible. The best example of that truth can be found in Matt. 26:39. In that verse, Jesus' flesh sought release from the cross, but His Spirit willingly accepted the cross and its implications. As a result, He now has a name above every other name (Phil. 2:9). He became one of us to show us when you believe, there is no failure in God!

Prayer—"Dear God, thank you for every resource available through Christ; your love for me is my strength."

APRIL 20

John 1:14—"The Word became flesh and made His dwelling among us . . ." (NIV)

The word 'dwelling' refers to Jesus 'pitching' His 'tent' among us or 'tabernacling' with us. It implies that God through Christ, set up shop on Earth for the purpose of experiencing life with us as one of us, while at the same time seeking to ultimately redeem our sins and reconcile us to God. So it was a visit, but with a purpose; God was not on a vacation looking to relax, He was on a mission looking to redeem. That's important, because where Hebrews 4:16 talks about coming boldly to the throne of grace, we can because God has been here and knows from "first hand" experience what we are saying when we pray.

God's pitched His tent here before. In Ex. 40:34, God filled the "tent of meeting" with His presence. When He did, Moses and the people responded with reverence. The point is what Ex. 40 hinted at, was completely fulfilled in Jn. 1:14, because there is no higher form of God tabernacling with His people than to become one of them. Israel could not approach God in Ex. 40:35, but now since the word became flesh, we can touch and be touched by God. When we seek God as Christians, we have unfettered access now because Christ has opened the door through His incarnation; He became flesh to secure our unending access to God.

Prayer—"Heavenly Father, thank you for your boundless love and for "pitching your tent" among us to provide the resource of prayer."

APRIL 21

Matthew 7:12—"So in everything, do to others what you would have them do to you . . ." (NIV)

This verse is a summary of everything Jesus has said between Matt. 5:1-7:11. In the previous verses, Jesus spoke of murder, revenge, and judging others, among other things and here in vs. 12, offers a summary of the ethic He's offered as a standard for His followers. Essentially, Jesus says, "if you don't remember the specifics of what I've offered as relationship principles, then just treat others as you wish to be treated." Jesus merely simplifies His teaching so all can benefit through application.

What is of great importance is to note that Jesus, according to Matt. 5:1-2, was speaking to disciples in Matt. 7:12. This helps us know that Jesus expects a distinctive attitude and behavior from His followers, otherwise, it's difficult to claim Him as Lord and His word as truth. That's why Peter refers to Christians in I Pet. 2:9, as a "chosen people, a royal priesthood and a holy nation". Christians are a 'marked' people, who should reflect the image of Christ and the influence of the Holy Spirit. We 'represent' the savior of the world and should, therefore, be examples of the pattern He set. When I was a teenager, my father never failed to remind me of my name so I would remember I represented more than myself. It's a little easier to treat others appropriately when you remember 'who' you are and 'whose' you are.

Prayer—"God, help me be gracious to others, even as you've been gracious to me."

APRIL 22

Matthew 7:12—"So in everything, do to others what you would have them do to you . . ." (NIV)

Jesus suggests in this verse that we see our relationships through the 'needs' of those we are relating to; that if we focus on ourselves, we usually tend to be selfish in our interactions with others. Obviously, Jesus is the best example of selflessness. In Matt. 20:28, He declared He'd come into the world for the purpose of humankind's liberation; that His work was directed toward others, and not Himself. Why was Jesus comfortable not seeking His own satisfaction? Because He knew (faith) that His Father would supply His needs, because His Father 'knew' what He needed. It's not very difficult to reach out to others or sacrifice when you begin with the assumption that where God guides, He provides.

What Jesus does here is put a positive spin on what had been stated negatively previously. Earlier, a Rabbi had said in essence, "if you hate it, don't do it to anyone else," That angle allows you to do nothing and be satisfied, but Jesus' approach calls for Christians to initiate good things with others, because that is God's pattern. Like the prodigal's father (Lk. 15), God doesn't wait when He sees you turn toward Him; He runs down the road to meet you and initiates forgiveness. This is what He calls us to do as we relate to others.

Prayer—"Father, help me treat others as you've treated me; your grace is the basis of my salvation."

APRIL 23

Matthew 7:12—"So in everything, do to others what you would have them do to you . . ." (NIV)

The word 'everything' in this verse is significant. It implies that Christians cannot choose the people or circumstances in which to reflect the example of Jesus Christ. Previously, in Matt. 5:47, Jesus said if you are kind only to those you like, how is that different from what others are doing? Jesus is saying it is characteristic for anyone to feel a bond or sense of camaraderie with people who share a common space with them and respond warmly to them, but that's what everyone does. Christians must do more than what is accepted or expected, because we are called to know and model the highest standard (righteousness). We must have an undiscriminating love, which finds its model in Jn. 3:16, recognizing God as an 'everybody' God (so loved . . . 'world'), and an 'anybody' God (that 'whosoever'). This is our calling.

Obviously, according to our verse for the day, love is the basis of relationships and our goal should be to respond to each other as God responds to us. That is only possible as we acknowledge our need to 'reproduce' God's nature in our examples and maintain a 'focus' on Him, which keeps us in proximity of Him, whether we are at home or among others. The only way to maintain the 'everything' of vs. 12 is to keep God close at all times.

Prayer—"Dear Lord, my desire is consistency in thought and action; guide my work and my words."

APRIL 24

Psalms 1:1—"Blessed is the man that walketh not in the counsel of the ungodly . . ." (KJV)

The word 'blessed' in this verse is a plural reference, implying that the individual in this verse is supremely fulfilled; that there is not an area in his life that God has not touched. Obviously, this Psalm means to convey that when God and His word are given preeminence the result is not just fullness, but overflow. It's a precious thing to experience God at that level; it produces the kind of peace so few people have, yet it's available to any and all.

Have you ever visited someone's home and discovered a door or two closed while you were there? Generally, it means those rooms were not 'presentable', so they were withheld from your observation. What this Psalm implies is that God is uniquely able to bless us in all areas and aspects of life, because there's nothing about God that He has to withhold from us; nothing is too hard for Him because He's self-existent with an unchanging nature. God can afford to be fully exposed without diminishing Himself. My greatest desire is to know Him so intimately, that I feel both the freedom and the urge to completely trust Him with all my concerns because then and only then will I find a plurality of His presence that satisfies my soul. Have a great day today!

Prayer—"Heavenly Father, expand your presence in my life; take control of my thoughts and actions."

APRIL 25

John 16:33—"These things I have spoken unto you, that in me ye might have peace . . ." (KJV)

Jesus is concerned that every follower of His has peace. Spiritually speaking, peace is a state of mind which allows believers to approach every circumstance with an understanding of the challenges and the available resources. The intent of Christ is to help us avoid panic. Panic is generally a myopic emotion, which concentrates so much on the problem that it becomes larger than it really is, because it focuses on the problem alone; it makes it impossible to identify help and our access to it. Jesus' success was related to the peace which comes from lateral and vertical vision; He looked out and saw the problem, but He also looked up and saw the power.

You can have that peace. It's not a freedom from enemies, but from anxiety; it's not an absence of conflict, but the assurance of an ongoing presence. It's that presence which calms fears and produces courage. I learned years ago, when you sit next to an older woman in church there are usually greater resources beside you. Most older women have tissues, safety pins, peppermint, and needles with thread right in their purses; they're prepared for anything. That's what it's like having Christ beside you; He's got everything, so you can relax. That's real peace!

Prayer—"Dear God, thank you for Christ and thank you for peace!"

APRIL 26

John 16:33—" . . . In the world ye shall have tribulation . . ." (KJV)

In this verse, the "ye shall have" is written in the active tense, suggesting that challenges are an ongoing reality for believers, like the barking dog that won't go away. The problem so many Christians face is the denial of this reality; the mistaken assumption that faith is a barrier to conflict. Faith does not deny or eliminate challenges; it accesses the resources to overcome them. So the issue for us is not the possibility of problems, but readiness for their inevitable manifestation.

John 16:21 refers to tribulation as being like the labor of childbirth, which is unpleasant while it's happening, but a blessing in its result. Therefore, what Jesus implies here is that the tribulation we experience is just the final step in the process of our blessings; it is pain with a purpose. If I could see my problems in this way, I'd have less trouble with my trouble! What does the doctor say, when a woman is in the final moment of childbirth? He says 'push'. That's what Christ calls us to do when we are in the throes of our most trying moments—push! If you do, watch God deliver a blessing you'll never forget. Have a great day!

Prayer—"Lord, I understand trials will come; remind me of the peace in your presence."

APRIL 27

John 16:33—"These things I have spoken unto you, that in me ye might have peace. In the world ye shall have tribulation; but be of good cheer; I have overcome the world." (KJV)

As you begin your day remember Jesus declares here that you can have 'peace' in spite of the ongoing problem with conflict that every Christian has. The reason is Jesus Christ has 'already' overcome the world. The word 'overcome' in the text is written in the perfect tense, implying Jesus' victory as a once and for all accomplishment. It's important to know though that Jesus did not say He'd obliterated or erased our challenges, but that He'd handled or subdued them. Obviously, this means our challenges will continue, but without the power they sometimes appear to have because of Jesus' victory on Easter weekend.

How is that good news for us? It's because Jesus says in this verse that His victory is our victory; that because we are "joint heirs" with Him (Rom. 8:17), we can claim His resources as ours, no matter the circumstance. It is the responsibility of a translator to take the language of one and make it meaningful to another. That is how you and I are able to inherit power and purpose from God. Our relationship with Christ translates the power of God into an inheritance for us, so that nothing can limit us when it comes to God's will for us. I praise God today for Jesus Christ and His sacrifice for me!

Prayer—"Heavenly Father, thank you for the assurance today, that victory is already mine."

APRIL 28

Matthew 7:7—"Ask and it will be given to you; seek and you will find; knock and the door will be opened to you." (NIV)

Each of the verbs in this verse (ask, seek, knock) is written in the present tense implying that prayer is a continuous action, requiring a persistent spirit. Literally, the verse suggests "keep on asking, keep on seeking . . .". This means the most important thing you can do in your prayer life is be consistent in your approach and persistent in your attitude. It's persistence that releases the intent of God, not because God is reluctant, but because persistence reveals the intensity of our hearts toward God in our relationship with Him.

Some years ago, I attended a child's birthday party at which was hung a piñata. Piñatas are goody-filled objects which must be struck over and over again to release the contents. That's what this verse teaches us about God's blessings; that believers must connect again and again with the will of God through prayer, not because God's willingness is an issue, but for the purpose of developing discipline 'through' prayer. If there's some purpose God's revealed for your life and you've yet to realize its fulfillment, remember, keep on asking, keep on seeking and keep on knocking.

Prayer—"Dear God, thank you for being my Heavenly Father and for teaching me discipline as your child."

APRIL 29

Joshua 1:3—"Every place that the sole of your foot shall tread upon, that have I given unto you . . . " (KJV)

These are the words of God to Joshua when he prepared Joshua to assume leadership of Israel following the death of Moses. God implies that success for Joshua would not be accidental, but incidental; that it would come purposely as the result of Joshua satisfying certain criteria. Success was literally 'bequeathed' or 'willed' to Joshua. The terms of a will are generally executed upon death, or maturity, but the point is the bequeathal contained in the will is yours even before you possess it, and waits only for the fulfillment of the required terms. For believers, it means God's will for Christians is success, with the criteria being a love for and commitment to God's word and will.

That's the message God conveyed to Joshua in Chapter one. God said in verses seven and eight, if Joshua was attentive and obedient to His word, then Joshua would have the right to claim God's promise and serve Israel effectively. Obviously, for Joshua then and us today, the study and application of the word of God is the key to recognizing and realizing the best life that God has to offer.

Prayer—"Heavenly Father, it's my desire to follow your will by loving your word; teach me your ways."

APRIL 30

Joshua 1:7—"Only be thou strong and very courageous, that thou mayest observe to do according to all the law, which Moses my servant commanded thee: turn not from it to the right hand or to the left, that thou mayest prosper whithersoever thou goest." (KJV)

As God prepared Joshua to lead Israel, He attached complete success to complete obedience. Notice the words 'all' and 'whithersoever' in our text verse. The reason God expected complete devotion from Joshua was because God had given Joshua complete provision. God promised Joshua property (vs. 2-4), presence (vs. 5), and prosperity (vs. 6-9) in 'orienting' Joshua for this job promotion. What God promised Joshua was comforting, but more importantly, it was comprehensive because God left no stone unturned.

Of course, for us this means God expects our complete devotion to Him, because He's provided redemption for us through Jesus Christ, but also ongoing resources which are accessed through faith and prayer. All these principles can be found where Joshua found his encouragement; in the word of God. God told Joshua to 'meditate' on it (vs. 8), which is to rehearse the truth of God over and over again so it becomes intellectually known, but also spiritually applied. Your success today is attached to your attitude about God and His word. Read it to be wise, practice it to be successful!

Prayer—"Dear God, help me be strong through your word and remind me of its power and purpose."

MAY 1

Matthew 7:24—"Therefore, everyone who hears these words of mine and puts them into practice is like a wise man . . ." (NIV)

This verse is an invitation to make what God says paramount, without restriction or reservation. Jesus promises when we do so, we will be examples of wisdom or 'skillful' living. Because of the 'nature' of Jesus, His words are more than vehicles of communication; they are actually reservoirs of power from which we can drink deeply and be blessed. Jesus told a Samaritan woman that His words, when followed, have a life-altering capacity (Jn. 4:13-14); the capacity to change a person fundamentally, rather than superficially.

Because of the identity of Jesus Christ, His word is powerful enough to bless anyone (everyone) who hears it and embraces it as eternal truth. That's why the invitation in this verse is unrestricted. Christ does not have to limit His invitation, because His power to bring change is unlimited. The only restriction God has placed on His word is an unbelieving heart. That's why John said that all those who believe receive the power and access of adoption into God's family. The result is, when the adopted child speaks, he/she no longer speaks alone, because they no longer stand alone. Give God's word its proper place today and watch God respond to your wise choice.

Prayer—"Dear God, thank you for a word which never fails, and always addresses my concerns and conditions."

MAY 2

Matthew 7:24—"Therefore, everyone who hears these words of mine and puts them into practice is like a wise man . . ." (NIV)

What Jesus commends and commands in this verse is wise living, and it is not, according to this verse, just about hearing, but heeding as well. Jesus refers to hearing 'and' doing as a model of wisdom. This means according to the Bible, that to be wise, is to be discerning and discernment involves the ability to separate truth from error, and then act on that truth. Matthew 13:44 refers to a man who looked for value, recognized it when he saw it, and took steps to make that which was valuable (treasure) a part of his life. What wisdom does is recognizes value, calculates the response necessary to possess it, and proceeds to invest whatever it takes, acknowledging it as worthy of the time and effort.

What God says is of premium value and requires absolute commitment to truly possess it. Most people would give great priority to God's word if they understood its latent power and advantages when it's applied. I remember reading the story of a man who took a cross country flight without eating because he didn't know the meal was included in the cost of the flight. Isn't that true of many of us? We miss the benefits due us as children of God because we fail to apply all that God says.

Prayer—"Heavenly Father, thank you for your word and for its power to bless and deliver."

MAY 3

Matthew 7:24—"Therefore, everyone who hears these words of mine and puts them into practice is like a wise man . . ." (NIV)

Let's conclude with this verse today. Jesus says specifically that the most important word you can hear is 'His' word. It suggests He has an exclusive understanding of truth, and the standard by which it is measured. The reason many were amazed at Jesus' teaching (Matt. 7:29), was because He taught from a perfect knowledge and not as one who had been taught Himself. You and I must admit that often what we say is an opinion and not necessarily a fact, because sometimes, like a filter in a clothes dryer, we are waiting to be cleaned so we can 'process' truth with greater clarity.

The difference between Jesus and the prophets is the difference between "thus saith the Lord", and 'being' the Lord; one word is a filtered word, while the other is direct. The word of Jesus Christ is to be valued because it is a direct word. He is the master type and everything else is just a duplicate. As we place ultimate value on His word, we cannot help but discover its ability, when applied, to influence thought, speech and action in a powerful way. Give His word your highest priority and watch it transform your life and relationships.

Prayer—"Dear God, your word is my light and lamp; keep me in the brightness of your revelation."

MAY 4

Matthew 7:1—"Do not judge, or you too will be judged . . ." (NIV)

The context of this verse reveals not a prohibition of judging, but a prohibition of being judgmental. The Bible requires us to make judgments; to know the difference between good and evil, or to recognize a false prophet. These things require discernment and the exercise of judgment. What Jesus does refer to in this verse is the spirit which induces us to take the place of God as if our word is the final authoritative word. It is very easy to be judgmental in our relationships and reactions because of our desire to feel better about ourselves by using another's perceived problems. The fact is though, that God knows more about others than we do, because God alone can see the heart (I Samuel 16:7). Our judgments are generally based on actions without any idea of intent or motive, so judgment in reality, is reserved for God alone.

Additionally, if God is the final judge of all things and people, then 'everyone' will be judged by God. This means we would do well to be consistently introspective and examine ourselves. It's called 'inventory' and that's what businesses use to identify their progress and profit since the last inventory. Judging is important because it reflects discernment, but don't forget who the final judge is.

Prayer—"Heavenly Father, help me see clearly as I look at others, so I may never assume what you alone truly know."

MAY 5

Matthew 7:1, 3—"Do not judge, or you too will be judged . . . Why do you look at the speck of sawdust in your brother's eye, and pay no attention to the plank in your own eye?" (NIV)

Again, this is a call from Christ not to judge, but to avoid a judgmental spirit, or to stand in God's place as the final authority on someone's example. According to Jesus in this passage, the judgmental person has a problem with vision and perception; that's why there's a reference to what he/she 'sees' when looking at others. Judgmental people are hard on others because they are often blind to their own faults.

The problem of judgmentalism is contained in the words 'speck' and 'plank' in Matt. 7:13. It means that judgmental people minimize their own problems while maximizing the faults of others. When we observe the implications of the speck/plank reference though, we come to understand that judgmental people generally have far worse challenges to deal with than the people they criticize. What a lesson that is for every Christian; that there is always so much to attend to in our own development, to spend inordinate time pointing out other's problems. What a reminder of grace as well; that all of us would be nothing without the love of God through Christ at Calvary. Thank God for Jesus!

Prayer—"Dear God, thank you for the cross and remind me of my need for its saving power."

MAY 6

Matthew 7:1-2—"Do not judge, or you too will be judged. For in the same way you judge others, you will be judged . . ." (NIV)

This problem of judgmentalism is a problem of assuming the place and authority of God, who alone has the final word. Jesus says the mistake judgmental people make is an error of 'standard'; judgmental people set a standard which is not of God and yet become the standard by which their own lives are evaluated and judged. Think of it; to unfairly judge another's life and then have that same unfairness applied to you. That's exactly what Jesus is referring to in these verses.

The danger judgmental people face is facing their faults without the benefit of the grace they deprive others of. Think of a world without the invaluable experience of grace; a world where every mistake is magnified and unforgiven; a world where every lapse in judgment is excessively criticized and shared with anyone willing to listen. That's a world without grace and that's the kind of world judgmental people create for themselves. The truth is, God's love for me is so boundless and His grace so free, that I must spend my time praising Him, examining myself, and identifying how I can help rather than hurt others.

Prayer—"Father, remind me of life's reciprocal nature that my life may mirror your love for all."

MAY 7

Matthew 7:1, 5—"Do not judge, or you too will be judged . . . , first take the plank out of your own eye, and then you will see clearly to remove the speck from your brother's eye." (NIV)

Let's conclude today with the issue of the judgmental spirit. We've already established that judging is sometimes necessary, while the judgmental spirit is forbidden. This mean that Christians are not called to overlook sin in others, but to minister to themselves first, so that they may be helpful to others. The reality is, every Christian is called to minister to others; that's why Jesus washed His disciples feet just before he was arrested and crucified (Jn. 13:4-9), but we cannot effectively minister to our neighbors when our own problems produce hurdles too difficult to overlook and overcome.

The call of Christ to every Christian is to lay him/herself bare before God, seek healing and forgiveness, accept God's grace and release, and then go to the rescue of others trapped by their trials. It is only through an awareness of my faults and God's forgiveness that I can learn to be charitable, based on God's charity toward me. Remember the instructions you receive on a flight: if there's a loss of pressure and the masks drop down, put yours on before you attempt to assist others!

Prayer—"Dear Lord, help me like Hezekiah, to set my house in order; I want to be helpful to others."

MAY 8

Proverbs 26:20—"Without wood a fire goes out; without gossip a quarrel dies down." (NIV)

The writer of Proverbs here reminds us of the power of words, by referring to the potential of gossip. He says that the capacity of words, when used as a negative personal reference, have the power to produce and maintain a quarrelsome and contentious atmosphere. Literally, gossip chokes the life out of relationships and results because of its poisonous influence on both. It's like carbon monoxide, which at certain levels is extremely dangerous to your health and is compounded by it's undetectability to both the eye and nose.

In the body of Christ, what gossip does is produce an atmosphere in which the intent of God cannot thrive. What God intends for the church is unity and fellowship, but neither can be realized in an environment characterized by bad words and feelings, which lead to a lack of trust. This verse suggests that Christians not add fuel to the fire of fractious relations, by misusing the power of words. It's best for Christians to speak words which edify and listen to words which educate.

Prayer—"Heavenly Father, teach me to hear and speak words which glorify you and your kingdom."

MAY 9

Genesis 1:3—"And God said, let there be light, and there was light." (NIV)

Some years ago a brokerage firm called E. F. Hutton used an advertising slogan which said, "When E. F. Hutton speaks, people listen". It was a reference to the credibility of E. F. Hutton as a brokerage firm in handling the funds of their investors. Obviously though, the slogan also referenced the words of E. F. Hutton's representatives as being meaningful and consistent when applied. Genesis 1:3 refers to what God says as credible and meaningful because His words are powerful enough to create, even with nothing to begin with. As far as we are concerned, words are God's gift to us, because they were God's original vehicle for creating and communicating, and God intends for us to continue to use words to create relationships, but most importantly, to speak to Him.

Words therefore, are powerful; they provide the bridge for interaction between sexes, races, and nations. They are the reason some marriages last and others don't; they can defuse an explosive situation or add fuel to the fire. It's obvious from God's perspective that we should use words to establish and maintain harmonious relationships; that explains why Jn. 1:14 says the word was "made flesh and dwelt among us". How will you use your words today?

Prayer—"Heavenly Father, help me speak words which draw others to you and declare your grace."

MAY 10

Genesis 1:1—"In the beginning God created the heavens and the earth." (NIV)

The reference to 'heavens' and 'earth' in Gen. 1:1 implies God made everything above and below. It means God 'completely' created; that everything has its genesis, or beginning in God. That's an important principle for us, because obviously nothing can be detached from God based on this verse; everything is part of the created order. For you and I, this verse is important, because if God was in any way limited in creation, then our prayer lives would be restricted to only the things God has control over, and that would force us to look for other options about other issues.

In God's 'complete' approach to creation, he addressed the issues of form on days 1-3 and the issues of fullness on days 4-6. This means that God built the house, then filled the house to make it livable. How wonderful that God thought of everything for us and then responded by making our world completely ready for our occupancy. God still maintains that kind of relationship with us today. He has a purpose for each of us and therefore, will not send us anywhere without giving us something to do when we arrive. God has a purpose for you and has provided both means and method for achieving it. If you seek Him through prayer, you'll discover how 'completely' He cares.

Prayer—"Dear God, identify your purpose for me; lead me in the way everlasting."

MAY 11

Genesis 1:2—"Now the earth was formless and empty . . . and the Spirit of God was hovering over the waters." (NIV)

According to Genesis, the first thing God addressed in the earth was its lack of form and fullness; the absence of order manifested by a chaotic condition. God did so through an act of preparation referred to in Gen. 1:2, where the author says the Spirit of God was 'hovering' over the waters (NIV). In this account of creation, God's Spirit is His outgoing creative and sustaining energy which prepares the subject (Earth) for the purpose of God. After the Spirit 'hovered', God began to speak and creation ensued. This is a great principle for us regarding God's Spirit; He, like John the Baptist acts as an "advance man" clearing the way for God, so His will can be accomplished. It is suggestive about how God works and helps us understand some of what we experience as both purposeful and preparatory.

Additionally, the word 'hovered' has a maternal meaning, referencing a mother hen or bird hovering over her eggs or incubating them until it's time for new life to begin. That's what God's Spirit does for God's children, to prepare them for a blessing from God. If we could appreciate this revelation, it would do much to help us patiently wait on God and realize His purpose and power in a meaningful way. Let's look forward to revisiting this tomorrow.

Prayer—"Dear Lord, thank you for your creative power and its transforming influence on my mind and heart."

MAY 12

Genesis 1:2, 3—" . . . And the Spirit of God was hovering over the waters. And God said, "let there be light", and there was light." (NIV)

Let's return to this passage today. Note, after the Spirit of God 'hovered', Gen. 1:3 begins with "and God said . . ." This implies that God literally called creation into being by virtue of the power of His spoken word. There is a sense of anticipation in vs. 3, suggesting as I have previously said in this devotional, that words have power. They have power because Genesis reveals words are pregnant; they have the potential to create or produce life. Isn't it significant that when we refer to a pregnant woman we use the word 'expecting'? There is something within her we expect to manifest itself in the fullness of time. Therefore, when God speaks, believers should expect something to happen because what God says has life giving power.

For today's focus, this means there is no distinction between God's words and deeds. God speaks into your circumstance and transforms it because there is no difference between what God says, and what He does! Why is that important? Because sometimes we speak and see the fruit of our lips, but if our words have any power at all it's because we were working with a pre-existing condition conducive for our use. Remember, when God spoke, He spoke to chaos and gave it order. If your life is out of order today, consult Him through prayer and His word and watch Him create anew.

Prayer—"Heavenly Father, speak to me; reassure me of your abiding love and abundant grace.

MAY 13

Isaiah 40:28—"Hast thou not known? Hast thou not heard that the everlasting God, the Lord, the Creator of the ends of the earth, fainteth not, neither is weary? There is no searching of His understanding." (NIV)

How would it be if in operating your car, you never had to check your fuel gauge? What a blessing that would be! It would imply that no matter how far you had to go, or how long it would take you to get there, you'd never run out of the resource necessary to reach your destination. That's exactly what Isaiah says about God in today's verse; God never runs out of the fuel that meets the demand of our faith. Why is that? Because God is self-existent and doesn't depend on anything or anyone to help Him be who and what He is. Further, because He's self-existent, God never lacks for anything and can therefore concentrate on meeting the needs of those who do lack—namely us.

I remember paying off a credit card debt and how wonderful it felt to put an issue (debt) 'behind' me. This verse implies that every believer has that same privilege available right now. Because of the unlimited resources of an unfailing God and the right to go to Him at any time, we can leave our concerns with Him, put our issues behind us and move on to the next challenge with the scent of victory in our nostrils. Praise God!

Prayer—"Dear God, I praise you for who and what you are, and I thank you for what that means to me."

MAY 14

Isaiah 40:29—"He giveth power to the faint; and to them that have no might He increaseth strength." (KJV)

Verse 28 of Isaiah 40 says that God has no peer; He's everlasting, the creator of all things, untiring and unfathomable. What an awesome combination of attributes, but vs. 29 is even more encouraging because it says this God of awesome power also has a willingness to use His power to our benefit. The reality is, its one thing to know God as a judge, but quite another thing to know Him as a Father. How reassuring it is to pray with the certainty that the object of my petitions has unlimited resources and unlimited love for me. It transforms prayer from a daily drudge to a daily delight!

Beyond God's willingness to share with His creation though is the wisdom to give us exactly what we need when we need it. That's why you see the reference to power and strength. What we need most in these times of conflict and challenge is resources which can internally fortify us and equip us for the ongoing fight of faith. I know you have times when you are tested, but remember, "He gives power to the faint . . .". Let that be your reason for getting up, getting out, and getting on.

Prayer—"Heavenly Father, I find joy in your resources and your willingness to put them at my disposal."

MAY 15

Isaiah 40:29—"He giveth power to the faint; and to them that have no might He increaseth strength." (KJV)

The most maddening thing about relationships sometimes, is the inconsistency of people we relate to on a regular basis. It keeps you off balance, never knowing what to expect. Isaiah 40:29 says God's willingness to share power and strength with us is not occasional, but consistent; that God is like that all the time. God's consistency is tied to the lack of 'tense' with Him; He's the same "yesterday, today and forever" (Heb. 13:8), because yesterday, today and forever are all the same to Him (Ps. 90:4). So this supply of strength and power is continuous on God's part, based on His nature.

All this from God the Father, because of our relationship with God the Son. The book of Hebrews has much to say about Jesus Christ as our High Priest (Heb. 7:24), and that truth relates directly to this perpetual supply of vitality from God. The implication is that Jesus has an ongoing priesthood because He lives forevermore and therefore, has no need to consider the transfer of that priesthood. This means for as long as we live, we have the security of knowing the effectiveness of our prayers, because we never have to change the name by which we pray (Jesus). The strength and power of Isa. 40:29 is consistent, because God settled the issue of consistency when He gave His Son the "name above every other name".

Prayer—"Heavenly Father, release to me today what you have always given me; your strength and power."

MAY 16

Isaiah 40:29—"He giveth power to the faint; and to them that have no might He increaseth strength." (KJV)

This verse says what God shares is perpetual and that's encouraging, but the next question is, "what does He share?". Isaiah says He shares power and strength. The power referred to here is the capacity to "bear up" when we begin to falter under life's pressures. It's when things seem to pile up in a short amount of time and you begin to say, "If it's not one thing, it's another."

When it happens like that, you don't have an appetite, can't sleep, don't want to get up, and don't feel like talking to anyone. That's the time when you need a resource of power outside yourself. What God does is give us the capacity to handle these pressures by reminding us how our problems compare to Him and His resources. It really comes down to an emotional/spiritual emergency based in the 'mind'. Our thoughts during these times often give too much credibility to our problems by 'perceiving' them as bigger than God. When God gives us power, He literally 'clears' our minds by standing next to our problems to bring clarity of perception. Whenever I see God and my problem side by side, I'm always reminded that "I can do all things through Christ, which strengtheneth me" (Phil. 4:13). I can face each day with the joy of the Lord, who is my strength and my Savior. Fight on!

Prayer—"Dear God, your keeping and sustaining power, is my confidence and strength."

MAY 17

Isaiah 40:29—"He giveth power to the faint; and to them that have no might He increaseth strength." (KJV)

Not only does our God give us the capacity to emotionally "bear up" under our stresses (power); He also increases our strength. This reference to strength implies the physical ability necessary to meet the demands upon us. It means God addresses both our durability and stability. Have you ever in the middle of your day felt drained and asked God for strength? The reason you were able to finish out the day, was because God heard you and fulfilled the promise of Isa. 40:29; He literally 'increased' your strength.

Notice in this verse that God 'gives' and 'increases' with reference to power and strength. This means God gives us what we don't have (power) and multiplies what we do have (strength), so that the entire scope of our needs are addressed by His resources and willingness to share them. That means God is a "full service" Savior. I've noticed recently that most auto repair shops now specialize in car service needs, but that places like Goodyear still advertise themselves as full service auto shops, meaning whatever your car needs, they can address it. That's what Isa. 40:29 says; that God meets every need we have by giving us what we don't have and multiplying what we do. Our God is a "full service" God!

Prayer—"Dear God, I praise you for the gifts of power and strength; they encourage me as I begin my day."

MAY 18

Isaiah 40:30—"Even the youths shall faint and be weary and the young men shall utterly fall." (KJV)

In the movie, "Magnum Force", Clint Eastwood uttered the memorable line "a man's got to know his limitations". He could not have spoken truer words as it relates to Christians or anyone else. Our ability to access what we need to live successfully, depends on our capacity to identify our limitations. Isaiah 40:30 addresses the reality of our limits by making reference to those regarded as most vigorous among us; it suggests that even those in peak physical condition have their limitations. 'Youths' is a reference to young males and "young men" is a reference to the choicest human specimens, such as soldiers or athletes. This verse declares that even these impressive people are subject to uncertainty and failure.

This truth is important because it teaches us to look for help outside ourselves; it teaches us to pray! Until I acknowledge my limits, life is just an endless cycle of fits and starts in which I alternate between hope and frustration. What I need is a means by which I can free myself from mood swings and experience a sense of joy and peace unaffected by my challenges and undiminished by time. It all begins with knowing I shall at some point be "faint and weary", and finding strength and rest in God.

Prayer—"Dear God, you alone are my help and strength; you are the refuge to whom I run."

MAY 19

Mark 1:17—"Come follow me", Jesus said, "and I will make you fishers of men". (NIV)

The call of Jesus to Peter and Andrew was a call to discipleship; a call to advance beyond a saving faith by following in Jesus' footsteps. It's the same call Jesus makes to every Christian. Jesus calls us, not merely to believe, but to have a relationship with Him that issues in our growth and development.

Notice that Jesus initiates the process of discipleship. He did not leave it up to Andrew and Peter, because the necessity of having disciples was too important to leave it to chance. Jesus understood the tendency of men to be spiritually lost or lazy, so He took matters into His own hands realizing humanity's salvation was at stake.

I read not long ago a reference to the playing and performance of music as a "perishable art"; meaning it's something which must be passed on to each generation, so that its beauty and creativity is always appreciated. Jesus could not allow the gospel message to die with Him; He treated discipleship as a 'perishable' enterprise which needed to be passed on so succeeding generations would know the love of God. Christ is still initiating the call today for followers who will perpetuate His message. What will your response be?

Prayer—"Heavenly Father, help me hear and heed your call, that your world will continue to receive your message."

MAY 20

Mark 1:16-17—"As Jesus walked beside the Sea of Galilee, he saw Simon and his brother, Andrew casting a net into the lake, for they were fishermen. "Come follow me", Jesus said, "and I will make you fishers of men". (NIV)

Let's continue with the theme of discipleship today. When Jesus calls men and women to follow Him, He calls people who are already busy. Jesus' aim is not to create energy in us, but to redirect it. I know men who are reluctant to work, but would never admit it. They always depend on others to do the things they should do themselves, whether it's preparing a resume, checking the want-ads, or being sure to get up on time. Jesus didn't need men he had to motivate; He needed men who were already motivated and just needed some direction for their lives.

Across the years, dams have been created as barriers to redirect the flow of water, for the purpose of providing a more stable living environment or to create electrical energy. That's exactly what Jesus had in mind when He called Andrew and Peter. Jesus' intent was to take their energy, redirect it through His example and produce stronger men who would make a more influential and spiritual impact on their kindred and culture. He's calling you and I today to put our lives in His hands and be redirected through His standard for the purpose of transforming the world around us.

Prayer—"Dear God, plant your word in me and re-focus my attention on your will."

MAY 21

Mark 1:17—"Come follow me", Jesus said, "and I will make you fishers of men". (NIV)

I remember some years ago my eldest daughter telling my son to take out the garbage and him ignoring her voice. A few moments later she told him, "daddy said take out the garbage", and his response was immediate. Of course, the difference was the authority behind the command. There is authority in Mk. 17; it's the voice not of a prophet, but of God Himself speaking. Jesus did not tell Peter and Andrew in this text to follow God, but to follow Him, because Jesus was God. So Jesus here does not point men to truth, but to Himself, because He is truth (Jn. 14:6).

Because Jesus speaks with divine authority, it implies His message has absolute clarity; it doesn't require a cosigner, but merely application to test its effectiveness. Once the authority issue is settled, you and I can get down to the business of developing intimacy with God, because more than anything, the Lord calls us to a relationship. What God wants most is for us to know Him in a way that gives us confidence about our challenges and produces the peace that can only come from an inextricable connection to Him. He's calling today; what will you do? Will you trust Him and follow or doubt and miss your opportunity?

Prayer—Dear God, your voice is the sound of music, and I await your direction for me today."

MAY 22

Mark 1:17-18—""Come follow me", Jesus said, "and I will make you fishers of men". At once they left their nets and followed Him." (NIV)

The response of Andrew and Peter to Jesus in Mk. 1:18 implies that Jesus calls men and women to abandon their trust in everything that would compete with Him as their absolute resource. Verse 18 says, "they left their nets . . .". Those 'nets' were trusted as the means by which Andrew and Peter paid their bills and fed their families. Let's be clear here though. Jesus was not issuing a call to stop working, but to trust Him more than their jobs or the relationships they'd previously cultivated. This call was not about employment, but trust, and in whom to place our ultimate trust.

It's really just a matter of 'prioritizing'; of giving our relationship with God the highest place in our lives. The same principle can be found in Matt. 6:33 where Jesus says, "seek ye first the kingdom of God . . .", or where Jesus commends Mary in Lk. 10:42 for choosing the "good part". God fully expects us to live and work in the world; He just wants us to remember this is a temporary situation that we can expect to exit from at some point when He calls us from labor to reward. Let your motto be, "I work horizontally, but I live vertically."

Prayer— "Heavenly Father, help me put first things first; help me live with your will as my goal!"

MAY 23

Mark 1:17—"Come follow me", Jesus said, "and I will make you fishers of men". (NIV)

Again we're devoting our morning time to this verse because Christ issues a call to everyone regardless of rank or race. This call to discipleship is a call to find our identity and support in Christ alone. That means at the point you accept Christ as your savior, your family name and employment become secondary in terms of your security and trust. You must identify yourself as a 'Christian' first, before you declare your earthly name or employment connection. Why is this important? Because Christians must learn to trace their roots deeper than a name or company; they must acknowledge that we were initially made in God's image and that He supplies identities and jobs.

Our greatest sense of security can only be found in Christ because every earthly tie is precarious at best and subject to fail us at some point. I find my confidence and identity in Christ because His resources are greater and unfailing, and His promises are guaranteed. I follow Him because His is the path of perfect peace.

Prayer—"Dear God, help me follow the path of your Son as I begin today's journey."

MAY 24

Mark 1:16-17—As Jesus walked beside the Sea of Galilee, he saw Simon and his brother Andrew casting a net into the lake, for they were fisherman. "Come follow me", Jesus said, "and I will make you fishers of men". (NIV)

The men Jesus called to be disciples had no special training or preparation prior to Jesus calling them. Jesus didn't go to the local seminary or even to the temple to find disciples; He walked along selecting men who were going about everyday ordinary responsibilities. There obviously was a method to this madness. I believe Jesus understood how hard it can be to train people who are, by their estimate, already trained. These would be people, perhaps already so full of themselves, that filling them with His grace would have been nearly impossible. Jesus needed men who were conscious of God yet open to a fresh revelation from Him.

Not long ago, I repotted a plant in my office. I did so because there was no longer room for the roots of the plant to stretch and grow. I didn't cut off the roots; I just gave them a new and more expansive environment. Jesus didn't ask Andrew and Peter to relinquish Judaism; He merely 'repotted' them to give more room for their roots. That's the essence of His call to us today; not to change who we are, but to re-channel it by 'repotting' us.

Prayer—"Dear God, plant me in the soil of your salvation and bring fruit from my faith."

MAY 25

Mark 1:17-18—"Come follow me", Jesus said, "and I will make you fishers of men". At once they left their nets and followed Him. (NIV)

Verses 18 and 20 of Mark 1 indicate the responses given by Andrew, Peter, James and John to Jesus' call to discipleship. The response of Peter and Andrew in vs. 18 was prompt ("at once . . ."); the response of James and John in verse 20 was complete ("left . . . father Zebedee . . ."). This is the reaction God desires and expects when He calls us into service; prompt and complete commitment.

We should respond promptly to God, because we have no idea when and where future opportunities will present themselves. I read recently of a man who noticed an excellent gasoline price at a gas station but waited an hour to fuel his car, but the price had risen ten cents per gallon by the time he returned. The point is to take advantage of opportunities before the price goes up.

Our response to God should also be complete, because God does His best work in and through us when we give Him complete control. The image of the Greek god Atlas struggling to hold the world up is a reminder that we cannot tackle our problems by ourselves. My mother taught me to sing, "He's got the whole world in His hands" and that's how life is best handled; leave it completely in God's hands.

Prayer—Dear God, I've heard your call; help me to trust you with all my concerns."

MAY 26

Roman 8:28—"And we know that all things work together for good to them that love God . . ." (KJV)

When I was four years old, I picked up a newspaper and saw a picture of two men shaking hands, but had no idea why. There was a caption under the picture, but because I couldn't read, the picture made no sense to me. By the time I was five, my mother had taught me how to read and I was able to connect words with pictures and make intellectual sense out of visual images. Life is meaningless until you can "make sense" out of your experiences.

Paul suggests in this verse that making sense out of life begins with understanding the relationship between God and what you go through; that there is no circumstance for believers that is not overshadowed by God and touched by His influence. Paul states this principle with confidence because he begins with the words "and we know". Obviously, Paul is implying that Christians have somewhere they can "hang their hats"; we hang our hats on the knowledge that God works 'through' both our ups and downs to produce a beneficial result for us. That's the kind of truth that settles the mind and allows for the peace which produces progress. Begin your day today knowing God is working in your behalf.

Prayer—"Dear God, thank you for your grace; it connects me with an ultimate blessing in spite of my challenges."

MAY 27

Roman 8:28—"And we know that all things work together for good to them that love God . . ." (KJV)

I remember once taking my family to an amusement park some years ago and one of my daughters was unable to enjoy a ride because of a height limit attached to it. This meant there were a number of people in the park that day excluded from the ride because they were too short. The words "all things" in this verse mean that in God's grace for us, He doesn't exclude any circumstance from His promise to provide the best for us. "All things" means the whole of life and that's important because life is made up of a multitude of experiences, many of which are challenges or changes.

Why is that so important to me? Because I know the recipe for my success must include even the most unpleasant experiences and I need to know that God is not limiting the issues I turn over to Him based on size or severity. The truth is, the most intense of my challenges are actually necessary to my success because when God exercises the promise of Rom. 8:28, that's when my praise is greatest! I'm happy to say I can give God anything and trust Him to produce what's best for me.

Prayer—"Heavenly Father, I give my life today and all its challenges to you; I know you'll do what's best."

MAY 28

Roman 8:28—"And we know that all things work together for good to them that love God . . ." (KJV)

Let's see what additional nuggets we can mine from this well known verse. Paul suggests that for believers nothing can touch them without first "passing through" the will of God. This means God literally inspects our experiences before they come to us. The tragedy of 9/11/01 was the result of a failed inspection process in some of our nation's airports. That led to more intense security measures since that time. This verse assures believers that God does not fail us in the area of screening our experiences to assure us that even in the most trying of times He's guiding and providing for us. You can find this principle in God's relationship with Job as He encountered Satan in Job's behalf in Job 2:6.

What God does for us can be found in the words of Paul in I Cor. 15:55, where Paul declares that death has no 'sting' because of Jesus' death on the cross. Jesus then absorbed the penalty of death, so that our dying would not ultimately harm us. What a joy it is to know that nothing can get to me without first passing through God's will and He would never allow more on me than I can bear.

Prayer—"Heavenly Father, I praise you for your love and provision. You are my guarantee of peace."

MAY 29

Exodus 14:10—"As Pharaoh approached, the Israelites looked up and there were the Egyptians marching after them. They were terrified and cried out to the Lord." (NIV)

It's obvious, based on the Israelites reaction, they expected the journey to Canaan to be easier. What the Bible and history teaches us is a far different truth. Israel had begun a journey, and journeys are different in nature from strolls. A stroll is an aimless walk with no particular direction or destination in mind and always ends up where it began. A journey on the other hand always ends differently than where it begins and has built-in twists, turns, hills, and other challenges along the way. These challenges are built in for the same reason a woman has labor pains (Gen. 3:16); God has determined to help up appreciate our blessings by installing burdens as our road to reward.

Think of this issue of labor pains. Doctors say that labor pains are caused by physical factors like muscle cramping, but if a woman can learn to breathe properly she can mitigate 'some' of the pain by increasing the flow of oxygen to her muscles. This principle applies spiritually to Christians as well. When we are challenged emotionally, we must learn to 'breathe' as Christians relying on the breath of God (Holy Spirit) to supply energy and confidence just when we need it. It will not eliminate the problem, but it will give us the strength to go through.

Prayer—"Dear God, turn my burdens into blessings and help me to apply the truth of your promise into victory."

MAY 30

Exodus 14:10—"As Pharaoh approached, the Israelites looked up and there were the Egyptians marching after them. They were terrified and cried out to the Lord." (NIV)

Challenges often affect Christians negatively in that sometimes they long for days and times that God has no desire for them to go back to. That's what happened with the Israelites in Ex. 14:11-12 when they complained to Moses about being 'stuck' in the wilderness, as Pharaoh approached. At that moment, they were feeling what they left behind was better than what they had.

Israel was ignoring three things. First they were forgetting what God had already done. Through the plagues (Ex. 7-11), God had proven Himself, and the memory of God's power was an essential for their journey, just like soap and toothpaste.

Secondly, they were overlooking the nature of Pharaoh, who had proven stubborn, but was like a toothless lion trying to defeat a mighty God. Remember, Satan only left Jesus for a season in Lk. 4:13.

Finally, they ignored that life is process and each step we take has its own test before we move on. Paul reminds us to 'press' toward the Mark (Phil. 3:12) and when we do so in faith, God will put markers on the side of the road to identify our progress.

Prayer—"God, keep walking with me as I walk; your presence keeps me strong."

MAY 31

Psalms 106:1—"Praise ye the Lord. O give thanks unto the Lord, for He is good; for His mercy endureth forever." (KJV)

Worship is an objective-subjective experience. Objective, because we think about God, but subjective, because we think about ourselves as well. True worship requires the right balance between the two. It begins with the objective (God), because God is the focus of it; we respond to Him with worship as we think of His love, grace, and mercy. We achieve the highest intent of the objective aspect of worship when we worship for God's glory only because God's 'worth' is the basis of worship.

The subjective aspect of worship (me) is important as well, because my concern is that my worship be pleasing to God. My sense of self in worship has much to do with how well I 'receive' in worship and with the quality of my worship. When Isaiah said, "woe is me", in Isaiah 6:5, it was a reflection of his sense of inadequacy in the presence of God, but it was also the basis from which he could begin to truly worship. Isaiah received what he needed that day because the subjective aspect of worship involves self-examination while the objective aspect involves forgiveness and healing. I encourage you to worship God and discover His goodness and grace.

Prayer—"Dear Lord, you are worthy to be praised; enter my heart and lead me throughout the day."

JUNE 1

Psalms 106:1—"Praise ye the Lord. O give thanks unto the Lord, for He is good; for His mercy endureth forever." (KJV)

The attitude we bring to worship helps us achieve the maximum in this objective-subjective experience. Our attitudes include emotions, feelings, thoughts, ideas, will and commitment which determine the 'quality' of our worship. When Paul said, "your attitude should be the same as that of Christ Jesus . . ." (Phil. 2:5, NIV), he was referring to the importance of a Christian's attitude.

I would like to spend these next few days with you talking about attitudes necessary for authentic worship. The first attitude is adoration. Adoration is the point from which worship commences. It's impossible to worship God without first adoring Him, because adoration insures that the 'roots' of worship are deep. Adoration guarantees that worship will be treated not as a habit, but as holy; not as routine, but as righteous. The fact is, when you adore someone you don't have to be convinced to do something nice for them; you do it naturally, based on the affection you feel for them. What adoration says is, "I stand in awe of God's might, majesty, provision, protection and I worship Him". It's just a simple matter of thinking of all God is and all God means, and letting God know how that makes you feel. That's worship!

Prayer—"Dear God, remind me today of all you mean to me; I praise you for your many benefits and blessings."

JUNE 2

Psalms 106:1—"Praise ye the Lord. O give thanks unto the Lord, for He is good; for His mercy endureth forever." (KJV)

Besides adoration, no one can truly worship God without a sense of gratitude. Gratitude is similar to adoration, because both of them consider what God has done. What gratitude does is celebrates the generosity of God after His blessings have been acknowledged and accepted. Gratitude is important because it will not allow me to remain in sorrow and despair; it reminds me that God has been good to me in spite of any challenges I may be having.

Our verse for the day refers to the steadfastness of God; that's the root of my gratitude. It reminds me that even when my boat begins to be rocked by waves, God is still on board and His presence is my confidence. That's a reason to rejoice, praise, and give God thanks. It's for that reason the old gospel song "the storm is passing over" has so much meaning here. Most importantly, the gratitude which produces worship comes from being aware of God's redemptive love; the free gift of salvation to those who believe on Christ. Someone once said to me, "thanksgiving makes everything taste better". He must have been thinking of what sugar does when added to lemons and water; it sweetens the mixture and makes it delightful and refreshing!

Prayer—"Heavenly Father, I praise and thank you for every blessing. Keep reminding me of your goodness and grace."

JUNE 3

Psalms 106:1—"Praise ye the Lord. O give thanks unto the Lord, for He is good; for His mercy endureth forever." (KJV)

Worship also requires a penitent attitude. Penitence comes from acknowledging and accepting ourselves as sinners in the presence of a perfect God. It is this attitude in worship that positions us for grace and power, which produces spiritual equilibrium. In Lk. 7:38, when a woman anointed Jesus' feet and cried in His presence, it was because she recognized 'whose' presence she was in and her penitent spirit led to her act of worship.

Penitence is difficult however, because it's more than eating humble pie; it's more than saying "I'm sorry"; it's actually a death to the will of self, so God can have complete and absolute control. Of course, this requires humility and our best example of humility is Jesus Christ, who willingly died for our sins even though He'd done nothing wrong. John says in I Jn. 1:9 that it is this penitent spirit God faithfully forgives and cleanses. While penitence is challenging, it's ultimately rewarding because the true richness of repentance is the assurance that God will not fail to forgive and restore.

Prayer—"Heavenly Father, I approach you in reverence and awe; thank you for forgiveness and mercy."

JUNE 4

Psalms 106:1—"Praise ye the Lord. O give thanks unto the Lord, for He is good; for His mercy endureth forever." (KJV)

Let's see today what other attitude/ingredients are necessary for worship. Worship also requires an attitude of dependence. It's the childlike approach to God which recognizes the need to ask God for His blessings and favor. Jesus acknowledged that principle in the "disciples prayer", when He taught us to ask God for "daily bread" (Matt. 6:11, 12). True worship acknowledges the needs of time can only be met by the resources of eternity. The parable of the Prodigal Son (Lk. 15) is instructive here because it teaches us that certain aspects of our relationship with God do not change; you may grow taller and stronger, but you still need your Heavenly Father's care and keeping.

Some years ago, I read the story of a great concert organist who forgot he could not exercise his gift without help. It was during the time when pipe organs required someone to sit behind the organ and pump wind into the pipes. The organist insulted the man who pumped the wind and when he began to play, no sound was heard. He quickly realized how important this obscure man was to his performance. True worship cannot take place without acknowledging our unseen God, who makes all things possible.

Prayer—"Dear God, you are the source of my supply; I rest my hopes in your sufficiency."

JUNE 5

Psalms 106:1—"Praise ye the Lord. O give thanks unto the Lord, for He is good; for His mercy endureth forever." (KJV)

Worship also requires submission or surrender. That's the attitude which says nothing is more important than God's will or purpose, and that nothing produces my highest welfare better than God's will. When we worship, it should be because we recognize a mind sharper than ours and a power greater than ours, and have a desire to submit to that mind and power. Mark 14:35-36, suggests that Jesus would've preferred a way other than the cross, but He was fully committed to doing the Father's will. As a result of His willing submission, Phil. 2:9 says Jesus now has a name above every other name.

This means therefore, that the richness of submission is that it releases all God intends for you, whatever your circumstance. Three Hebrews named Shadrach, Meshach and Abednego (Dan. 3:16-25) submitted to God and experienced divine fellowship and deliverance; Paul and Silas submitted to God (Acts 16:16-36) and experienced His power and deliverance. It is impossible to truly worship without a spirit of submission.

Prayer—"Lord, I give you my thoughts and actions today; use me as your instrument."

JUNE 6

Psalms 106:1—"Praise ye the Lord. O give thanks unto the Lord, for He is good; for His mercy endureth forever." (KJV)

Let's wrap up with this verse today. I pray it has inspired you as it has me. Finally, you cannot truly worship God without a spirit of commitment. Commitment is the climax of worship, because it opens the door to doing the will of God by applying the benefits of the worship experience. The committed Christian sees the folly of participating in and enjoying worship without translating its principles in daily activities. It would be much like having a well or spring, without ever drinking from it.

Isaiah is a great example of this truth. Isaiah 6:8 says that the prophet made a commitment to God, based on a previous appeal, but not without first worshipping God in vs. 5. When worship is authentic, the worshipper then focuses on God and that focus clears everything else out of the way, so that God's will is spotlighted and the appropriate response can take place. This allows the believer to concentrate on achieving the purpose of God. Worship therefore, does not take place in a vacuum; it should always lead to an action rooted in a consciousness of a gracious and loving God. Praise the Lord!

Prayer—"God, I praise you for all you are and all you've done; I commit to your will today."

JUNE 7

Hebrews 11:1—"Now faith is the substance of things hoped for, the evidence of things not seen." (KJV)

One of the things faith requires us to do is move beyond the logical; to sometimes do the thing that, humanly speaking, doesn't make sense. The reality is, much of what constitutes our relationship with God is illogical. The doctrines of the trinity, virgin birth, and atonement are all illogical, yet a reality for us, because we embrace them through faith. When Mary McLeod Bethune arrived in Daytona Beach, Florida, she had only $1.50 in her purse, yet she still succeeded in starting a college for African-Americans.

Everything God asks of us is not illogical, but sometimes God requires us to step beyond the ordinary, because He's promising an extraordinary result. When Jesus turned water into wine (Jn. 2:1-11), it required the servants present to follow unusual instructions, but that was the only means to address the need at that point. It's often the illogical gesture in God's kingdom that opens the door to the miraculous because such a gesture is rooted in obedience and a right relationship with God. Are you ready to step out on faith today?

Prayer—"Dear God, speak to me; remind me of your presence and strengthen my faith."

JUNE 8

Matthew 25:21—"Well done, good and faithful servant . . ." (NIV)

How you see yourself is always important in determining the fulfillment of your purpose in God. The failure of many is related to attaching too much credibility to themselves, and overlooking God as the source of all success. Our verse today is a part of the response of the master in the parable of the talents. This parable has lessons about responsibility, trust, giftedness, risk and reward, but there's another truth which requires our attention. The master in this verse refers to a man who has just experienced success as a 'servant'. The implication is, there are no categories with God, and we do our best in His service when we identify ourselves only as servants.

In the temptation experience of Jesus in Matt. 4:1-11, the issue of Jesus' identity came up in His conversation with Satan, but it wasn't an issue with Jesus himself. He knew who He was, what His purpose was, and saw Himself as a servant of His Father's will (Mk. 14:36) and as a result, He has a name above every other name (Phil. 2:9). It is this servant spirit that pleases God and produces the fulfillment of God's purpose in the believer's life.

Prayer—"Dear God, help me know myself, that I might be the person you desire."

JUNE 9

Matthew 25:14—"Again, it will be like a man going on a journey, who called his servants and entrusted his property to them . . ." (NIV)

Everything about our lives; our gifts, abilities, successes and failures is in reality a trust. We have been given the opportunity to make something out of ourselves by redeeming our time and talents. What God expects is to see progress through growth and development as we move from station to station. The key to our success is to begin by acknowledging that all we have and are, comes from God and belongs to God. Beginning there, helps us feel a greater sense of urgency about our gifts, and God's return to assess us.

When I was a teenager, a couple on my street asked me to watch their children while they went to dinner and a movie. Babysitting merely requires that you return something exactly like it was given. According to Jesus in this parable, God does not call us to babysit His gifts to us, but to risk them in righteousness; not to bide our time, but to build on the foundation of our faith by using His resources to advance ourselves and our society. This is the call to every believer; to risk resources for God, knowing God will provide the power. Take a chance for God today and watch Him do the rest!

Prayer—"Heavenly Father, all I have is yours; multiply it that your kingdom might be blessed."

JUNE 10

Phil. 3:14—"I press toward the mark . . ." (KJV)

Sometimes I ask myself "where does the time go?" As a parent, I've at times been so busy helping to raise my children that I didn't notice how much time had passed, until they began to take on some responsibilities I'd previously shouldered. I just wish those years didn't seem like such a blur of grades and graduations.

I believe God intended it that way though. God wants us to 'use' the past, rather than dwell on it to teach us the value of the present and the promise of the future. God doesn't mind our reminiscing; He just doesn't want us pitching our tents in yesterday, because that hampers our best efforts today. The best thing I can do with yesterday is apply its lessons today, so I don't repeat avoidable mistakes.

I believe Paul gives us direction as it relates to handling the past; he says we should "press towards the mark", because life is more about where you're going than where you've been. I have some wonderful memories, but I've learned that the past is just a repository of resources to draw from when I'm challenged by my circumstances, and if I can translate yesterday's information into today's application, I can find success. I encourage you to press on!

Prayer—"God remind me of your promise and power that I may face each day confidently."

JUNE 11

Isaiah 55:—"For my thoughts are not your thoughts, neither are your ways my ways", declares the Lord," (NIV)

Every year, somewhere in the world, a tragic event takes place, manifested as a natural disaster, such as hurricanes, tornadoes, earthquakes, floods, etc. It is during those times when people most often question the purpose, presence and providence of God. I suppose it's because during times of severe upheaval it's difficult to sense God's presence and concern. What every believer must learn is 'why' God chooses to relate to us and why He does it 'like' He sometimes does. Is it to prevent disasters from happening or to provide us with resources for life's unexplainable events? If you chose the former, then get ready for disappointment and disillusionment because challenges will never cease. If you chose the latter, then you will always have a well of resources available no matter the circumstance.

I do not belittle the world's tragedies; I only seek to avoid allowing anything to be bigger or 'seem' bigger than God. I try never to forget that Adam's sin resulted in built-in conflict (Gen. 3:17-19) for humanity, which helps me get on with the business of equipping myself for each day's affairs. The fact is, I can't explain some things, but I can trust God to "supply all my needs, according to His riches in glory". (Phil. 4:19)

Prayer—"Dear Lord, you are my peace; you remind me of your guiding hand in all my experiences."

JUNE 12

Psalms 119:105—"Your word is a lamp to my feet and a light for my path." (NIV)

On August 14, 2003, New York City experienced a major electrical loss resulting in a blackout. My sister, who lives in Brooklyn, told me about some of her experiences during that time. She referred to the shutdown of businesses, city services and the looting which invariably occurs. She said the darkness was so thick, you literally could not see directly in front of you if there was no moonlight. The effect of a blackout is it paralyzes the area affected by the lack of power.

Our verse for the day (Ps. 119:105), suggests life to be a paralyzing experience without the information and inspiration that comes from the word of God. The implication is that you can neither see where you are or where you are going without God's word. The true value of the Bible is its timely and timeless applications; it speaks to the contemporary circumstance, although its stories are ancient. Obviously, there is nothing new under the sun (Eccl. 1:9). The key to success in life is identifying both source and resource. That's what the word of God addresses; it reminds us that God is both source and resource for believers and His word is the written guide which illuminates that truth.

Prayer—"Heavenly Father, thank you for the light of your presence and the gift of your son."

JUNE 13

Psalms 119:105—"Your word is a lamp to my feet and a light for my path." (NIV)

Although this verse is a reference to the value of God's word, it is not a 'worship' of the book, but of the Lord of the book. The psalmist does not say 'the' word, but 'your' word meaning he's directing his comment to God. This means the psalmist values his relationship with God more than the 'word'. It is as if the psalmist is saying, "Lord, I wouldn't have this word if it wasn't for you".

The expression "it's the thought that counts", expresses the same principle. It refers to the giver more than the gift. Not long ago, one of the members of the fellowship I serve gave me a book as a gift. While I am sure the book is a good one, I appreciate the giver more, because the book suggests something special about our relationship. So while I value and appreciate the word of God (Bible), I appreciate God more for thinking enough of me to give me a guide for my daily choices and challenges. I praise God that He didn't just make me, then push me into the world and say, "go for it". My God gave me a road map to lead me to my destination and if you have a relationship with Him, that same resource is yours today.

Prayer—"Dear God, I love you, I praise you, I adore you. You are the strength of my life!"

JUNE 14

Psalms 119:105—"Your word is a lamp to my feet and a light for my path." (NIV)

This verse is so rich with eternal truths, it deserves another day of thought and study. The Psalmist indicates here that God is faithful in maintaining His covenant with us. God promised to bless all people through Abraham (Gen. 12:3), and kept that promise by providing us, the sons and daughters of Abraham with a timely and timeless word; a word both 'fresh' and 'relevant' for the times we live in.

What the Bible does, is documents the promises of God and shows Him keeping those promises as we move from testament to testament. In addition, we also verify the faithfulness of God in keeping His word as we trace and track our own experiences in applying God's word. I have a 1985 BMW for which I have a title that documents my ownership. It certifies that no one can contest my relationship with that car. God's word documents my relationship with Him to the extent that no one can contest it. Once I confessed and believed on Jesus (Rom. 10:9), His word became the document which guaranteed my salvation. I trust you will continue to take the time each day to read and apply this divine document to each experience.

Prayer—"Dear God, your voice is my call and your word is my direction."

JUNE 15

Psalms 119:105—"Your word is a lamp to my feet and a light for my path." (NIV)

I thought it interesting that this reference to God's word is not as a lamp post, or lamp stand, but more like a torch. This means that the word of God is not something which 'points' us in the right direction, but which we 'carry' to give us continuous light and guidance. The implication is, to make progress, you must see both where you are and where you are going, and God's word meets both of those needs. That's why it's important to read the word each day for fresh revelation and inspiration.

Remember, God gave Israel daily bread (manna; Ex. 16:31), and told us to pray for daily bread (Matt. 6:11), so obviously God desires that we address our daily needs by giving His word a daily commitment of time. The main principle is the daily 'need' for God. I can remember driving at night and thinking of the continuous need for light to insure my safe travel. There were times when other cars were around me, and I could have cut off my lights and followed them, but since that wasn't always the case, I needed my own lights. That's why the word of God is so important as a personal possession; at some point it's no one but you and God, and when that happens, you'll need the light of God's word to see you through.

Prayer—"Heavenly Father, continue to shine your light on my path and give me your direction."

JUNE 16

Psalms 119:105—"Your word is a lamp to my feet and a light for my path." (NIV)

I would like to use today and tomorrow to finish our devotional look at this verse. What the psalmist says God's word provides, is diagnosis (lamp) and prognosis (light). The lamp is for the purpose of showing me where I am and what my next step should be, while the light is for my path, to show me what my general direction is or should be.

Let's begin with the light—the reverse order. What the light (word) does not show is every twist and turn in the road; it provides only a general sense of direction. That's important because if we knew where every challenge was, we'd be apt to set up camp in places God only intended as rest stops. God's word tells us we're lambs among wolves (Lk. 10:3) and subject to tribulation (Jn. 16:33), but it does not say when or where. That's general information (light) without specific revelation (lamp). Consequently, the Bible tells us not to be unequally yoked (2 Cor. 6:14), but not who to marry; it says our bodies are the temple of the Holy Ghost (1 Cor. 6:19), but doesn't say "don't do drugs". What God does expect of us is to use the general principles of His word by applying them in specific situations.

Prayer—"Lord, thank you for the light of your word and its power to direct."

JUNE 17

Psalms 119:105—"Your word is a lamp to my feet and a light for my path." (NIV)

We left off yesterday looking at God's word as a light and today want to see His word as a lamp. Again, the light is a general reference, while the lamp is specific. As a lamp, God's word shows me where I am right now and what my next step should be, because sometimes I need immediate and specific help from God. Sometimes I need for God to speak in more than general terms, because there have been times when I had the light I needed, but was still confused, because I didn't know where I was or what the next step should be.

Not long ago I was watching a movie where a son was following his father, but at a certain point was afraid to proceed. Despite the father's urgings, the son would go no further, so the father reached back and took the sons' hand and led him to safety. That's what the psalmist means as he distinguishes between the lamp and light of God's word; sometimes we're content with the general principles of God's word, but other times we need God to reach back for our hand to give us 'specific' guidance. I'm sure glad God is willing to be there whatever my need may be!

Prayer—"God, I begin this day with the assurance of your presence and purpose through your word."

JUNE 18

Hebrews 11:6—"And without faith it is impossible to please God." (NIV)

In Matthew 13:44, Jesus says the Kingdom of Heaven (reign of God) is like a treasure. He implies that possession of that treasure is worth everything, because the man in the parable sold all he had to secure it. The obvious implication is that our success in life is in our positioning to benefit from "kingdom' resources. Consequently, we must do all we can to establish citizenship in this kingdom and that requires learning by what means and methods we can 'please' the King.

Hebrews 11:6 provides the answer to the question. It says that faith is the one action on the part of humanity, which has the unfailing potential to please God; faith is the one thing which commends us to God. When we exercise faith or take God at His word, it opens the door to the resources of God and makes them accessible to every circumstance. I have never left a grocery store with items which haven't been paid for. The store owners will not allow me to leave without me exchanging my money for their goods. Heb. 11:6 says God will not transact the business of blessings with us, until we exchange our faith for His favor.

Prayer—"Heavenly Father, help me to increase my faith, that I might please you."

JUNE 19

Hebrews 11:1—"Now faith is the substance of things hoped for, the evidence of things not seen." (KJV)

Hebrews 11:6 says faith is an absolute in our relationship with God, but Heb. 11:1 explains the nature of faith and I hope to explore that nature briefly with you for the next few days.

The author begins by referring to faith as 'substance'. This word means "to stand under", or 'support', implying that our relationship with God rests upon, or is supported by our belief about God and His Son; that faith is something upon which a relationship with God can be built and built up. We must not overlook the word 'hope' though. In this devotional verse, it doesn't refer to an uncertain desire or wish, but to an expectation or desire based upon an assurance related to the character of God.

Our author is reminding us of the right as believers to have expectations of God, knowing that our faith in Him makes our hopes real and substantial. I once spent money I didn't have expecting a friend to repay a debt, which he didn't. I've come to realize only God has the credit and credibility to give substance to my expectations. Have faith!

Prayer—"Lord, I trust your resources and righteousness as the means of my success."

JUNE 20

Hebrews 11:1—"Now faith is the substance of things hoped for, the evidence of things not seen." (KJV)

The author of Hebrews also describes faith as 'evidence'. The word 'evidence' means 'conviction' or 'proof'. This definition has a legal flavor. It's a reminder that evidence leads to proof or conviction. Consequently, as physical eyesight produces the evidence of visible things, so faith is the spiritual organ that enables believers to identify the invisible order.

Some realities are unseen because they belong to the spiritual realm, but others because they lie in the future. In either case, faith is the means by which we see and respond to those realities. The word 'evidence' is also important in this text because some things which are objects of our faith are not a part of the things we hope for. This means that some realities are beyond even our imaginations because our God is able to do things beyond all we can ask or think (Eph. 3:20). That's why faith is so important; it enables us to move beyond the limited range of our thoughts and makes a reality out of what only God could've thought of. Praise God for a great imagination and for the faith to identify it!

Prayer—"God, I thank you for my faith and for your willingness to reward it."

JUNE 21

Hebrews 11:1—"Now faith is the substance of things hoped for, the evidence of things not seen. For by it the elders obtained a good report." (KJV)

Let's finish our devotional look at this verse today. Our author says that the faith of the elders of the past produced for them a "good report". This is a reference to the Old Testament heroes he mentions in verses 3-40 of Chapter 11. What he means is that people like Abraham and Moses received a witness about themselves, because of their faith. So as we read about Abraham and Moses they witness to us because God witnessed to them and about them. The Bible is literally God's report or witness about those who exercised faith in Him.

Let me illustrate it this way. When your child brings home a commendable report card, it is a testament to the good work your child has done; yet it is also a testament from your child's teacher. The report card is actually bearing witness about your child, in the teacher's behalf. We admire Abraham because God commended him through His word. How does this truth apply to you? If you want God's commendation; if you want God's blessing; if you want God to make a difference for you, then you must exercise faith! God does reward those who diligently seek Him and His will.

Prayer—"Dear God, my faith is my foundation; thank you for your constant strength and support."

JUNE 22

Phil. 1:21—"For to me to live is Christ and to die is gain." (NIV)

As Christians, it never escapes us that we are citizens of a kingdom and the values of that kingdom are different from the values of the world. There are many things about this kingdom which are paradoxical, yet purposeful; down is up, death is life and humiliation is the basis of exaltation. For believers, that's an encouragement, because we often feel inadequate or impotent in the face of our challenges, and need to know that the material for our miracle is actually contained within the deficiency of our circumstances.

More importantly though, God needs us to know that our limitations do not limit Him; that they are opportunities for Him to show the abundance of His resources for every situation. So, while some experience may make us feel inadequate, or at a loss, the paradox is that we are really at our best in those moments if we are "leaning and depending" on God. When that happens, God is pleased, because He knows He'll get the glory; that men and women will see our good work, yet glorify 'His' name. Take heart in the sufficiency of God to make all things "work together" for good.

Prayer—"Dear God, I praise you for your ability and willingness to make the most out of my mess."

JUNE 23

2 Corinthians 4:7—"But we have this treasure in jars of clay." (NIV)

It's interesting and paradoxical that many of us keep our treasures or valuables in safe deposit boxes or vaults, because we don't believe we have the capacity to keep our valuables safe and secure. Yet God places His treasure (the gospel) in people, without concern for its preservation. He does so because God knows that in spite of our deficiencies, He has the power to 'keep' His treasure secure even though we leak and break easily.

This verse is intended to produce humility in those who serve or 'minister' in the kingdom of God. Paul refers to those who minister as earthen vessels or jars of clay. The implication is that metal vessels can be repaired and glass vessels can be melted and reformed, but jars of clay when broken, must be thrown away. This indicates the limited value of the vessel; clay vessels chipped and leaked easily and were not attractive, but they were functional. Yet their lack of value never detracted from their contents, which means that our lack of comparative value with God's message does not hinder God from investing in us. What a joy to know that in spite of my weaknesses, God loves me enough to trust me with the treasure of His truth.

Prayer—"Heavenly Father, open my heart to receive your word and my mouth to share it."

JUNE 24

2 Corinthians 4:6— "For God who said, "Let light shine out of darkness," made His light shine in our hearts to give the light of the knowledge of the glory of God in the face of Christ." (NIV)

In this verse our understanding of its meaning hinges on the word 'knowledge', because when properly acted upon, knowledge produces fruitfulness in our personal experiences. That's why Paul refers to knowledge as a 'treasure' in vs. 7. It is so, because this knowledge Paul refers to is a revelation of the glory of God as manifested through Jesus Christ.

Notice that Paul refers to the original creation, implying that God exercised a second creation through Jesus, illuminating mankind in a different way with the intent being to dispel ignorance this time as opposed to darkness the first time. This means that in the first creation, God created time, and in the second creation, God created salvation. In both creations, darkness is dispelled; in the first, it is a personal word "let there be light", but in the second, it is a personal act "God shone in our hearts . . .". This verse reveals the extent God is willing to go to help us be all He envisions us to be. Why not use this knowledge of Him today to brighten your world and fulfill His will?

Prayer— "Lord, thank you for knowledge and thank you for the wisdom it produces."

JUNE 25

*2 Corinthians 4:6-7—"For God who said, "Let light shine out of darkness,"
made His light shine in our hearts to give the light of the knowledge of
the glory of God in the face of Christ. But we have this treasure in jars
of clay . . ." (NIV)*

Yesterday, I suggested that Paul refers to the knowledge of God as a
treasure, but I'd like to fully address that thought in today's devotion. The
knowledge of God is a treasure, because when I see and know God, I see and
know myself better. When Isaiah saw God in Isaiah 6, that knowledge of
God was the catalyst for Isaiah identifying his own problems and positioning
himself to commit more fully to his prophetic work. The same was true of
Job in Job 42:5-6 and Peter in Luke 22:54-62. Each of these experiences was
a revelation, which led to redemption and victory.

When I see and know God through Christ, it helps me understand that
I am impotent to save myself, but that Jesus has done the necessary work to
make my salvation possible. Additionally, if I just walk in the fullness of the
work of Christ, I can appropriate His victory into my experience and know
that God sees me through the eyes of His son at Calvary and regards me as
righteous because Jesus has paid my debt. What a joy to know I don't have
to 'create' a path; just walk in the one Jesus has already paved!

*Prayer—"Dear God, help me know today how much you've done for me
and how to continually access my blessings."*

JUNE 26

2 Corinthians 4:7—"But we have this treasure in jars of clay . . ." (NIV)

It is important, as we finish our look at this passage, to recognize the value of God's word and the comparative value of ourselves as the vessels which carry it. Without that acknowledgement, the true source of our power will be obscured. If I smile genuinely when I feel like crying the world should know it's not me, but the Christ who lives in me. Some years ago, I moved into a new home and for the first several months there, I received mail for the previous owner. I never opened or tampered with her mail; I promptly found out her new address and sent her the mail myself. That's how I see my ministry and my relationship with God; my success in life is all due to Him, so I try to make sure I don't accept any mail (praise) that's due to Him alone. When I do receive praise, I just try to leave that mail unopened and forward it on to God.

This section in 2 Cor. 4 is all about showing the true source of power, so the world will be attracted to the one who makes all things possible. What good does it do to have a beautiful, expensive car, but have no battery? It puts things in perspective doesn't it? The source behind my smile, my victory and my deliverance is God. To Him be the glory!

Prayer—"Heavenly Father, I rest in your assurance and victory; thank you for all things great and small."

JUNE 27

2 Corinthians 4:6-7—"For God who said, "Let light shine out of darkness," made His light shine in our hearts to give the light of the knowledge of the glory of God in the face of Christ. But we have this treasure in jars of clay . . ." (NIV)

So far, in our devotional look at these verses, we've come to understand that the knowledge of God is a treasure and God has placed this treasure in us, although like clay pottery, we are leaky and easily broken. It's good to know in spite of our weaknesses, we are still the object of God's desire. What these verses teach is that more than anything, God wants functionality from us; He wants us to fulfill the purpose for which we were created, which consequently, spreads His message and gives Him the glory.

Sometimes, people create financial difficulties for themselves by buying a car they can't afford, when the object is transportation, not prestige. The object is to arrive reliably rather than making a 'personal' statement as you go. What God wants from Christians is not a personal statement, which lifts them up, but the functioning of faith that focuses on and elevates the cross. I never pay attention to a drink vending machine until I see a sign on it which reads "out of order", because that means the machine is not fulfilling the purpose for which it was created. God says He wants us to recognize that we leak and break easily, but what marks us is not our appearance, but our failure to fulfill His purpose for us.

Prayer—"Dear God, my joy is to do your will and to spread your word; make me your example."

JUNE 28

Luke 9:6—"... He gave them power and authority to drive out all demons..." (NIV)

In this passage, Jesus was sending out his twelve disciples on their first mission without Him. It was an apprentice experience for them; a "getting the feet wet" experience. It was important for them to know that they were well equipped for this responsibility, so Jesus indicated they had power and authority over 'all' demons. I think that word 'all' is significant for this text. It meant for them and for us that no enemy is stronger than God and no power is greater than God's power.

Why should this matter? Occasionally we meet with circumstances which are out of the ordinary in terms of intensity. When that happens, it's important for we who follow Christ, to know that His power and presence is more than enough for the most difficult of times. I remember once turning on every light and appliance in a room at home just to see if the circuit for that room could handle a heavy electrical demand. I discovered it could, even though the demand was out of the ordinary. The same is true of our relationship with God; even when the demand is great, there's more than enough in the circuit of faith to supply our every need.

Prayer—"God, keep me plugged into your power and ready me for every challenge."

JUNE 29

Luke 9:3—"He told them, "take nothing for the journey . . ." (NIV)

When Jesus sent his disciples out for the first time, he told them to take nothing for the journey. Essentially, Jesus told his disciples to take no supplies with them. Obviously, the Master wanted his followers to know that God would provide for them if they gave Him complete and utter trust. It's difficult to concentrate on our responsibilities and consequently give our best effort when we are distracted by a concern for provision. Jesus was commending to them then, and to us today, the absolute dependability of God when we trust Him with a "whole heart".

Later in Luke 22:35-38, Jesus said it was alright to carry supplies, but here in Luke 9, the disciples needed the revelation, which only trust in God can produce. I remember the story of a boy who saw a sign saying "*handful of cherries, 5 cents*". The boy asked the grocer for a handful of cherries and the grocer told him to help himself, but the boy refused. The boy understood what we sometimes do not; he knew that the grocer's hands were bigger, so he waited for the 'man' to give him a handful! How much more successful we would be if we trusted the hands that created all things to supply our needs!

Prayer—"Heavenly Father, I await your provision and guiding; your hands are big enough."

JUNE 30

Matthew 13:11—". . . the knowledge of the secrets of the kingdom of Heaven have been given to you, but not to them." (NIV)

For some years, American Express used the slogan "membership has its privileges". It was a reference to all the benefits exclusively available to American Express cardholders. Those benefits could only be accessed by establishing and maintaining a relationship with American Express. In the context of this verse, when the disciples asked why Jesus taught the people using parables, Jesus said it was for the purpose of providing benefits for those who had chosen to establish and maintain a relationship with him.

Apparently, what American Express views as a business principle is also a spiritual principle. There are certain blessings related to the kingdom of God, which can only be experienced by those who have become kingdom citizens. It's not a matter of prejudice or preference, but positioning; God doesn't love one any more than another. In His kingdom when we position ourselves rightly with Him, we can expect to receive whatever His intent for us is. You can begin this day with the confidence that comes from knowing that the only issue with your blessings is your proximity to God.

Prayer—"Dear Lord, thank you for showing me your way and will; I seek to walk your path for me."

JULY 1

Matthew 13:11—"... the knowledge of the secrets of the kingdom of Heaven have been given to you, but not to them." (NIV)

When Jesus' disciples asked Him why He taught using parables, He replied that His parables had a two-fold purpose; to reveal and conceal. Jesus' intent was to reveal the secrets of God's kingdom to those following Him and to conceal those secrets from the unresponsive. He accomplished this two-pronged agenda using one expression—parables.

Even though Jesus used parables to conceal a truth, it was not His desire that the mystery of a parable be permanent to the unresponsive. Ultimately, Jesus hoped that those who heard Him, but didn't understand, would be moved to investigate His meaning by following Him further, and seeking clarity. Christ wants us to know that God's kingdom is a treasure (Matt. 13:44), which requires digging to uncover and appreciate, and when we do, we become beneficiaries of multiple blessings. Remember, God doesn't want anyone to perish (2 Pet. 3:9), so it's important to God that we discover His benefits and take full advantage of them. What Christ does, is like my mother's example, who when I was a child called me to the table for dinner, but if I didn't come when she called, led to a missed opportunity. He's calling you today; what will you do?

Prayer—"Heavenly Father, I praise you for opening the way to me. I will take advantage of your gifts to me."

JULY 2

Luke 2:52—"And Jesus grew in wisdom and stature . . ." (NIV)

Growth is a sign and symbol of health. Physically, it means the body is being served well internally. Sometimes, when a child doesn't grow it means there is a deficiency in the pituitary gland, which secretes growth hormones and prevents the body from growing as it should. God has never intended believers to remain stagnant spiritually, just as He designed the body to grow physically. Remember, growth is generally a sign of good health.

The growth of Jesus referred to in this verse, is the result of His awareness of His identity and purpose, meaning Jesus knew who He was and what He'd come to do. That awareness was manifested in verses 49 and 51, where Jesus acknowledged His "Father's business" and was obedient to His parents, even after identifying an awareness of His mission. So growth is essentially the result of finding your purpose and focusing on it and maintaining right relationships with others, even as you pursue the will of God. This will allow for vertical (God) and horizontal (others) success, which is God's intent for every believer.

Prayer—"Dear God, my desire is to grow into the person you intend, that I may fulfill your will."

JULY 3

Acts 6:3—"... full of the Spirit ..." (NIV)

When men were chosen in the early church to help solve a conflict regarding ministry to widows, one of the criteria for service was to be "full of the Spirit". This is a quality not only necessary for church leadership, but for everyone who represents Christ in every generation. Whatever influences us most, determines our thoughts, actions and reactions. As 'kingdom' ambassadors, we must determine to be spiritually minded at all times.

The word 'full' suggests that there should be no room for anything else to diminish and dilute our thought processes as we seek to serve God and His world. When Paul said, "don't be drunk with wine, but be full of the Spirit" (Eph. 5:18), his meaning was, whatever you're 'full' of will influence you and, whereas wine can impair you, the Spirit of God will empower you. This verse is a reminder to give God complete control and watch Him use us for His kingdom and glory. It doesn't take much information from each day's headlines to know God needs more people full of the Spirit to reverse the tide of evil prevalent in our world. God needs you!

Prayer—"Lord, I pray for your complete control over my actions and attitude; use me for your glory."

JULY 4

Ecclesiastics 11:1—"Cast your bread upon the waters, for after many days you will find it again." (NIV)

The word 'cast' in this verse is interesting because it means something more specific than the first interpretation suggests. It does not refer to 'throwing' away, but to 'sending' away with the expectation of return. It is to release with a confident expectation. It is true that the 'waters' cannot be predicted, but for believers, the unpredictability of the waters doesn't diminish the level of expectancy. My father "sent me away" to go to Morehouse College in 1972 and although he had no idea how things would turn out, he was confident that things would go well, because he trusted that God would bless the investment.

The reality is, the waters in this verse represent the unknown, but that's where the faith of the believer is supposed to take over. What faith says, is that the uncertainty of the waters is under-girded and controlled by an unchanging God, who works all things "together for good" (Rom. 8:28). In Bible times, people threw seeds into the Nile River, which were brought back to shore and planted during the annual season of overflow. When you invest your life with God, you can expect a season in which that investment pays off.

Prayer—"Dear God, thank you for the principle of seed time and harvest time; I trust your seasons."

JULY 5

Ecclesiastes 11:1—"Cast your bread upon the waters, for after many days you will find it again." (NIV)

The word 'seasons' is important to a Christian, because it speaks of the unchanging nature of God. It implies that we live in a kingdom with unchanging laws and standards, and while we are subject to hurricanes, tornadoes and storms, the fact that they are seasonal reminds us that "trouble don't last always". That's why this 'casting' of bread could never be a waste for a believer; it is a calculated gesture, based on the nature of God, whose consistency is our basis of faith. When I cast my bread upon the waters; when I invest my life in God, I do so expecting the best in return, because God never fails.

I have observed people through the years tell others to withhold their money from their churches, because of some perceived problem with those who counted or handled funds. My problem with that kind of response has always been that everything we have belongs to God, and the potential for our harvest is always contingent on recognizing God's ownership of all things by giving Him what belongs to Him and leaving the rest in 'His' hands. Our concern should never be with the 'waters', but with the 'bread' and its potential to be multiplied in God's hands (Jn. 6:9).

Prayer—"Heavenly Father, teach me to value your gifts and use them wisely."

JULY 6

Ecclesiastes 11:1—"Cast your bread upon the waters, for after many days you will find it again." (NIV)

As we continue our devotional look at this verse, it's important to know the word 'bread' in this verse refers to "bread-corn", which does not mean the finished product (bread), but the seed or grain which produces it. This means that the things we invest in God, or give to God, have not reached their full potential at the time of their offering. In 2 Cor. 9, Paul refers to giving as 'sowing', because there is always the expectation of a return or 'harvest', when you invest (sow) in God.

Additionally, Matt. 13:8 refers to sowing in "good soil", which when added to this verse means that all giving should be thoughtful and calculated, considering it's potential to bless the kingdom of God, as well as the giver. This obviously means that the decisions we make with regard to living and giving must not be done haphazardly, but following prayer and meditation. This will insure that what we do is maximized for God and reaps a harvest worthy of a benevolent God. What will you give today and with what attitude will you present it?

Prayer—"Dear Lord, I present my all to you today; multiply my offering for your kingdom."

JULY 7

Ecclesiastes 11:1—"Cast your bread upon the waters, for after many days you will find it again." (NIV)

"After many days" in this verse is a reminder of the patience necessary to realize the harvest of God after you've given Him your best. That's difficult in this hurried, pragmatic age, so we must ask ourselves, how can Christians appropriate the truth of this verse and learn the value of patience? It begins with understanding that in God's kingdom the return is always greater than the investment. When Jesus said, seek first God's kingdom and everything you need, will be added . . . (Matt. 6:33), He was suggesting the vast potential of God's kingdom to bless us when we invest in God.

The key is, to remember while you are waiting, something unseen is going on. That principle is what produces fruit from a single seed. Once the seed is planted, it's penetrated by water, split open and activated by the moisture, nourished by the soil and after "many days", you see the evidence of an unseen process. That's how God works with our investments in His kingdom; all we need do is trust that after we have placed it in His hands that He will keep His promise to bless and multiply. Will you trust Him to bless your offering today and wait patiently for the return?

Prayer—"Heavenly Father, help me to wait on you and know you are at work in and around me."

JULY 8

Ecclesiastes 11:1—"Cast your bread upon the waters, for after many days you will find it again. Whoever watches the wind will not plant; whoever looks at the clouds will not reap" (NIV)

In this passage, verse four seems to suggest that there is no 'perfect' time to invest in God; that believers must look upon each day as an opportunity even if the circumstances suggest otherwise. The farmer knows that there is a season for planting and even if the winds are boisterous and the clouds are threatening, he must plant anyway, expecting a harvest at the right time. That is what God calls upon believers to do; to invest in Him, although the prospects look unfavorable, knowing that God, who can 'create' by the power of His words, will work all things "together for good".

This means Christians are called upon to act on imperfect evidence; to move anyhow. Christians must always recognize the "substance of things hoped for and the evidence of things unseen". When we do, there will always be a return address on our faith and God will return it to us, better than when sent.

Prayer—"Dear Lord, I thank you for every blessing and for your unfailing faithfulness."

JULY 9

Matthew 13:44—"The kingdom of Heaven is like treasure hidden in a field. When a man found it, he hid it again, and then in his joy went and sold all he had and bought that field." (NIV)

Jesus says here that what God has to offer is a treasure worth having; so much so, that everything else can be abandoned because it's worthless in comparison. It is difficult for many to accept this truth, because they become so attached to 'things' or 'people'. It's only a matter of perspective though, because if relating to God is a treasure, then no risk is involved because God is the answer to everything you'll ever need.

Still for many, reluctance remains because they see a relationship with God as a subtraction factor, based on 'abandoning' things and people for God. They've yet to see that God 'completes' life rather than subtracts from it; that God guarantees 'fullness' of life for believers. Remember, God did say when we seek His kingdom and righteousness, 'everything' we need is added unto us (Matt. 6:33).

Prayer—"Heavenly Father, your kingdom is my treasure; you are my only resource."

JULY 10

Matthew 13:44—"The kingdom of Heaven is like treasure hidden in a field. When a man found it, he hid it again, and then in his joy went and sold all he had and bought that field." (NIV)

The man who found the treasure in this parable, found it accidentally. He was not looking for a treasure; he was just going about his daily business. That's an important lesson, because it means that people who discover valuable things, generally do so as a result of being busy. Idle people rarely find anything of value, because they're not in 'position' to discover anything. People like Moses, David, Peter and John were already busy when God called them to a life of greater value and purpose. God still operates by that principle.

Additionally, don't miss that in this verse, the man referred to, found this treasure in an ordinary field, meaning we must learn to look for the outstanding in ordinary places and spaces. This text helps us become sensitive to God, who chose a manger, rather than a mansion to manifest Himself on earth. With that in mind, don't ignore the little things today; God may be sending you a treasure!

Prayer—"Thank you God, for your richness and redemption; your glory is my goal."

JULY 11

Matthew 13:44—"The kingdom of Heaven is like treasure hidden in a field. When a man found it, he hid it again, and then in his joy went and sold all he had and bought that field." (NIV)

Why did this man go to such lengths to possess the treasure? Obviously he knew he couldn't enjoy the treasure's benefits without owning the treasure himself. He knew the difference between observing and owning. Observing allows you to enjoy visually, but owning allows you to experience personally. The tragedy of so many in our churches today is contentment with observing what happens at church, without personally experiencing it first-hand. God wants to manifest himself in a special way, but too many are satisfied with church as a spectator sport.

If many would see the church as more than a 'field' and recognize the hidden treasures of worship, study and service, the church would be a more exciting place to worship and learn. Everything about the kingdom of God is rich and rewarding and when that treasure is discovered, nothing compares to the feeling of having God close and connected at all times.

Prayer—"Dear Lord, I love the benefits which come from knowing you and having you direct my life."

JULY 12

Matthew 13:44—"The kingdom of Heaven is like treasure hidden in a field. When a man found it, he hid it again, and then in his joy went and sold all he had and bought that field." (NIV)

Jesus said in Matt. 6:10 that the kingdom of God comes, when God's will is done on earth as it is in Heaven. Coupling that with our devotional verse, those who do the will of God are the people who possess the treasures of Heaven. This parable in Matt. 13:44 is about discovering the richness of God, by an exchange of wills; yours for His. The only questions is, is it worth it to make the exchange? Obviously it is, because a 'treasure' positions you to replace anything given up, but also to access other blessings you couldn't have dreamed of otherwise.

The only question is, are you willing to go that far? Are you willing to buy the 'field' to have the treasure? The field represents all the baggage attached to the treasure, but its still worth it. When my mother comes to visit me, not only is she welcomed in my home, but whatever baggage she has with her as well. That's the essence of commitment. That's what we must do to possess the treasure of God; we must accept whatever baggage God brings (trials, tests, etc . . .), knowing it's worth it just to have God around.

Prayer—"Dear God, I accept you and all you bring, because life would be worthless without you."

JULY 13

Matthew 13:44—"The kingdom of Heaven is like treasure hidden in a field. When a man found it, he hid it again, and then in his joy went and sold all he had and bought that field." (NIV)

Some years ago, I recall seeing a man on a beach using a metal detector, scouring the sand for valuables. I assumed he generally found nothing, but on those occasions when he did, he had to dig to find whatever it was. In our last devotional look at this verse, I find this principle to be true; the value of a relationship with God and the benefits of His kingdom require a little more than a cursory look; the true treasure of Heaven requires a search beneath the 'surface' of life.

Like the man on the beach, if we find the wealth of God, it will be in the places which are common to life, but often overlooked by the multitudes that miss the presence of God everyday. You'll find God and His riches in a smile, handshake or gentle breeze, but those are the circumstances that are often passed over as mundane or meaningless. The treasures of God are rarely in a display case or on a shelf, but they are accessible to those who look for God with the unwavering conviction that the life of God can be found in every experience.

Prayer—"Dear God, my joy is in discovering your presence as I live each day; help me be sensitive to your Spirit."

JULY 14

Matthew 7:24-26—"Therefore everyone who hears these words of mine and puts them into practice is like a wise man who built his house upon the rock. The rain came down . . . , but everyone who hears these words of mine and does not put them into practice is like a foolish man . . ." (NIV)

The two men in this passage represent all people. Consequently, Jesus is implying that all people will eventually find themselves in a storm and no one is exempt. Where many believers fail, is in the area of the "real issue". Some people believe that where storms are concerned, avoidance is the issue and while I am sure some storms can be avoided, I am also sure that some storms are coming regardless how you live or think. In Mk. 6:45-51, the disciples experienced a storm as a result of obedience, rather than disobedience. That's a great lesson for us all.

If the issue is not avoidance, then it must be preparedness. The foolish virgins in Matt. 25 were foolish because they knew the bridegroom was coming, didn't know when, but left home unprepared anyway. It would be foolish to leave home driving with a nearly empty gas tank, facing unpredictable traffic and hope you get to your destination. This text suggests that every believer should be prepared for all of life's uncertainties by maintaining consistent contact with Christ.

Prayer—"Heavenly Father, help me establish your word as my priority and guide."

JULY 15

Matthew 7:25—"The rain came down, the streams rose and the winds blew and beat against that house . . ." (NIV)

Since conflict is inevitable for believers, there must be a purpose for these challenges. Based on this parable of the two foundations in Matt. 7, tests obviously come to expose the strength or weakness of the thing being tested. Hot hardness in metallurgy is the ability of a metal to retain it's hardness at a high temperature. Fracture toughness is the ability of a metal to resist further cracking after a crack has started. Impact toughness is the ability of the metal to resist fracture under impact. This means that heat, cracks and impact 'expose' the strength of the metal and if it fails the test, the metallurgist does further work to improve the strength of the metal. That explains why believers experience challenges; God wants to expose our strength or weakness and help us draw closer to His image.

The bottom line is, there are certain truths about ourselves we'd never know if we were never tested. So while I may not enjoy my tests, they do help me eliminate self-ignorance, and identify my resources in God. The result is, I become a stronger and more knowledgeable Christian while reflecting the difference Christ makes to those who trust Him unwaveringly.

Prayer—"Father, help me accept and understand the nature of life and remind me of your abiding presence."

JULY 16

Matthew 7:26-27—"... Everyone who hears these words of mine and does not put them into practice ... fell with a great crash." (NIV)

In this parable of the two foundations, Jesus refers to the gravity of His advice and the consequences of ignoring it. He refers to the house of the man who ignores Him, as falling with a 'great' crash. Obviously, failing to hear and heed the Savior has grave implications. The great crash in vs. 27 refers to a house that cannot be repaired. It's like a wrecked car that's been totaled; there is no hope for its restoration. The context of this parable has to do with withstanding the coming judgment of God and how our obedience affects it, but within our current context, it refers to our ability to withstand the everyday storms of life. Jesus suggests that when God's will is our priority, none of life's challenges can produce an unrecoverable fall.

Remember, the crash was not related to materials used, but to the foundation laid. The meaning is, you can have everything one can want, but without Jesus as your foundation, all of life becomes precarious and subject to a crash. As you begin your day "build your hopes on things eternal; hold to God's unchanging hand,"

Prayer—"Lord, I rest on the foundation of your will and word."

JULY 17

Matthew 7:24—"Therefore everyone who hears these words of mine and puts them into practice is like a wise man". (NIV)

In all phases of life, the primary ingredient for success is obedience. As a child, life at home was at its optimum when what I did was pleasing to my parents. The same is true as a student in school or as an employee at a job; your success at either location rests on pleasing the one given authority for you. That's the principle Jesus addresses in this text; that success 'rests' on obedience. Jesus was a perfect example of this truth. The Bible shows us that the reason Jesus was raised from the grave (Matt. 28:6), and has a name above every other name (Phil. 2:9-10), was because He was obedient to the will of God (Matt. 26:42).

When God referred to being "well pleased" with Jesus Christ, it was a father expressing pleasure in a son who was obedient to the father's will. When that happens, it positions the son to receive everything the father intends to give the son. That's the concern of Christ in this parable; that believers learn to value His word, so that life can release to them every blessing God has in store. It reminds me of a song I heard as a child "if you live right, Heaven belongs to you".

Prayer—"Dear God, I purpose today to be obedient to you; use me as your instrument."

JULY 18

Matthew 12:50—"Whoever does the will of my father in Heaven is my brother and sister and mother." (NIV)

Let's address the issue of obedience to God again today. Jesus says in this verse that our 'kinship' with him is based on obedience; that the true family of God, are those who do God's will. Remember, to be related or 'kin' with someone is to share a connection with them that goes beyond friendship. It means there's a biological connection, or a connection produced through birth. Because of that genetic connection, you look like your kin or you inherit mannerisms from them. Jesus' implication here is that those who are obedient to God are so, because they look, think and act like Jesus and those examples are inherited through the new birth. (Jn. 3:3)

People who've seen me and my mother say I look like her. It's apparent to them that we are connected by birth. God wants the same to be true in our relationship with Him. He wants people to say "you look like your Father", because He wants our example to reflect Him, so that His name is glorified and His kingdom advanced. What will you do today that will be an expression of God in your life? Will you make Him look good?

Prayer—"Dear God, help me show your love and grace wherever I go, so the world will see you in me."

JULY 19

John 8:32—"... the truth will set you free." (NIV)

In Luke 15, Jesus refers to three things lost and found: a sheep, a coin and a boy. In these parables, Jesus talks about how they became lost. With the sheep, it was distraction; with the coin, it was another's influence and with the boy it was willfulness. In each scenario, we are led to believe that the things lost were of value and therefore, needed finding. The issue therefore, was never 'how' they became lost, but that being lost is terrible and being found is cause for celebration.

People and objects are not the only things that are lost; sometimes truth gets lost amid the daily bustle of activities and challenges. When truth is lost, it's really not very important how it happened, it's only important that truth is recovered, because truth liberates us to fulfill the vast potential God sets before us. Truth is the basis of our freedom, because it loosens the bonds of ignorance and error, and sets us on the road to our destiny in God. The most important aspect of truth though, is that it is divine in nature. Jesus said, "I am the way, the truth and the life" (Jn. 14:6). If you really want the truth, look at the life and words of Jesus, believe on Him and be free!

Prayer—"Heavenly Father, feed me truth; liberate me from self and sin."

JULY 20

Isaiah 40:28—"Hast thou not known? Hast thou not heard?" (KJV)

The words 'known' and 'heard' in this verse are written in the perfect tense in Hebrew, suggesting that the information referred to was already known in such a way that it could not be taken away. There are things Christians know in such a way that no storm or difficulty should ever be able to affect. When I was growing up, I often heard deacons at my father's church sing a song of which one of the verses said, "you can't make me doubt Him; I know too much about Him". It references that when you know some things about God unequivocally, that knowledge provides an unshakeable foundation.

When I'm tempted to doubt or fret, I should ask myself questions based on what I've already known and heard. I should ask myself, "How has God handled these kinds of circumstances for me in the past?" If God blessed me then and He's the same yesterday, today, and forever (Heb. 13:8), then what's to prevent Him from doing the same thing for me today? I'm sure you agree with me that our unchanging God stands ready to help us today just as He did yesterday. Go in peace!

Prayer—"God, remind me of those things I sometimes forget that I might live in victory."

JULY 21

Isaiah 40:28—"Hast thou not known? Hast thou not heard?" (KJV)

As a believer, what should I have known and heard? What should I not forget that will help me avoid the stress that comes from the struggle? In the context of verses 27-31 of Isaiah 40, I should know something about the nature of God and how it's manifested. I should know that God's nature is eternal, that He rules sovereignly and that He exercises absolute authority and power. Within those descriptions is the answer to our times of discouragement and despair. If God's eternal, there's never a 'time' when He's unavailable, because He's not confined by time or space. If He rules sovereignly, then we can carry all our concerns to Him, because the buck stops there. If He exercises absolute authority and power, then no circumstance is beyond His ability to control.

Most significant for us though is because of our covenant relationship with God, every resource related to His attributes is at our disposal. That access to God is further compounded by His desire and 'willingness' to bless us, based on His love for us. When I read Isaiah 40, I come away with the assurance that God is not too great to care about me, but He is too great to fail me.

Prayer—"Lord, I find peace in who and what you are; go with me as I begin a new day."

JULY 22

Isaiah 40:28—" . . . the Lord, the creator of the ends of the earth, fainteth not, neither is weary . . ." (KJV)

At the time of this writing, I'm approaching the age of fifty. I've noticed a physical difference in myself as a result. There are some things I don't do as well as I used to and that's to be expected. The truth is, it is characteristic of every created thing to eventually wear out. This verse in Isaiah is a reminder that God, because He is not a 'created' being, is not subject to the limitations attached to the created order. Isaiah 40 says that God is self-existent and therefore, dependent on no one to help Him be who and what He is.

Obviously, God does not, according to this verse, get faint or tired from the execution of His responsibilities, or weary and gasping for air from exhaustion. That means it's impossible to "wear God out". Why is that meaningful? Because it means God never has to abandon or postpone His plans while He recovers or regroups for strategy. That's the blessing for every Christian; that even when we are faint and weary, our God is right there with resources undiminished by use and uncorrupted by time.

Prayer—"Dear God, I praise you for your consistency and concern; you are my rock and fortress."

JULY 23

Isaiah 40:28—"... there is no searching of His understanding..." (KJV)

In this verse, Isaiah refers to the impossibility of understanding fully the mind of God. It suggests that while the created order is subject to tests which provide a scientific understanding of it, that the mind of God is beyond scientific examination and discovery. Consequently, because God is not a created being, the means we use to acquaint ourselves with creation, cannot be used on God.

The Bible does suggest that we can know God (Jn. 10:14), but that knowledge of Him is relative, based on the limitations of our own minds (1Cor. 13:12). So 'knowing' God does not rest on creation, but on divine revelation. All we know about God comes from what He has made known about Himself, because only God, as our creator, can 'translate' truths about Himself to our level. We would do well to remember that God is infinite and we are finite; God is universal and eternal, while we are local; God's ceaselessness always has Him ahead of us, no matter our achievements. The good thing is, the difference between us and God does not make Him prohibitive toward us; He loves us so much, that as we submit to Him, the wealth of Heaven becomes ours.

Prayer—"Dear God, guide my thinking, that even in my limitations I may be in your will."

JULY 24

Matthew 14:28—"Lord, if it's you," Peter replied, "tell me to come to you on the water . . ." (NIV)

I've always thought it intriguing when watching a horror movie, that people hear an ominous sound then walk in the direction of that sound. It seems a foolish response to me, considering the lack of knowledge related to the circumstance. There is however, a more important truth about relating to the unknown, which comes directly from the word of God.

What the Bible teaches, is that believers can have victory rather than defeat in areas of the unknown, based on the presence, power and permission of Christ. Matthew 14:28 is a part of the episode in which Jesus walked on the water. In verse 28, Peter asked for permission to walk on the water to Jesus. For Peter, it was an untried and unknown experience, but because Jesus gave Peter permission, it was a risk worth taking and Peter was initially successful based on that permission. One of the things this passage suggests is that our relationship with the unknown should always be based on our relationship with Christ, because only He can guarantee our ultimate success and victory. Today may be an unknown quantity for you, but walk in the victory of a resurrected Lord and watch Him make the difference.

Prayer—Father, I don't know what my future holds, but I know my future is in your hands."

JULY 25

1 John 1:2—"... now are we sons of God, and it doth not yet appear what we shall be ..." (KJV)

This verse of John's suggests that once we become God's children, our relationship with the unknown or the future changes. It changes because of our relationship with God, so there must be something about God that enables us to face our tomorrows with confidence. We must admit, that even after the fact and act of salvation, we do not possess any greater knowledge about the future than before, so we must look to God as our resource.

Christians can be confident about the future because of God's relationship with all things unknown. Psalms 139:1-4, 7-10 speak clearly on God's relationship with the unknowable, because those verses refer to God as omnipotent, omnipresent, and omniscient. Those characteristics of God give us confidence, because as our Father, He will not withhold good things from His children. The parable of the prodigal (Lk. 15), is God's reminder to us of how he sees us and of the ongoing access to His resources, which is our promised benefit. Today may be a new day, but we serve a timeless and timely God, who's been where we're going, and He has made provision for our journey.

Prayer—"Heavenly Father, I find confidence in the promise of your protection and provision."

JULY 26

1 John 1:2—"... now are we sons of God, and it doth not yet appear what we shall be ..." (KJV)

I never purchase milk without looking at its freshness date because that date indicates how long the milk's been on the shelf and what its life expectancy is. The reason I love this verse is because it reminds me there's no freshness date on God or His ability to meet my needs and fulfill His promises. God's blessings and gifts are timeless, and therefore undiminished by time or usage. I can expect that God will continue to transform me into what He's purposed me to be, as I yield to His will.

This verse suggests that because I'm God's child, there's continuity between my present and future state, based on the quality of what God has reserved for me. My continuity in life rests on the fact that God's love works visible, transforming results in His children. This means I'm not what I used to be; I'm evolving into a better version of myself and can tell the difference. It's still me, but God's producing some things in me that couldn't have come otherwise. Sometime ago, I took a timed released capsule which releases its active ingredient gradually to prolong its effect. That's what God is doing for believers; He's timing the release of some blessings to insure an 'eternal' influence on our growth.

Prayer—"Dear God, I thank you for all you see in me and all you do for me."

JULY 27

Genesis 1:3—And God said, "let there be light", and there was light. (NIV)

I remember reading about a man interviewing for an important corporate position wearing a jogging suit. Of course he was not seriously considered for the job. His mistake reflects how important first impressions are; how the first thing you do sets the tone for all that follows. In the Ten Commandments, God refers to Himself first, as well as in the Lords Prayer. This reflects the preeminence of God for us as believers.

Our text for the day says God's first command in creation was, "let there be light". Because this command was a separation of day from night, God was in effect creating time; God was creating order and structure. This is meaningful because, sometimes our circumstances seem "out of order", and we need to know that God can speak order into our chaos and create peace. Since God's 'word' has that kind of power, all that remains is to apply His word to the condition. I remember my mother applying salve to a wound when I was a boy. The salve protected the wound, keeping germs out, so the inherent healing process could take place. That's what the application of God's word does for believers; it provides an orderly environment, so the will of God can take place in the believer's life.

Prayer—"Dear God, my greatest comfort and security is in your word, and its power to transform."

JULY 28

Genesis 1:3—And God said, "let there be light", and there was light. (NIV)

I think it's interesting that God created light in Gen. 1:3 and created the sun in Gen. 1:14-16. God's intent was to create time in vs. 3, and provide us with a way to tell time in vss. 14-16. Obviously, God said let there be light before creating the sun to prevent us from worshipping the sun as a god itself. The meaning is that the sun is 'created' like everything else, therefore only God is worthy of our worship. This of course, leads me back to the word of God, which alone can create order out of disorder, and that helps me focus on God alone as my resource for life.

The book of Genesis is about beginnings and ascribing everything to God. So it helps me understand that while the sun 'gives' light, that God 'is' light and in Him is no darkness at all (1Jn. 1:5). What I am suggesting, is that it is the presence of God alone that makes the difference for us, and when we allow competition for God or substitutes for Him, the result is impotence and failure. There are many things in my life I enjoy and appreciate, but nothing can take the place of God. He alone satisfies me!

Prayer—"Dear God, I take joy and pleasure in your complete ability to meet all my needs."

JULY 29

Genesis 1: 4—And God said, "let there be light", and there was light. God saw that the light was good . . . (NIV)

Verse 4 of Genesis 1 says that God saw that the light was 'good'. The word good in this verse means beneficial, because nothing God created was for Him. Man was last in the created order; everything which preceded man was 'for' man. The word good meant good for man. Further though, by God making a qualitative statement regarding light or order, God was saying that light was totally fit for its purpose.

As we read on in Gen. 1, we discover other acts of creation which God refers to as good. God does this to help us differentiate between ourselves and Him in assessing what's really good. In Gen. 3:6, Eve attempts to attach goodness to what she sees, and the result is the introduction of sin to humanity. The point is, only God is qualified to give true assessments of life. Since that is so, it's important as believers to see life through God's eyes, so we may avoid overestimating the things God is not impressed with. Ultimately, because human goodness must be related to divine goodness, we must always seek a standard which reflects a kingdom that's not of this world.

Prayer—"Lord, I desire to see life through your eyes that I may live with a standard of excellence."

JULY 30

Genesis 1:3—"And God said . . ." (NIV)

When I was in high school, we had a debate team, which was well known in the city for its proficiency in interscholastic competition. The goal of a debate team is to win its argument by speaking persuasively for its perspective. This is accomplished by using the power of words. Words are so powerful, that arguments can often be won, even when the perspective presented is untrue. What is unique about Genesis 1 is that only God speaks, because no one can debate with God using words; God's word in reality is both question and answer.

In Genesis 1, when God spoke, there was no intermediary; no one He needed permission or assistance from. God's word was and is law and life. That's why what God says and said is so important for us today. His word has the capacity to alter or transform circumstances for believers, so that what appeared to be an obstacle becomes an opportunity for victory and God's glory. Whether our challenges are related to our jobs, relationships, church, health or finances, there's a principle in God's word, which when applied, can create newness of life and plant the seeds for a harvest of success.

Prayer—"Dear Lord, keep speaking and I will hear, trust, and obey."

JULY 31

Isaiah 40:31—"But they that wait upon the Lord shall renew their strength . . ." (KJV)

God has made promises to those who trust Him and patiently wait on Him. One of those promises is found in our devotional verse today. He says patient Christians have their strength renewed. The word 'renew' means to put on 'fresh' strength; to exchange our depletion for God's fresh supply. I use my cellular phone regularly and as a consequence, the battery gets low, which means the phone has a limited ability to fulfill its purpose. When that happens, there's no need to throw the phone away; I connect it to an electrical adapter, which renews my battery and allows my cell phone to again be used.

That is the principle in this verse. God understands we run down in the process of doing His will, and promises those who trust Him can find refreshment and recovery through a relationship with Him. What recharges us is prayer, because it 'connects' us with God and positions us to draw from His deep and eternal resources. Not long ago, I was at a diner having a cup of coffee. When my cup was nearly empty, the waitress came along and asked if she could 'freshen' my cup. That's what God does in our low moments; He offers to freshen our cups. If I were you, I'd let God do a work of renewal today.

Prayer—"God, sometimes my cup runs low; I'm so thankful you're always there to restore my loss."

AUGUST 1

Matthew 4:19—"Come follow me," Jesus said . . . (NIV)

I once saw a racehorse that did not leave the gate when the bell sounded. The horse was in the right place, at the right time, but never fulfilled his purpose. The intent for the horse was not to remain at the gate, because that's just the starting point. That's something for every believer to ponder, because when we become stagnant believers, we miss the joy of the journey and the thrill of victory; we forfeit the things made available to us by God, which are only accessible as we 'follow' Him.

The message for every believer is to never remain at the point of belief in Christ; to follow Him as He leads, because His path for us, while filled with challenges, has the promise of victory and personal fulfillment. How does the process of following begin? It starts with 'learning' from Jesus; reading His word and meditating over it, so the Holy Spirit can provide insight and interpretation. As we read and meditate, we become more knowledgeable about God and more perceptive of His will. As a result, growth takes place and the example we set takes on greater influence, because Christ is shining through more and more. So don't stop now; press on!

Prayer—"Dear God, I long to know you better each day; help me follow your footsteps."

AUGUST 2

Matthew 5:1—"And seeing the multitudes, he went up into a mountain: and when he was set, his disciples came unto him." (KJV)

I've always thought it interesting that in this verse the multitude is distinguished from the disciples. The implication is that Jesus left the crowd to teach the disciples. Why is that? The crowds followed Jesus around, but the disciples followed Jesus. The multitude followed Jesus around because they were attracted to his miracles; the crowd was hungry for miracles, but not discipleship, because it involved commitment and responsibility.

The difference is, when you follow someone around, you have the option of 'exiting' the highway wherever you choose, but when you truly follow someone, their destination is your destination. Following Jesus involves rejection, suffering and sacrifice; that's why many preferred to just follow him around. Following Jesus involves taking "his yoke upon" you and that's why many preferred to follow him around. Consequently, Jesus must make a distinction between the crowd and disciples, because not everyone is committed to the road he travels. Which category are you in?

Prayer—"God, help me to truly commit to your will for me; help me be steadfast."

AUGUST 3

Matthew 5:2—"He opened his mouth and taught them . . ." (KJV)

Why did Jesus teach his disciples? Because every disciple needs training. They needed this training because Jesus was introducing them to a new kingdom in which the standards and values were different from those they'd been taught. Jesus needed them to know what life in this kingdom was like, because his first message was "repent, for the kingdom of Heaven is at hand" (Matt. 4:17). The master understood without his guidance, these disciples would be rudderless and therefore unable to navigate their course in the uncharted waters of kingdom ministry.

Every new responsibility requires a period of orientation. This is necessary, because at some point we'll be required to do the job on our own. It's like riding a bike; at some point the training wheels come off and you have to do it alone, based on the training received. Training is for the purpose of preparedness. I value private and corporate Bible study, because that's when God prepares me for future challenges, so whenever he "opens his mouth", I try to be there to hear and heed.

Prayer—"God, as you speak, I pledge an attentive ear and a receptive heart."

AUGUST 4

Phil. 4:19—"And my God will meet all your needs according to His glorious riches in Christ Jesus." (NIV)

The key to a life relatively stress free as a believer, is the confidence that God has both the ability and attitude to address any of life's circumstances; to know you can place your family, job, finances and relationships in his hands, and expect God to work "all things together for good". When matters are 'confidently' placed in God's hand, you can expect the maximum benefit as a result of your trust. Sometimes, as I notice the word 'all' in this verse, we fail because we limit God to certain areas of our experience and forfeit specific intended blessings from God. It's like keeping money under a mattress, which places your money at risk to thieves, and forfeits the interest available through a banking institution.

Why is it important to trust God with everything? Because God can multiply fish and bread, give the blind sight and resurrect the dead. In others words, nothing's too hard for God, because He is both self-existent and self-sufficient; He never has to reach outside himself to do his job. You can begin this day with the certainty that if you trust Him, he'll meet every need.

Prayer—"Dear Lord, I place all matters in your hands, believing your provision is all I need."

AUGUST 5

2 Corinthians 1:3—"Praise be to the God and Father of our Lord Jesus Christ, the Father of compassion and the God of all Comfort..." (NIV)

I love this verse because in it, Paul praises God for who He is, rather than what He's done. That's important, because it means God is to be praised primarily for His nature and characteristics. There are times when we don't feel especially thankful, mostly because nothing particularly noteworthy has happened (a faulty perspective) and during those times, it's important to remember the difference between God and others, and praise Him for who He is.

When I think about it, if I had a hard time identifying His current blessings, I'd still be happy just to have someone like Him in my life. The fact is, every blessing is tied to his nature, so my primary reason for praise is related to Him rather than what He's done. What He's done wouldn't be possible if He wasn't who He is. Praise shouldn't be based on a contingency; it shouldn't require having to come up with some recent reason. It should rest alone on the ongoing faithfulness and love of God, who's the same yesterday, today, and forever.

Prayer—"Dear God, praise is my joy because you are 'who' you are; you are my sustainer and redeemer."

AUGUST 6

2 Corinthians 1:3—"... the God of all comfort ..." (NIV)

The word comfort in this verse literally means 'encouragement'. Paul does not mean rescue from discomfort, but the tools and training to handle every uncomfortable circumstance; that's what God provides for believers. That principle shines through in John. 6, when Jesus would not allow the disciples to dismiss the crowds at the end of the day, but commanded them to participate and invest in the crowd's feeding. That's how God does it; He produces growth in us by giving us encouragement 'in' the circumstance, revealing the inherent resources available in seemingly hopeless situations.

'All' comfort implies that no circumstance is beyond God's ability to encourage us, but also that God is the only one who can do it. That settles an important question for us; it means we don't have to worry about the scope of God's power, but only our position to receive it. The issue never is God, or even the situation; it's always us. We must never fail to ask ourselves, "what am I doing that either promotes or prevents God's will being done in my life?" when that question is sincerely asked and addressed, you can open the door for God to encourage you!

Prayer—"Heavenly father, I thank you for the comfort of your presence and provision."

AUGUST 7

2 Corinthians 1:3—". . . the God of all comfort . . ." (NIV)

I saw a movie some years ago, where a pilot and co-pilot operating a passenger jet were murdered. Landing the plane became the responsibility of one of the flight attendants, who had no previous flying experience. Someone in the flight tower was summoned to talk the flight attendant through the landing process. What I noted was, that the stewardess had every resource the pilot had, but because she was unfamiliar with the process, she had to be 'encouraged' and 'instructed' to discover she could do it. Continuing from yesterday's devotional, it's important to see during times of stress, that the issue never is the circumstance, but us and how we respond.

Let me refer again to the movie. The gentleman who talked the flight attendant through the landing process gave her technical and moral (spiritual) support. That's why the "God of all comfort" is important to us each day. When we are challenged, he speaks to us as God and as man; as Christ at the right hand of God and as Jesus who lived with us at this level. That means God speaks to us from a depth of understanding. I'm glad God knows us in this way. It means we can never present a need to God, with which he is unfamiliar. Thank God he knows us better than we know ourselves.

Prayer—"God, I praise you for your knowledge of all things; your knowledge comforts and reassures me."

AUGUST 8

2 Corinthians 1:3-4—" . . . the God of all comfort, who comforts us in all our troubles, so that we can comfort those in any trouble . . ." (NIV)

As we have spent the previous two days examining the all-inclusive comfort of God, it's important to study 'why' God comforts us. Obviously, God considers it a waste, if his comfort ends with us; God encourages us, so we can encourage others. This means believers are not called to be receptacles, but channels by which others receive what God has done for us; we are to be bridges for the blessings of God. Therefore, when God encourages us and 'talks' us through our problems, He's showing us where the handles are. Handles are strategically placed on luggage to make it easier to carry. God doesn't remove the need for luggage; he just shows us (comfort) how to 'carry' our problems.

As a result, it's then our responsibility to show others where the handles are; to say to others "this is what got me through", or "this is what brought me out". All of my life is an example of the comfort of God, who points out what I could never see on my own and gives me power to appropriate his blessings. That's a comfort to my soul!

Prayer—"Dear Lord, help me channel your presence in my life, so others may be blessed."

AUGUST 9

Matthew 16:24—"If anyone would come after me, he must deny himself and take up his cross and follow me." (NIV)

I'm a big fan of the TV show '24'. In it, a government agent (Kiefer Sutherland), has the responsibility of protecting the nation from terrorists and their threats against America. In certain episodes, a high priority alert is issued, and when it is, all employees at the agency are obliged to suspend their current activities and concentrate on the matter which commands the priority. In this verse and its context, Jesus says discipleship, or our relationship with him is of the highest priority; to the extent that if it were to come down to a choice between him and anything else, He should be the choice.

This is so, partly because Jesus' main concern is the kingdom of God and its establishment on earth. Remember, the kingdom of God exists wherever God's will is done on earth as it is in Heaven (Matt. 6:10). Further, the kingdom of God is eternal and offers benefits unavailable through any world system or society. But Jesus also refers to discipleship as a priority, because only He can help us succeed in life to the level of fulfillment we seek. It's only by His example and the faith we attach to him, that we achieve our destiny.

Prayer—"Lord, as my priority and provider, I trust you in all things."

AUGUST 10

Luke 9:57-58—" . . . a man said to Him, "I will follow you wherever you go." Jesus replied, "foxes have holes and birds of the air have nests, but the son of man has no place to lay his head." (NIV)

When Jesus spoke his reply to a man's offer in vs. 58, it was within the context of his ministry being rejected in verse 53 of the same chapter. Obviously, Jesus wanted the man to understand the inherent possibility of failure and rejection in Christian discipleship, and decide whether he could pay that price. Failure, as a part of the process of discipleship, is not a unique principle. Failure is actually a part of everything we attempt to do. How many get a hit on the first swing, or walk without first falling? This means we should never be afraid of failure.

For believers, failure is not fatal or final. Within the circumstances of failure for God's people, the seeds of victory and achievement are sown. That's why failure for us is an opportunity to become more intimate with God and experience the power of his resurrection. Failure is not final. Jesus was laughed at by neighbors, had his sanity questioned by family, betrayed by friends, traded and crucified by his countrymen, and still he was raised with a name above every other name. Whatever you do today, don't give up; help is on the way!

Prayer—"Dear God, I praise you for the promise of victory in spite of failure; I will not give up."

AUGUST 11

Luke 9:58—"Jesus replied, "foxes have holes and birds of the air have nests, but the Son of man has no place to lay his head." (NIV)

Have you ever been in a supermarket check-out line and discovered you didn't have enough cash to purchase everything you selected? At that point you probably began to look for the thing you could do without. Everyone is guilty of underestimating the cost of something at some time in their lives, but Jesus wants us to avoid that mistake when it comes to discipleship. Jesus always urged people to count the cost before following Him, so He tempered the enthusiasm of would-be followers with a dose of reality. His intent was not to discourage discipleship, but to produce genuine commitment.

Much of what we hear these days in preaching and teaching, refers to the benefits of discipleship, but not the burdens; that information is either neglected altogether, or placed in the "fine print". As a result, some Christians end up disillusioned and confused because no one told them the path of discipleship is rewarding, yet difficult. I would encourage you to be an informed Christian, if you expect to serve God to the best of your ability.

Prayer—"Dear God, show me clearly the power and problems of my path that I may serve you effectively."

AUGUST 12

Luke 9:57-58—" . . . a man said to Him, "I will follow you wherever you go." Jesus replied, "foxes have holes and birds of the air have nests, but the Son of man has no place to lay His head." (NIV)

The man in verse 57 makes a wonderful pledge to Jesus, but he was both overconfident and under-informed. That's why Jesus responded as He did in verse 58. The man had no idea what 'wherever' meant when he pledged unconditional loyalty to Jesus. For him, 'wherever' was purely geographical with no experiential implications. For Jesus, wherever included Jerusalem, where betrayal and crucifixion awaited Him. Jesus' response in verse 58 was intended to reveal to this would-be follower the cost involved for all those who seek to be Jesus' disciples.

This is important information. It suggests that the pledge of discipleship is like joining the army; you know beforehand the possibility of combat as an enlisted soldier. The same principle applies to marriage. Part of the marriage vow includes the phrase "for better or worse", implying every couple should expect and prepare for the worst. Jesus' concern here is that every believer be aware of the nature of discipleship and make their decisions based on that information.

Prayer—"Lord, keep my heart and mind as I seek to follow you; your presence reminds me of my need."

AUGUST 13

Luke 9:59-60—"He said to another man, "follow me". But the man replied, "Lord, first let me go and bury my father." Jesus said to him, "let the dead bury their own dead, but you go and proclaim the kingdom of God." (NIV)

Here is the case of another would-be disciple. This man's response to Jesus is an example of delayed commitment. His reply was "first let me", with 'first' being the operative word here. The word first implies, I'll have a relationship with you, but something else is first in my life. That's why Jesus responded as He did, although the Master's remarks do seem callous and cold. Understand, this follower offered a contingent discipleship; he said I'll follow you 'when', 'after' or 'if'. He offered Jesus a secondary status in His life and Christian discipleship doesn't work as a hobby or part-time pursuit.

What Jesus suggests here and to every disciple is that nothing, not even family considerations, can substitute for our relationship with Him. Jesus wants us to always fulfill family obligations and responsibilities, but never to the extent that family members, take the place of God. It was God who created the family and as we remain mindful of that, we create an environment in which the family can thrive.

Prayer—"Heavenly Father, teach me your ways for serving both above and below to your glory and honor."

AUGUST 14

Luke 9:61-62—"Still another said, "I will follow you, Lord; but first let me go back and say goodbye to my family." Jesus replied, "no one who puts his hand to the plow and looks back is fit for service in the kingdom of God." (NIV)

Jesus' main point in this encounter is how much looking back can hamper the disciple's progress. Again, Jesus' words sound unfeeling, but an important principle is being shared here. Do not overlook Jesus' reference to the 'kingdom' here. The meaning is that the kingdom is urgent because its God's desire that His will be done on earth as it is in Heaven (Matt. 6:10), and nothing's more important than that. What this man and others like him needed to know is that it's impossible to be saved and go back to "business as usual"; Christ calls us to be "new creatures" with a new agenda.

Additionally, Jesus knows this man's heart. Jesus knows if this man goes home, he and his family will find multiple reasons to forego his desire to follow Jesus. I recently read about a man who didn't want his father to kill the family cow when he was a boy. The cow was slaughtered and the boy did enjoy the hamburger. He said he learned from that experience that there are no "sacred cows" in the life of a believer; that only God is holy. I hope you find the same to be true and will make God your first priority.

Prayer—"God, I worship and adore you; help me keep you where you belong."

AUGUST 15

Isaiah 40:31—"But they that wait upon the lord shall renew their strength;
they shall mount up with wings as eagles . . ." (KJV)

The phrase "mount up" in this verse refers to 'soaring', implying that Christians can pass over certain circumstances as an eagle soars above the elements of a storm. Eagles have the unique ability to use thermals or warm updrafts of air to fly above atmospheric conditions, while conserving energy through a limited need for wing use. Basically, it means that eagles can use the circumstance they're in to reach their destination. What this means for believers is that they can find deliverance from their problem, not by its absence, but by incorporating their relationship with God into the circumstance itself. Therefore, our prayer should be "Lord give me strength", rather than "Lord remove my burden".

This reference to eagles is not just about flight; it's also about sight as well. It refers to the bald eagles' ability to see ahead and to the side at the same time. Believers "mount up with wings as eagles" through the Spirit's gift of discernment to those who "wait on the Lord". This discernment allows us to see as God sees that we may identify things as God does, and draw His strength as our resource. The promise of God for you today is flight and sight. With those gifts you can soar to unexpected levels.

Prayer—"Lord, I praise you for every blessing; for the gifts you give to
strengthen my walk with you."

AUGUST 16

Isaiah 40:31—"But they that wait upon the Lord shall renew their strength; . . . they shall run and not be weary . . ." (KJV)

The promises of God guarantee consistent progress for those who rest their hopes on God. As we continue our devotional look at this verse, God promises that the faithful will "run and not be weary". The word run makes reference to life's exceptional circumstances and our needs during those times. Those are circumstances when more than the usual energy must be exerted. Athletes who train for the Olympics would consider the running of the event as the exceptional circumstance and all other times as training to prepare for it. What God promises is, when your time comes and more than usual is required of you, He will make sure you have what you need.

I remember having difficulty some years ago passing a truck on a two lane highway. My problem was, I was traveling uphill and driving a four-cylinder car. I didn't have the power I needed for the exceptional circumstance. I now drive a six-cylinder car and don't have that problem any more. My point is, most of life only requires four cylinders, but sometimes the circumstance requires six cylinders and that's when God supplies believers with the power they need to overcome their challenges. God's promise to you is that He knows, He cares and He responds.

Prayer—"God, I thank you for grace and power for every day. I live each day with faith."

AUGUST 17

Isaiah 40:31—"But they that wait upon the Lord shall renew their strength; . . . they shall walk and not faint."(KJV)

If God grants us power for the exceptional challenge (run), then he also supplies our needs for the daily grind (walk and not faint). Paul perhaps had the daily grind in mind when he encouraged believers not to be "weary in well doing" (Gal. 6:9). It can be difficult sometimes to maintain with consistency the obligations which become routine to us. The problem is the sameness of daily life can at times lead us to think we're making no progress. When that happens, we tend to become discouraged. What God does is a two-fold blessing: first he energizes us as we maintain our focus on him, and second, he puts little signs here and there to reveal the progress we're making.

The key is to remember even though it sometimes looks as if no progress is being made, that God is doing an unseen work, which can only be realized by those who persevere. So don't allow any challenge today to intimidate or discourage you. God has what you need, whether it's encouragement for your everyday woes, or power for the unusual difficulty. Wait on the Lord!

Prayer—"Heavenly Father, grant me knowledge and wisdom today that I may live life to the fullest."

AUGUST 18

John 14:1—"Let not your heart be troubled: ye believe in God, believe also in me." (KJV)

Transitions are extremely difficult for some because they often require us to do what we've been doing in the absence of some seemingly necessary component for our success. Jesus in this verse addresses the anxiety that comes from a transition in our discipleship experience. He spoke these words to His disciples as He drew close to His time of crucifixion. What Jesus hoped those disciples and we would learn is that transitions are important, inevitable and necessary; they allow believers to understand that God's presence and His promise (the word) are all we need for any and every circumstance. We begin to appropriate His resources as we move beyond wondering how to carry on without the thing we thought we couldn't do without.

To begin addressing personal transitions, believers must come to the conclusion that every experience in life is for the purpose of preparing us for inevitable transitions. That means every circumstance drives us to and readies us for transitions. Transitions therefore, show us how well we've understood the previous events of life and how far we've come as a result. Remember, God is leading you, and whenever He leads, He will insure your time is not wasted.

Prayer—"Lord, thank you for the encouragement I find in your word and your presence."

AUGUST 19

John 14:1—"Let not your heart be troubled: ye believe in God, believe also in me." (KJV)

Let's continue for a few days with this devotional passage. When Jesus spoke these words to His disciples, it was the result of a comment He made to them in Chapter 13, in which Jesus referenced His impending departure. The disciples apparently couldn't fathom maintaining their ministries in Jesus' absence; they felt feelings of inadequacy and loneliness, which Jesus addressed in John 14. Jesus' response in essence was, "set your heart at ease". Jesus did not necessarily expect His words to be fully comprehended here; He did expect His words to be more meaningful later. Sometimes what we hear are just seeds to be harvested when our heads are clearer.

Discipleship requires a focused spirit. It requires we focus on God and what He has said. When we focus on our troubles, the troubles get between us and God, but when we focus on God, He's the closest thing to us and we have immediate access to God's power to comfort and deliver. The key is to remember that it is impossible to fulfill the demands of discipleship, if we are ruled by our emotions. Today may offer you a great challenge, but focus on God and don't let your heart be troubled.

Prayer—"Dear God, I rest on your strength as my comfort and assurance."

AUGUST 20

John 14:1—"Let not your heart be troubled: ye believe in God, believe also in me." (KJV)

This verse is a call to all disciples to 'maintain' their faith in the face of any and all challenges. In essence, Jesus was saying to His disciples, "keep it where it is". That's maintenance, and the same principle applies to the smooth operation of our automobiles. We practice regular maintenance on our cars because it insures that they run with optimum efficiency, but also because we are required to drive in all kinds of conditions. Jesus is saying to His followers here, "maintain your faith", because at its optimum it won't fail you and will allow you to 'function' in any type of circumstance.

This verse is essentially a call to follow the pattern of Jesus, who never denied the reality around Him, but never forgot the power available to Him. In John 6, Jesus was well aware of the multitude present, but also aware of the resources available to feed that crowd once the bread and fish was placed in God's hands. The same power is available to you today as you go out to fulfill your call. This is God's world and you are God's child; claim your victory!

Prayer—"Heavenly Father, give me your power and presence that I may be assured of victory."

AUGUST 21

John 14:1—"Let not your heart be troubled: ye believe in God, believe also in me." (KJV)

I hope you're not tired of this verse yet. I find it to be a treasure trove of inspiration. Jesus sought to comfort His disciples in this verse by giving them a double imperative. He called upon them to trust God, as well as Him. The implication was that trusting in Him was no different from trusting in God, because He and God were no different in personality or purpose. Jesus meant that trust in Him was not an 'addition' to trusting God, because Jesus 'was' God (Jn. 1:1). Yet Jesus does distinguish between faith in Him and God, because we must never forget that we trust God because He supplies our needs and we trust Jesus Christ, because He gives us the access to those supplies.

Jesus' words of comfort here, are intended to lead His disciples to evidence confidence; to be reminded of what Jesus Christ has already done, and to draw their confidence from that unchanging example. Jesus was attacked and abandoned, yet he was resurrected and now has a name "above every other name" and that's a reason to feel confident and secure.

Prayer—"Dear God, you are worthy of praise; you assure me of every necessity and my access to it."

AUGUST 22

John 14:2—"I go to prepare a place for you . . ." (KJV)

As we continue with this passage, note that Jesus bases His call to confidence on the assurance of divine provision for His disciples. He says His leaving is for the purpose of providing for them something they could not have otherwise. Every believer eventually learns that the events of life, whether pleasant or unpleasant, are woven into the fabric of our ultimate benefit. This is an important truth, because it helps us avoid overreacting and stressing to the point of worry. God wants us to understand that He knows our situations and has provided for us.

When I was in elementary school, I lived across the street from my school. Because I was in such close proximity, I went home for lunch every day. My mother always had my meal ready and on the table when I arrived home. She knew when I was coming and how long I had to be there. Jesus expresses that same truth here. He says God knows your condition and your seasons and has already prepared a table before you even if it's in the presence of your enemies (Ps. 23:5). Rejoice, because Jehovah-Jireh has supplied the need.

Prayer—"God, I thank you for the blessings you've already bestowed; you are my creator and sustainer."

AUGUST 23

John 14:2—"In my Father's house are many mansions: if it were not so, I would have told you. I go to prepare a place for you."(KJV)

The word 'mansions' in this verse has confused so many believers. The remedy for that confusion is to have an understanding of the root meaning of the word. The word mansions in this verse, is derived from a word which means 'remain'. It implies permanence as opposed to space or square footage. This is important because, if all Jesus did was provide us with more room to run around Heaven, then He did not really address our deepest need. What you and I need most is to be assured that what Christ provides cannot be taken away and that we have unbroken fellowship with Him as a result of His work.

So don't think of Heaven as a picturesque space or place, but as unbroken fellowship with God; not in terms of square footage, but as an unalterable relationship. What difference does it make to have all the space you want, but without the joy of relational sharing? Jesus said He was preparing a place for us that we might know what it's like to be in His company, and never hear the word goodbye again.

Prayer—"Dear God, I thank you for your love and company; your presence in my life is my greatest strength."

AUGUST 24

John 14:1—"Let not your heart be troubled: ye believe in God, believe also in me." (KJV)

In John 11:33, 12:27 and 13:21, Jesus is described as troubled. His confidence though, came from the conviction that His Father's purpose and power was greater than the things which troubled Him. What we see in this verse is Jesus' words to help disciples confront and conquer their own troubles.

In vs. 2 of this chapter, Jesus, when speaking of the purpose of His departure said, "if it were not so, I would have told you." His implication was that His word is credible enough to stand on its own and needs no validation from any other source. It reminds me of asking my Father years ago why I had to do what He said, and his response was, "because I said so". Jesus here embraces the same principle; whatever He says, is an authority of its own and needs no "propping up" by anyone else. Can you imagine the confidence which comes from knowing "if God said it, that settles it?" That's the security you and I can take into every experience, knowing God's word is enough to settle and satisfy any demand, when we believe.

Prayer—"Dear God, I trust your word above all; it creates and perpetuates alone."

AUGUST 25

John 14:2-3—". . . I am going there to prepare a place for you. And if I go and prepare a place for you, I will come back and take you to be with me . . ." (NIV)

In these verses, Jesus not only refers to the 'necessity' of His departure, but how essential 'He' is in this process of departure and preparation. There is a two-fold truth here. The first is that these kinds of transitions are necessary to our growth and development; the second is that without Jesus as the subject of this departure and transition, we lack the capacity to turn transition into triumph.

What that means, is that only Jesus, with the story of His conflict and victory on Easter weekend, can give us both the knowledge and assurance necessary to fight on in life even when the odds are against us. It's the story of a cross on Friday and an open tomb on Sunday that assures me that God always has the final word! How could we face our tomorrows, steeped in the unknown, if Jesus hadn't already gone ahead to provide and make those same resources available to us? Today may be a mystery to you, but I'm confident that our God, omniscient and holding the reigns of time in His hands, is waiting for you at each turn to give you direction and deliverance.

Prayer—"Lord, I praise you for what you've already done; your love has provided for all my tomorrows."

AUGUST 26

Job 1:21—"The Lord gave and the Lord has taken away; may the name of the Lord be praised." (NIV)

When I purchase items like milk or bread, I always pay attention to the freshness date on the packaging. That date is important because it means the product cannot be sold beyond that date. Of course, that implies as well that the milk has a shelf life to it, beyond which it loses its taste and health benefits. Isn't that true of life in general? All of us come into the world with a freshness date, beyond which we lose our usefulness. I thought I'd share some thoughts with you today, related to this principle of "freshness dates".

First, the difference between us and the milk is the milk comes with its freshness date, but we do not. We come into the world full of promise and potential, but we have no idea how long we have to fulfill or realize that promise. Secondly, if all the bread is not used before its freshness expires, it must be thrown away due to the presence of mold. What a truth for us! How many lives have been wasted; how many dreams unrealized because of the waste of time and opportunities? We would do well to do all we can while we can. Meet me tomorrow to continue this thought.

Prayer—"God, thank you for gifts and thank you for opportunities to use them."

AUGUST 27

Job 1:21—"The Lord gave and the Lord has taken away; may the name of the Lord be praised." (NIV)

Let's continue this discussion of freshness dates from yesterday's devotional. We are focusing our thoughts on the truth that all of us come into life with an expiration date and that we must do all we can to fulfill our potential at every opportunity.

Another truth which comes from the freshness date printed on a loaf of bread is that someone else determines what that date is. The person who bakes the bread or produces the milk determines its length of freshness. How important that is for each of us. When we develop a sense of consciousness about ourselves and life, we generally expect to live a long life with reasonable success. The fact is though, only God can determine the length of our days no matter how well we live or succeed; our "freshness dates" are solely a matter of His discretion and will. Job says in this verse that God gives and takes away. Since this is a divine prerogative, don't you think we should give God our best at all times? When I combine the grace of God with my own mortality, it encourages me to stay faithful and focused; that's the only way.

Prayer—"Heavenly Father, walk with me each day as I seek to be my best and do my best."

AUGUST 28

Hebrew 4:12—"For the word of God is living and active. Sharper than any double-edged sword . . ." (NIV)

In the literature of Greek mythology is the story of Pandora's Box. In that story, Pandora opened a box which unleashed all the evils we experience in the world today. One of the timeless principles of that story is that some things have tremendous potential for good or evil, but they can only influence our circumstances when they are provided the opportunity. The evils in Pandora's Box could never have affected the world if Pandora had kept the box closed.

Hebrews 4:12 says that the word of God has tremendous potential for blessing and benefit, but the truth is, until we open and apply the truths of scripture, we can never experience that benefit. The Bible is a treasure (Matt. 13:44), but what good is any treasure if it remains buried or ignored? Life's experiences are too variable to leave unused the power God makes available. I've discovered, as I hope you have, that I am too weak and powerless to overcome my problems by myself. I encourage you today to 'open' God's gift to you (Bible) and discover the joy of this eternal resource.

Prayer—"Dear God, I praise you for your word and its depth of meaning to me"

AUGUST 29

Hebrew 4:12—"For the word of God is living and active. Sharper than any double-edged sword . . ." (NIV)

The author of Hebrews refers to God's word as 'quick' or 'alive'. This means that what God says is never outdated or irrelevant. To be outdated is to be replaceable by something that serves the purpose better. Obviously, there is no difference in God's word now and when He first 'spoke' the universe into existence, or when Jesus spoke and the winds and waves obeyed Him. God's word then 'updates' itself not in its content or character, but in its ability to analyze and adapt.

In the 'Halloween' series of movies, Michael Myers was characterized as "pure evil" by his psychiatrist. That characterization was manifested by Michael coming back from situations no one else could ever come back from. The implication was that Michael could not be ultimately affected by the ordinary like other humans; that his life was not an ordinary life. What our author says in this devotional verse is that the word of God cannot be stifled or eliminated by the things of this life, because it has a life of its own, based on the life of Him who has no beginning and no end. You can always trust what God says, so spend your day confidently listening to God.

Prayer—"Lord, when you speak I am confident that all you say will come to pass; speak to me today."

AUGUST 30

Hebrew 4:12—"For the word of God is quick and powerful . . ." (KJV)

As we continue our look at this verse, note the author also says God's word is 'powerful', or active. That means that God's word speeds to fulfill God's intention when God speaks. That's what the author of Genesis implies when he says "God said . . . and it was so . . ." It also refers to Isaiah 55:11, which says God's word never returns to Him void. The implication is, when God utters a word of purpose, upon its return that word will have accomplished its goal; it doesn't come back empty-handed. In the parable of the talents (Matt. 25), the final man came back empty-handed (in terms of increase), because he reflects the difference between humanity and God; God never fails to achieve His purpose.

God's word then is self-fulfilling; it needs no assistance in producing God's intent. It's different for us though. When we speak, our words are 'potential', generally requiring assistance in their fulfillment. God's words are power, meaning everything needed to achieve His goals are already contained within His words. Many items purchased say "batteries not included" meaning potential is there, but not power. Not so with God; when He speaks the power is already there for those who believe. Why not trust Him to supply your needs today?

Prayer—"Dear God, speak to me, remind me over and over again what can happen through your words."

AUGUST 31

Hebrew 4:12—"For the word of God is quick and powerful, and sharper than any two-edged sword, piercing even to the dividing asunder of soul and spirit . . ." (KJV)

What a deep treasure this verse is. The word of God, "sharper than any two-edged sword" is a reference to the absence of dullness in what God says. It means by a single stroke, God's word can accomplish God's purpose using less words and less time than it takes us to do the same thing. More importantly, this verse says that the word of God gets right to the heart of the matter addressed. I remember as a boy watching the 'Ginsu' knife commercials. The Ginsu Knife was shown to be able to cut through just about any surface without losing its sharpness. This is what Hebrews 4:12 says about God's word; that no matter how many times you apply it, it never loses its ability to cut to the heart of human matters and bless the faithful.

Additionally though, don't fail to see that God's word cuts through every emotion we wrap and justify ourselves in, whether it's pride, anger, fear, stubbornness, unbelief or self-righteousness. The power of God's word is rooted in the spiritual and therefore, gets to the heart of any matter because all of life has a spiritual beginning. It's more than a joy to me to know I have a resource which never fails to help me know, interpret and apply truth. I hope you feel the same way!

Prayer—"Heavenly Father, I'm glad you know me as you do; your knowledge of me helps me know myself."

SEPTEMBER 1

Hebrew 4:12—"For the word of God is quick and powerful, and sharper than any two-edged sword, piercing even to the dividing asunder of soul and spirit, and of the joints and marrow, and is a discerner of the thoughts and intents of the heart." (KJV)

God's word is complete in its ability to analyze us because the penetration it executes extends to both the natural and supernatural. Hebrews 4:12 says it can divide soul from spirit, meaning the word of God can distinguish between our desires and our understanding. That literally means that what God says can breakdown how I interpret life, to how I processed the information when first received. Further, this verse says the penetration of God's word extends to the joint and marrow. This is a reference to the body's skeletal system and how joints, ligaments, and bones work together to allow us physical movement and range of motion.

What God wants us to understand from this verse is that God is so perceptive, that unlike those around us, He can clearly distinguish between our outward actions and inner thoughts. The implication is that sometimes our actions do not reflect our attitude. Obviously, God wants to encourage a harmony between the natural and spiritual components of man; that through that harmony our motives may be beyond question, and His kingdom and glory can be advanced.

Prayer—"Dear Lord, help me know you as you know me that my life may be pleasing to you."

SEPTEMBER 2

Hebrew 4:12— "For the word of God is quick and powerful, and sharper than any two-edged sword, piercing even to the dividing asunder of soul and spirit, and of the joints and marrow, and is a discerner of the thoughts and intents of the heart." (KJV)

While this verse has been important to us the past few days in helping us see God, it has more importantly helped us see how God sees us. God's ability through His word to judge our thoughts and intent suggests that God 'sifts' our actions because sometimes our motives are quite different. This is important because it's therapeutic for believers; it means that God's word not only exposes the attitudes, it also enables me through its principles to align my will with God's when He sees an intent outside His will for me.

Since God's word is that active and powerful, at some point all of us are confronted by the truth of God's word. His word is prophetic and searching and cannot therefore be avoided. The Bible says that in due season, all will acknowledge Jesus Christ as Lord; so too shall all of us face the distinguishing power of God's word. As a boy, I remember seeing a cartoon in which Daffy Duck was trapped in a house and couldn't escape Elmer Fudd no matter what he tried or where he went. God's word is a searchlight, which exposes human thought and action, but only for the purpose of God bringing out the best in us and bringing glory to Himself.

Prayer— "God, search my heart and expose me, that my life may reflect your grace."

SEPTEMBER 3

Ephesians 6:11—"Put on the full armor of God so that you can take your stand against the devil's schemes." (NIV)

No matter how well applied roofing material is placed on a roof, if water is allowed to sit on it, it will eventually find its way into the building. That's why every roof needs to have a drainage design, which allows water to flow off rather than sit on it. This principle is important for believers to maintain their strength and capacity during difficulty times. The point is, Christians must be careful not to remain in positions which eventually allow the enemy to have a stronghold and affect their relationship with God and access to His resources.

Addictions bear this truth out clearly. If an individual has been addicted to a substance and becomes rehabilitated, the worst thing a recovering addict can do is hang around people and environments which encourage the use and abuse of drugs. That's a "standing water" scenario in which the recovering addict is destined to relapse into drug abuse again. I believe that's why the psalmist suggests we avoid the counsel of the ungodly and standing in the 'way' of sinners; he obviously understands how important it is for believers to arm themselves against the many influences that can victimize Christians and hamper their walk with God. What do you need to do today to 'maintain' your walk in victory?

Prayer—"Heavenly Father, dress me for success today; help me fight the fight of faith."

SEPTEMBER 4

John 9:4—"As long as it is day, I must do the work of Him who sent me. Night is coming when no one can work." (NIV)

It is significant that one of David's greatest failures came at a time when he was idle (2 Sam. 11:1). Idle time is dangerous because it opens the door for choices outside the will of God. John 9:4 suggests that life is an opportunity for accomplishment and that opportunity should not be wasted, because it can't be recovered. Further, Jesus says since our opportunities are limited we must do all we can while we can. Isaiah implied the same when he said "seek ye the Lord while He may be found . . ." (Is. 55:6-7).

I discovered recently that cars are manufactured to run more efficiently when idling time is decreased, even in cold weather. The problem with an idling car is, it's engaged to do something it's not being allow to do, so air is polluted, gasoline is wasted and money is lost. God made us to work and idling is just as destructive in the spiritual realm as it is in the natural. It's harmful to us spiritually because we fail to influence the environment as the salt of the earth. It's harmful to me personally because I miss opportunities to exercise my gifts and experience growth. People who are idle should just wear a sign that says "out of order", because they fail to fulfill God's purpose for them. Don't let this be an unproductive day.

Prayer—"Lord, use me today to fulfill your purpose and bless others."

SEPTEMBER 5

Hebrew 10:25—"Not forsaking the assembling of ourselves together, as the manner of some is; but exhorting one another . . ." (KJV)

Kicking a live coal from a pile of hot coals, of course leads to the isolated coal quickly cooling and dying from separation. One of the Christian's necessities is to avoid isolation from those who share his/her faith. What fellowship with other Christians provides, is encouragement, assistance and accountability. Because God made us for fellowship, when it is absent, we are more susceptible to the things that weaken us spiritually. Hebrews 10:25 reminds us that it is impossible for believers to dash into fellowship occasionally, dash out and expect to experience the fullness of God's resources and presence. The problem with that approach, is the blessings of God are in a 'flow' and when we treat Him sporadically, we cut off His flow to us, which would otherwise be continuous.

Remember, Jesus taught us to pray for daily bread implying the need for 'fresh' blessings each day; so yesterday's blessings are inadequate for today's needs. I shop for food once a week, because I'm always in need of replenishing. God never set up life for us to receive everything all at once and that's why we must be consistent in worship and service. God is calling for people who are ready to give Him praise and glory consistently. That's the only way to experience the fulfillment of God's promises to His children.

Prayer—"Lord, remind me of the benefits of regular worship and fellowship; advance your kingdom through me."

SEPTEMBER 6

Hebrew 10:25—"Not forsaking the assembling of ourselves together, as the manner of some is; but exhorting one another . . ." (KJV)

I believe God has a concern for helping us maintain and preserve what He does for us through salvation. Consequently, He reminds us to spend time in the company of individuals who are of like mind. I remember my grandmother telling me years ago that when she made preserves, she boiled the jars and lids before canning the preserves. She boiled the lids because the heat softened the rubber on the lid and provided an airtight seal. The intent was to keep the ingredients in the jar fresh until the seal was broken. When believers forsake assembling with other believers, it's like opening the jar, letting air in and losing the 'atmosphere' of preservation.

The fact is, we as Christians need the regular assembling of ourselves (worship and study), because some of our resources can only come as we access them through fellowship. Additionally, our fellowship with others is a reminder that we are not alone in our experiences; that we have a common bond through a common belief and that commonality is a source of comfort and security as we 'collectively' praise God.

Prayer—"Heavenly Father, I thank you for my church and those who share my worship of you."

SEPTEMBER 7

Exodus 12:13—"The blood will be a sign for you on the houses where you are; and when I see the blood, I will pass over you." (NIV)

God here said He had a blessing for Israel, but the bestowal of it rested upon the evidence of Israel's obedience to God's command. If Israel here obeyed God, it would be an acknowledgement of God's covenant with Israel and their intention to recognize it through their actions. This is certainly an example of the blessings which come from obedience, but more importantly, it reminds us that what God really honors is not an action, but an attitude; God honors His spirit in us.

God has given a certain framework to life; He has set certain basic principles, which are unchanging and rewarding. That is of course beneficial, because it means God is consistent and we can faithfully depend on Him without fear of His failure or delay. It also means though, that God doesn't bend the rules just because we need a break. His standards are fair and righteous as are His ways. What it comes down to is, if God's will is our goal, righteousness will not allow us to choose another road, but grace does allow for a "change of lanes".

Prayer—"Father, I count on your faithfulness; I seek to be consistently where you desire."

SEPTEMBER 8

Genesis 2:18—"The Lord God said, 'It is not good for the man to be alone. I will make a helper suitable for him.'" (NIV)

One of the Bible's basic premises is that much of what God wants to do for us is related to our interaction with each other. That principle is as old as Cain and Abel (Gen. 4), and as late as the unforgiving servant (Matt. 18). Essentially, it means that none of us can expect God to bless us if we distance ourselves in work or worship; there is no fullness of inheritance for the isolationist. The only negative reference God made during the creative process was that it wasn't good for man to be alone, meaning we do better with God when we cheerfully cooperate with others like us. Apparently, the evidence that God is with us is the fruit of our relationships with each other (Gen. 1:28). God determined that the relationship between Adam and Eve could not be a success without harmonious interaction and reproducing their own kind.

Why is this 'fellowship' important to God? Because God is a God of fellowship. God has fellowship on the divine level between the Godhead (Father, Son, and Holy Spirit) and being made in His image, we lack fulfillment until we learn how to seek and enjoy the company of those who share our humanity. This may be a good day for you to open up your world and let someone else in.

Prayer—"Dear Lord, thank you for others like me and thank you for fellowship with them."

SEPTEMBER 9

Luke 6:37-38—"Do not judge and you will not be judged. Do not condemn and you will not be condemned . . . Give and it will be given to you. A good measure, pressed down, shaken together . . . For with the measure you use, it will be measured to you." (NIV)

These verses say the attitude God honors in His people is mercy, coupled with benevolence, because we must never forget that God has treated us with that same spirit. Further, these verses suggest that we must begin our relationships with each other under the assumption that none of us could survive the scrutiny of God if it were based solely on justice. I remember a teacher in high school once grading a class test on a curve. She realized if we were to do well on the test, we would need help from her; she coupled justice with mercy.

Jesus says in these verses don't 'judge' or 'condemn', because although God 'prefers' to act in mercy, when we put others on trial, we invite God to do the same with us. What Jesus forbids here is not the judicial system or church discipline, but the tendency to criticize and find fault in others. Essentially, God hates "status by negation", which is seeking to prop ourselves up by bringing others down. When Jacob left his encounter with God with a limp (Gen. 32:31), from then on, every step he took was a reminder of his tricks and schemes, but also of God's mercy. What would life be like if not for God's grace?

Prayer—"Dear Lord, teach me to treat others as I desire to be treated; remind me of your grace."

SEPTEMBER 10

Luke 6:37, 38—"... forgive and it will be forgiven. Give and it will be given to you ..." (NIV)

As we continue with these verses today, God calls upon us to imitate His character as we relate to each other. He calls for forgiveness and benevolence. God suggests that believers learn to let things go and reach out in addition. Forgiveness involves setting a person free from the past and the obligations of recompense attached to their actions; it is to release the past and any expectations you had related to the past. This forgiveness does not ignore the guilt or proclaim innocence; it merely releases the debt and moves on. The basis for this forgiveness is the measure of forgiveness and grace found in God's relating to us; He has forgiven us freely only because we have accepted the Lordship of His Son, Jesus Christ.

Jesus gets more radical here though. He says to not only forego the right to recompense, but to extend my hand in open-handed generosity to the guilty. That's difficult, because most of us, if we do forgive, prefer to walk away, but God won't let us forget that our blessings are not connected to isolation, but fellowship. That means then that reconciliation requires sacrifice and that reminds me of the extent God went to at Calvary to reconcile me to Him. Praise God!

Prayer—"God, keep working in me, so I may treat others according to your will and example."

SEPTEMBER 11

Luke 6:37, 38—" . . . forgive and you will be forgiven. Give and it will be given to you. A good measure, pressed down, shaken together and running over, will be poured into your lap." (NIV)

Jesus in Luke 6:38 gave His followers an incentive for going the extra mile in their relationships. He says horizontal benevolence produces a vertical blessing. The implication is that God responds to those who practice mercy and benevolence. The blessing is explained using images from a granary.

"Good measure" means "more than fair"; it refers to the kind of business practices that keep you coming back to the same company over and over again. Good business people understand the importance of cultivating relationships, because they value people more than profit.

"Pressed down" refers to the practice of insuring that the container holds all it can by pressing your foot or hand inside. "Shaken together" is for the purpose of filling in every empty space. Why does God respond to us in this way? It's because God wants us to keep coming back to Him recognizing His faithfulness and fairness, but also to remind us that this promise of blessing is contingent on how we relate to and treat our neighbors.

Prayer—"Dear God, your standard of love and grace is my goal; teach me to love as you have loved me."

SEPTEMBER 12

Matthew 26:50—"Jesus replied, "friend, do what you came for"." (NIV)

These words were spoken by Jesus when Judas betrayed Him in Gethsemane. The lesson contained within Jesus' response to Judas is, in spite of appearances, Jesus was in control of this scenario. Jesus was arrested because He deliberately refused to prevent it, understanding His role in securing our redemption through His sacrifice. The reality of Jesus' control in this setting is important, because believers must always believe that no circumstance is beyond God's control. To be secure in that knowledge, we need both sight and insight; we must look out and up if we are to face our earthly realities with heavenly confidence.

Jesus is a great example of looking out and up. He looked out and saw a multitude of thousands (Jn. 6), and two fish and five loaves, but looked up and saw divine provision and knew He had everything He needed to meet the challenge. It is the upward look that gives us the confidence that victory is ours. I remember seeing a little girl ask her father to lift her on his shoulders. The implication was she wanted to see life from His perspective. What a difference it makes to rest our concerns on Him and benefit from our Fathers' perspective!

Prayer—"Heavenly Father, stand beside me and through your presence give me assurance and victory."

SEPTEMBER 13

James 1:2, 3—"My brethren, count it all joy when ye fall into divers temptations; knowing this, that the trying of your faith worketh patience." (KJV)

Impatience is generally a sign of immaturity in the life of a believer. The result of immaturity is the loss of needed lessons that strengthen and stabilize us in our difficult seasons. In these devotional verses for the day, James suggests that believers must learn to consistently respond to their difficulties. That's what he means when he says "count it all joy . . .". This unwavering intensity of faith does not allow the 'joy' of it to be diluted by any other emotion which would inhibit faith's ability to bless us.

What James implies here is that God 'perfects' our faith through tests. I learned recently that test pilots check structure, instruments and other parts of planes before and during flights, as a means of determining the safety of an aircraft. James is saying here that real faith does not fly without the tests which prove its ability to handle that for which it was made. I said earlier that impatience is a sign of immaturity because it's like any child who can't sit still long enough to wait for the end result of a process. If you are aware of the Easter story, then learn to "count it all joy" on Friday, because when Sunday comes you'll see God always "works all things together for good".

Prayer—"God, I need more patience; I need the reminder of your unfailing power to transform my life."

SEPTEMBER 14

I Peter 1: 3, 4—"Blessed be the God and Father of our Lord Jesus Christ, which according to His abundant mercy hath begotten us again unto a lively hope . . . to an inheritance incorruptible . . ." (KJV)

When Peter wrote these verses, he suggested that God is worthy of praise even when believers are in the midst of trying circumstances, because God's realities are unaffected by what we go through. First, Peter says God is worthy of praise because of the new birth He's provided us. Birth exists for the purpose of introducing the child to a new level and starting that child on the path of growth and maturity. We have been born from above to mature us in the example of Jesus Christ.

Secondly, Peter says to praise God for our "living hope". The living hope is closely connected to our new birth because it refers to growth and maturity; it anticipates a better and brighter day based on the resurrection of Jesus Christ. This means we have reason to persevere because not even death could keep Jesus down.

Finally, God is worthy of praise because of our inheritance in Him. An inheritance is a gift which belongs to someone else, but is promised to us based on certain criteria being met. It's ours, but not without some indication of our readiness to receive it. Why should we praise God? Because He birthed us into a new life, assures us of victory, and holds for us a special blessing that no one can take away. Praise God!

Prayer—"Lord, thank you for every blessing, particularly the gift of salvation and promise of ultimate victory."

SEPTEMBER 15

I Peter 1:4, 5—". . . an inheritance incorruptible, and undefiled, and that fadeth not away, reserved in Heaven for you, who are kept by the power of God . . ." (KJV)

Let's continue with this passage from yesterday. Peter says God has an inheritance for every believer, but he takes a moment to describe the inheritance. First, Peter says what God reserved for us is 'incorruptible'. This means God's promise to us is not subject to rot or decay; it's not in anyway diminished by time, like all created things are, because God's gifts are eternal in nature like He is.

Then Peter says it's 'undefiled'. This means it's unstained and unpolluted by sin or anything detrimental to its makeup. Again, the gifts of God reflect His nature of holiness, which indicate the separation of God from anything unrighteous. God cannot give us or promise us anything, which could be less later, than it was when given.

Finally, Peter says God's inheritance is unfading, meaning unlike a flower, it doesn't wither or lose its beauty. All the characteristics of God's gifts are perpetual, because of the unchanging nature of God. The best part is this inheritance is 'kept' in Heaven, implying it will be there when we get there and we need not worry because verse five says we're being kept as well, so we can claim our gift at the appropriate time.

Prayer—"Heavenly Father, I praise you for keeping power and for promises you never fail to deliver on."

SEPTEMBER 16

I Peter 1:4, 5—"... an inheritance incorruptible, and undefiled, and that fadeth not away, reserved in Heaven for you, who are kept by the power of God ..." (KJV)

Let's go further with this passage today. Verse 4 says God preserves our inheritance, but verse 5 says God preserves us too. This means there's a balance between God's action on earth and His action in Heaven. God protects our future by preserving our inheritance, but He also protects our present by preserving us. The words 'reserved' and 'kept' in verses 4 and 5 are military terms which reflect how seriously God regards us and our inheritance. After the terrorist attacks of September 11, 2001, the heightened security in our airports was a reflection of how important the safety of airline passengers is. God feels the same concern for us, but at a higher level, and His concern is our security.

What does this mean for us? It suggests that although we experience conflict as believers and feel vulnerable, God will not allow our circumstances to overwhelm or overcome us. God is preserving us internally and protecting us externally, so that in due season He can give us what He's promised and we can enjoy the full measure of our relationship with Him.

Prayer—"Dear God, I'm sure of your protection and provision; I'm determined to stay close to you each day."

SEPTEMBER 17

I Peter 1:7—"These have come so that your faith . . . of greater worth than gold which perishes even though refined by fire may be proved genuine . . ." (NIV)

Peter says God's goal in allowing certain circumstances in the believer's life is to authenticate our faith. Why is faith so important? Because it is the one and only thing which connects us to God. Romans 10:9 and Hebrews 11:6 both say that faith establishes and maintains our relationship with God; it's what God looks for when we seek to access His benefits. The same principle can be found in Exodus 12:13, where the death angel looked for blood on the doorpost to authenticate a covenant relationship and "pass over" wherever he saw the blood. In the same way, God looks for our faith in His power and promise to validate our faith and give us what we need.

What God wants believers to see, is that any genuine thing can always be used for the purpose for which it was created. That's why counterfeit money has no real value; it may be used for a moment, but is soon discovered as valueless and discarded. Only faith in God has the capacity to serve us unfailingly, regardless the circumstance. I encourage you today to recognize every test as an opportunity to strengthen and validate your faith.

Prayer—"Dear God, help me to see you in every experience that I may show faith and courage each day."

SEPTEMBER 18

Genesis 1:31—"God saw all that He had made and it was very good."
(NIV)

As Christians and people made in the image of God, we look to the Bible, God's revelation of Himself, to instruct us in living up to God's standard. According to Genesis 1, God's example is a standard of excellence. Genesis 1:31 says God's standard of excellence began with the created order. Whether it was the world or sky or creatures, God declared each aspect of His creation to be good (Gen. 1:4, 10, 12, 18, 21, 25). In each verse good meant 'beneficial' or perfectly suited for its purpose.

Genesis 1:31 is God's overall assessment of His work. Obviously, the whole of God's work was very good, because God was good in the details (vss. 4, 10, 12, 18, 21, 25). God's concern was not just for a good result, but for a process which never overlooked or left out God's best. I can remember looking at a house once as a prospective new home. At first appearance, the home looked wonderful, but after a close examination, I discovered the 'detail' work was shoddy and I quickly dismissed both the home and the company which built it. God calls upon us to appreciate the importance of details and to strive to be excellent; that was His pattern in creation and what He expects from those of us who make up His kingdom.

Prayer—"Heavenly Father, excellence is my goal. Help me reflect your nature in all I do."

SEPTEMBER 19

Genesis 1:26—"Then God said, "Let us make man in our image, in our likeness . . ." (NIV)

I'd like to continue today with God's pattern and standard of excellence. Genesis 1:26 says God made us in His image and gave us dominion over the planet and everything in it. Remembering that God does all things excellently (Gen. 1:31), it seems obvious that when God gave man dominion, He intended for man to experience life as God experiences it, with the purpose being to help us be as much like God in the process of fulfilling our role as stewards for the earth.

God gave us dominion, but more importantly, He made us in 'His' image, meaning He made us to reflect Him in exercising our authority. The quality of any flashlight is not based on the bulb or battery, but on the reflector which surrounds the bulb. A quality reflector takes the light from the bulb, powered by the batteries, and sends that light out to reveal position and progress. It was God's intent in Genesis 1:26 to help us, through His image, to reflect Him in our relationship with the planet and all its creatures. God wants the light (example) others see in us to be a reflection of His glory (Matt. 5:16). When we are excellent in our example, it calls attention, not to us, but to God, who is excellent in every way.

Prayer—"Dear God, how excellent is your name in all the earth; help me to be like you."

SEPTEMBER 20

Genesis 1:31—"God saw all that He had made and it was very good." *(NIV)*

This verse says God is excellent in all He does. He also calls me to excellence, but in my pursuit of it, I discover the difference between me and God. In God's pattern, there's no deviation in the course God follows, because God has excellent results based on excellence in details. The difference with me is, I've had good results in my life, but my details have often left something to be desired. It's like a man who attempted to walk a straight line on the beach, but after arriving at the desired point, he looked back to a crooked path left behind. As I've said, I've had excellent results in my life, but my details reflect failure and weakness which the presence of God has help me overcome.

As we note the difference between us and God, it helps us maintain a pattern of excellence, because it keeps us confronted with God's standard. To effectively reduce the length of a drawn line without touching it, you must draw a larger parallel line next to it. That's what God does for us; He stands next to us (in Jesus) to show us how good we can be and how far we can go. God made us in His image to give us the capacity for excellence as we imitate His example.

Prayer—"Lord, your example is my standard for life; it's my desire to be more like you each day."

SEPTEMBER 21

Genesis 1:31—"God saw all that He had made and it was very good." *(NIV)*

Our God is excellent in all He does and I have an attitude of excellence, but I'm still a sinner, who needs God's grace. That's why Jesus died for me; to handle the details I'm powerless to accomplish. How did God do it? Yesterday, I shared with you the story of a man who tried to walk a straight line on the beach, only to discover a crooked path left behind him, in spite of his best efforts. What I didn't tell you was that as he lamented his ability to walk a straight line, the tide rolled in and washed away his crooked path. That's what God has done for us through Christ; He has washed our past away with the blood of His son and freed us to meet His standard through grace.

Because of this act of love, excellence is my goal; not to be the best at what I do, but to be the best I can be. That's why excellence is more important to me than success. Excellence is a reflection of the God who made me, so others can see Him shining through me.

Prayer—"Heavenly Father, as I strive for excellence, empower me by your Spirit and encourage me with your word."

SEPTEMBER 22

John 7:6—"Therefore Jesus told them, "the right time for me has not yet come" . . ." (NIV)

I remember reading some years ago, although I cannot remember the source, that "time is our education for eternity". The implication is that God desires we use time as our window to eternity, identifying God's purpose and plan for us. This means that time is too important to waste; it must be spent with an eye on those matters which are most important to God. Ovid, the first century author, once referred to time as a 'devourer', meaning time eats away at wasted opportunities such that they do not come our way again.

When Jesus told his brothers in John 7 that "the right time" for Him had not yet come, He was suggesting to them and to us that we should spend our time on the things which outlast time; that every decision we make should be based on seeing beyond the present moment. The fact is, everything we see is passing away because what we see naturally is not the highest reality. The ultimate reality is God and the resources of His kingdom. God gave us 'time' to identify those resources, so we might know the temporary nature of life in this world is not a reason to be discouraged. Begin your day by taking advantage of every opportunity to know God better; that's the best thing you can do with your time.

Prayer—"God, I thank you for the time you've given me; help me use it to your glory and honor."

SEPTEMBER 23

John 7:6—"Therefore Jesus told them, "the right time for me has not yet come" . . . " (NIV)

These are the words of Jesus to His brothers when they sought to rush Him to a Jewish feast. Jesus' response here indicated that He did not do things haphazardly; that 'timing' was important to Him because He sought to please God in all He did.

Note first, that time is different with God than us, because time is a created experience, and God who has no beginning or end, lives outside of time. This means we see life sequentially, but God sees all things at once. Obviously, because God can never be surprised, we do well to trust our 'times' to Him.

Secondly, Jesus is suggestive about His approach to time. He implies that His time was 'fixed'; that He was on a set plan from God. Gal. 4:4 refers to Jesus' coming into the world as being in the "fullness of time". This means that the mission of saving our souls was too important to approach without a divine sense of timing.

Finally, this verse suggests if time was important enough for God to step into through Jesus Christ, then it should be important enough to us to spend it well. Samuel Butler once said, "time is the only purgatory", meaning the time we have now is our only chance to get it right. How will you spend your time today?

Prayer—"Dear Lord, today is another chance for me; help me spend my time well."

SEPTEMBER 24

Acts 1:8—"... and you will be my witnesses in Jerusalem..." (NIV)

Jesus commissioned His disciples in Matt. 28:19, 20 to "go into all the world" and make disciples. It was His mandate to believers everywhere to value His story and to use that story to win others to His kingdom. In Acts 1:8, Jesus was more specific about the process of evangelism. He said to the disciples to begin in Jerusalem. He intended for the disciples to commence their ministries with those closest to them. The implication is, the criteria for success in ministry in the larger arena, is the measure of success achieved in the smaller setting, namely the home and extended family. If we are unable to influence and win those with whom we share the deepest intimacy, then how can we influence those with whom we are less familiar?

There's something else here though. This verse also says something about how we value or esteem those closest to us, meaning, if you have found the answer to life's greatest questions, surely you'd want to share it with those you love. The first thing most people do with good news is pass it on to those they share their closest bonds with. Jesus demonstrated that love principle, when on the cross, as He gave His mother to John and John to His mother (Jn. 19:26, 27). There is no greater example of love you can express than to say to your friends and family as the Samaritan woman, "come see a man ..." (Jn. 4:29).

Prayer—"Dear God, thank you for those closest to me and help me be to them what you've called me to."

SEPTEMBER 25

Mark 2:4—". . . they made an opening in the roof above Jesus and after digging through it, lowered the mat the paralyzed man was lying on." (NIV)

Mark 2:1-12 contains the story of a paralyzed man Jesus healed. The man was brought to Jesus by his friends, who let him down through the roof, after being unable to get him through the door because of the crowd. This man's friends did what it took to get him to Jesus because they had no idea whether the opportunity would be available later. What his friends understood was the nature of disease and deliverance. They knew the disease was grave and that deliverance is seasonal. That's important because God calls us to feel a sense of urgency with some of our friendships. That means that friendship brings with it responsibility and accountability, both of which require us to go beyond casual conversation.

The Good Samaritan (Lk. 10:25-37) teaches us that all men and women are neighbors and based on his response to the victim on the Jericho road, we should feel a heightened sense of responsibility to our friends. That 'sense' is rooted in love and displayed at Calvary, because Jesus says the greatest example of love lays down life for the sake of friendship (Jn. 15:13). What kind of friend are you?

Prayer—"Heavenly Father, help me show my friendship through the example of divine love you gave at Calvary."

SEPTEMBER 26

Mark 2:5—"When Jesus saw their faith, He said to the paralytic, 'son, your sins are forgiven.'" (NIV)

We've been looking at some principles of friendship as found in the Bible and how to apply those principles based on this story of four men who brought a paralyzed friend to Jesus for healing. Notice that Jesus observed the faith of the four friends, but spoke only to the paralyzed man. This obviously means there is a limit to faith and friendship; those for whom we pray and intercede are required to do some things for themselves if our prayers and God's purpose for them are to be realized. The Bible does teach that the prayers of the righteous avail much, but what those prayers avail is open doors, or opportunities that the object of our prayers must will to walk through. Jesus gave the paralytic an opportunity to show he had as much faith as his friends.

Additionally though, Jesus spoke to the paralytic, because He knew something that the four friends didn't; Jesus knew the man's condition was more spiritual than physical. Jesus knew this man would never walk again, if the didn't 'release' his past and look ahead. Because this paralytic attached his condition to past sins, he needed to know he was forgiven, if he was to access physical healing; he needed to know his soul was healed. You can live each day in the powerful presence of God if you learn to release the baggage of your past through Jesus' sacrifice at Calvary.

Prayer—"Dear God, I praise you for friends, but praise you more for my relationship with you."

SEPTEMBER 27

Mark 2:5—"When Jesus saw their faith, He said to the paralytic, 'son, your sins are forgiven.'" (NIV)

This man's friends brought him to Jesus for healing, but he received forgiveness in addition. I believe this passage says something to us about our expectations and intentions in the application of our faith. We must not forget as we observe this incident that when we exercise our faith, God answers through grace, and grace is always more than we expect or deserve. In the parable of the laborers (Matt. 20:1-16), the later workers received more than they expected, because they worked faithfully, relying on the master's will alone to compensate them. I remember some years ago being upgraded from coach to first class by a friend who worked for the airline, just because he wanted to do something nice for me. That's grace! That means that although faith writes a check, it's always grace that cashes it.

This passage teaches us that even in exercising faith, leave room for God to do what He wants. Some years ago at a church picnic, we discovered the ball field at the park we secured was too small for adults to play on. That limited our options. This passage teaches us to let God determine the space He needs to operate by expecting God to do the unexpected. When it comes to friends and family, rather than determining what they need as you pray, let God respond through grace and watch God abundantly bless!

Prayer—"Heavenly Father, your grace is not only sufficient, but more than I could hope for."

SEPTEMBER 28

Isaiah 40:8—"The grass withers and the flowers fall, but the word of our God stands forever." (NIV)

In 1996, George Plimpton wrote a book called *The X Factor*. Plimpton's book is an examination of the quest for excellence. In his book, he seeks to discover how two individuals can compete with each other with the same set of skills, yet one comes out clearly superior to the other. According to Plimpton, the reason is the "X" factor; it is the one quality which distinguishes highly successful people from everyone else. As a believer, I need to know if there is an "X" factor to insure my success as a Christian; is there in these changing times, something I can depend on to equalize me, even in the worse of circumstances? Isaiah 40:8 says the believer's "X" factor is the word of God.

As I look at Isaiah's assertion here, I'm led to conclude if just anyone were making this promise, I'd be justified in being skeptical, but because this promise comes from God, who has no limits, it's a word worthy of my trust. The implication is, whenever God's word is applied, no matter the circumstance, God who speaks and creates, can through his word, affect and alter the things which trouble me. I can confront confidently anything life produces, knowing God's word is equal to the challenge—His word is my "X" factor.

Prayer—"Dear God, my walk with you has taught me to trust your word; you speak and your will is accomplished."

SEPTEMBER 29

Isaiah 40:7, 8—"The grass withers and the flowers fall, because the breath of the Lord blows on them. Surely the people are grass. The grass withers and the flowers fall, but the word of our God stands forever." (NIV)

Note that Isaiah says we share a context with other life forms on the earth; we are like grass and other creatures which come from the ground (Gen. 1:24; 2:7) and are therefore inconsistent and unreliable. Our encouragement however, comes from knowing our God is distinct and different, and when He speaks His word is reliable.

Our greatest encouragement comes from the word 'our' in vs. 8, because it suggests that although I'm like grass, because Jehovah is my God, the stability of His word applies to me. Isaiah 40:8 is a covenantal statement, because it says God does not allow my creature status to exempt me from His resources; what's His is mine because I'm a joint heir (Rom. 8:17) with Christ. The key here is not the 'what' of my existence, but the 'who'. What I am is human, but who I am is God's child and even if I leave to go to the far country (Lk. 15) and come back to God, I find I never stopped being His child as He welcomes me home. What a joy it is for me to know that my weakness and frailty does not affect God or His relationship with me; He is "from everlasting to everlasting"!

Prayer—"Heavenly Father, remind me each day of your unchangeable nature and unfailing power."

SEPTEMBER 30

Ephesians 6:11—"Put on the full armor of God so that you can take your stand against the devil's schemes." (NIV)

The Bible suggests that Satan's attack on Christians is generally in the area of the mind. The mind is important, because for us, our minds constitute the image of God. God therefore, never by-passes the mind in communicating to us because He knows truth is our best weapon and resource. Obviously, Satan knows the same, so he uses deception and lies in an attempt to trick us. Let's spend a couple of days examining further why God uses truth to communicate with us.

First, truth is the 'essence' of God. When Jesus said He 'was' the truth (Jn. 14:6), His meaning was that more than knowing the formula for success, He 'is' the formula. He said, "I am . . . the truth . . .", because of His intimate knowledge of life's ultimate realities and His ability through His words and example to bring us clarity and power for all life's issues.

Secondly, God uses truth because the scriptures say He is the "Spirit of truth" (Jn. 16:13). The Spirit of God came to partner with Christ (Jn. 14) to further reveal the message and ministry of Jesus to His disciples. God's Spirit acts as a guide to direct us through the familiar and unfamiliar territory of truth. That's why the mind is so important; it is a battleground for truth and you must do your best to keep your mind "stayed on Jesus".

Prayer—Dear God, illuminate my mind, so my thoughts might be concentrated on your will for me."

OCTOBER 1

Ephesians 6:11—"Put on the full armor of God so that you can take your stand against the devil's schemes." (NIV)

As we began with this verse yesterday, we discovered the enemy's schemes concentrate on our minds, because they constitute the image of God. Truth therefore, is paramount to every Christian. Additionally, we discovered two reasons why God communicates with us through truth. Today, I'd like to mention two more reasons why truth is important to us from God's perspective.

The third reason God uses truth with us is because truth is liberating for believers (Jn. 8:32). Truth provides us spiritual freedom which liberates us from the 'dominion' of sin and allows us to 'become' all God has purposed us to be.

The final reason God works with us using truth, is because truth is unalterable. Facts may change, but truth never does. This means truth gives us stability and confidence in a changing world. If I've lost my job or have a bad relationship or a bad day, or I just don't see the light at the end of the tunnel, as a believer, truth says that God is still working "all things together for my good" (Rom. 8:28). Without the truth of God, I really don't know what I'd do. Thank God for truth!

Prayer—"Dear Lord, your presence is my most prized possession. Keep leading me with your truth."

OCTOBER 2

Ephesians 6:11—"Put on the full armor of God so that you can take your stand against the devil's schemes." (NIV)

We've already discovered that Satan's wiles confront our minds, because that's where God deposits truth. Further, Jesus says that Satan is both a liar (Jn. 8:44) and the father of lies. It's apparent that Satan uses lies for the same reason that God uses truth; to communicate with our minds for the purpose of influencing our thought processes and decisions. Satan's objective is to deceive the human heart and induce us to believe what He suggests, rather than what God declares. This is important, because sometimes we believe the lie and miss the blessing of God. Sometimes when you say to yourself, "my life will never change" or, "I'll never be happy", it's the result of believing the lie that God either doesn't care or that He cannot or will not help. Christians must always be careful to maintain their focus on the irresistible power of God and His willingness to bless His children.

The key truth here is that lies have a short shelf life, because they are eventually exposed. That's why lies must be dressed as truth and why Paul says Satan disguises himself as an angel of light (II Cor. 11:14). Satan knows he must 'trick' us to influence us, and he counts on a weak faith in us to achieve that goal. If we are to 'stand' against Satan's wiles, it will require a daily dose of faith, valuing each moment with God as our only and necessary resource.

Prayer—"Lord, I lift before you my mind and means; use both to your glory."

OCTOBER 3

Ephesians 6:11—"Put on the full armor of God so that you can take your stand against the devil's schemes." (NIV)

I remember as a boy hearing the words "counterfeit money" for the first time. I was told that counterfeit money looks like the genuine article (real money) and therefore requires a close examination to tell the difference. Recently, I discovered a website which offers comprehensive information for spotting counterfeit currency. The same principles apply to distinguishing between the lies of Satan and the truth of God. Oftentimes, lies sound like truth and are accepted as truth, only because they are not spiritually analyzed. There is a resource for analyzing the information we hear and it is the Bible. Through it, God helps us separate the counterfeit from the genuine article.

Why is this important? Because there are counterfeit churches, doctrines, messiahs, Christians, and ministers with which we must contend. It is a battle for the mind and requires the careful study of the word of God and an unwavering reliance on the Holy Spirit if we are to experience victory in this conflict. Counterfeit money may be exchanged at first, but eventually it is discovered and discarded. I pray each day for discernment and detection of false doctrine, but it begins with a love for the Bible, prayer and trusting the Spirit of God for insight and interpretation.

Prayer—"Dear Lord, speak to me and teach me to know the difference between truth and error."

OCTOBER 4

Ephesians 1:3—"Blessed be the God and Father of our Lord Jesus Christ, who hath blessed us with all spiritual blessings in heavenly places in Christ." (KJV)

In our battle with sin and Satan, Paul says in this verse, that believers have been secured through Christ, at a higher spiritual level. This means that from the moment we become saved, God positions us to see the true nature of life. The implication is that because life originates from the spiritual (Gen. 1:2-3), all of life is therefore spiritual at its root. Therefore, whatever my circumstance may be, as a believer, I must learn to see life from a spiritual perspective, because there's always more going on than my natural senses can identify. Nothing in life can be separated from the Spirit.

I remember watching a movie called "Thirteen Ghosts", in which the destructive ghosts of a haunted house could only be identified by wearing a certain pair of glasses. This meant that anyone in the house without the glasses was blind to its inherent dangers. How deadly and damaging it is to live life without the perspective which comes from a saving relationship with Christ. I'm glad He's provided a 'heavenly' place for me from which I can walk in vision and victory. He is truly my Savior!

Prayer—"Dear Lord, thank you for lifting my consciousness and placing my feet on the rock of your unfailing resource."

OCTOBER 5

Ephesians 6:12—"For our struggle is not against flesh and blood, but against the rulers, against the authorities, against the powers of this dark world and against the spiritual forces of evil in the Heavenly realms." (NIV)

I've always thought it was interesting that although Adam and Eve had the closest possible fellowship with God, when Satan came calling they fell hard anyway. I'm sure it happened because of all the resources at Satan's disposal in this verse. This lone verse is key for believers understanding both the nature of the conflict and how much we need if we are to live victoriously. Once the truth of this verse sinks in, it becomes clear that physical strength, natural weapons and natural resources have no effect on the outcome of this struggle.

That's why Paul suggests the "whole armor of God" in Eph. 6:13. As Christians, God seeks to help us avoid doing the first thing that generally comes to mind when we feel offended or threatened. Paul says many of our responses in life could be changed if we saw our struggles as spiritual in nature. The spiritual perspective makes us pray before we punch, and meditate before we seek another's destruction. How important it is to live each day looking beyond what we see and hear naturally, to allow God to identify the real enemy.

Prayer—"God, I thank you for discernment and for wisdom in responding to it."

OCTOBER 6

Ephesians 6:12—"For our struggle is not against flesh and blood . . ." (NIV)

So many times in my early adulthood I regarded people as enemies who needed to be defeated. As I became more familiar with spiritual warfare, I learned that people's actions may manifest evil, but that they are not my enemies, because there's warfare of a higher nature going on. What we must learn to do is pray for discernment that we might know the truth, engage in the real battle, and access the proper resources. In John 4, a Samaritan woman believed Jews were her enemies, then she met a Jew named Jesus, who brought her salvation. Even the prodigal (Lk. 15) in some sense saw his father as an enemy of his success, but he eventually "came to himself" and went back home.

When we learn to consistently and sincerely study and pray, God will help us see our real enemy, so we won't underestimate his capacity and our resources. The best truth is, God will show us our enemy is already defeated because no one can be God, but God. Satan, as a created being, is always subject to what God's will allows, and God will not allow him to defeat us as we walk in the victory of a resurrected Lord! This is God's world, we are God's children, and we are heirs of the Father and joint heirs with the Son!

Prayer—"Heavenly Father, I seek to take advantage of all you've made available; help me fight the fight of faith."

OCTOBER 7

Matthew 16:18—"... and upon this rock I will build my church ..."
(KJV)

I have a neighbor who takes very meticulous care of both his home and the landscaping around it. I'm sure he does so because his home represents him; it speaks for him to everyone who passes by and visits. The truth is, people attach credibility, or the lack of it to us, as they experience the people and places that represent us. It's important to note in this verse, Jesus' reference to the church as belonging to Him. He says 'my' church. He does not only mean His in terms of ownership, but also that the church speaks for Him on earth in His physical absence from the world. Because the church is His, He has a personal interest in what the Christian church is saying and how she represents Him. Isn't it true of most of us that we take a keener interest in the things we own as opposed to what we don't?

Yet Jesus' interest in the church is also about those who are a part of it. The church is a community of baptized believers, so when the church is blessed it means that those who make up the church are being blessed. Jesus' concern for His church is both external and internal. He wants us to develop greater intimacy with Him and His word and to represent Him as He deserves, in our daily actions and attitude. Are you committed to His church and do you reflect with clarity His love and grace?

Prayer—"Dear God, I thank you for the fellowship of other Christians and for the opportunities for service it presents."

OCTOBER 8

Matthew 16:18—". . . and upon this rock I will build my church . . ."
(KJV)

These are of course the words Jesus spoke to Peter after Peter's confession of faith in Caesarea Philippi. Jesus' words indicate a vision of His church as a community of individuals who would follow His teachings and be led by His representatives (apostles). The "will build" in this verse refers to an ongoing operation requiring a commitment from all those who claim discipleship in the body of Christ. Jesus did not say in this verse that He 'had' built His church, implying everything was done, but "will build" meaning the expectation of growth through addition or multiplication. This is an important truth for all of us who worship Christ and serve His church.

Every mandate Jesus gave the disciples concerning His church has the ring of expected growth to it; " . . . make disciples of all nations" (Matt. 28:29); "Ye shall be witnesses . . . uttermost parts of the earth . . ." (Acts 1:8); "Go ye into all the world" (Mk. 16:15). So Jesus does not call us to 'maintain' the church, which is to keep it where it is, but to grow the church, which is to give it back to Him better than we found it, unlike the third investor in the parable of the talents (Matt. 25:24-25). Because of who Jesus is, and what He's done, His church deserves our best.

Prayer—"Dear God, I give your church and her work my highest priority;
use me as your instrument."

OCTOBER 9

Matthew 16:18—". . . and upon this rock I will build my church . . ."
(KJV)

I mentioned yesterday that Jesus expects more than mere 'maintenance' of His church. That would be to keep the church where it is and return it as we received it. In Jn.14:12, Jesus suggested that the potential and promise of the church is greater in our time than it was in His. This is an important truth because Jesus doesn't want us setting limits on ourselves or His church. He implies that we (the church) can go as far as we allow the Holy Spirit to lead us. The fact is, Jesus was anticipating a day of completed work for the church when He returns to claim His bride. That day is referred to in Eph. 5:25-27.

In order to achieve that goal, Jesus has built His church on those who bear witness for Him. That's why after Peter's confession of faith in Matt. 16:16, Jesus implied that was what He needed to build His church on in vs. 18; but because this is a continuous process, Christ needs people in every age and era to be witnesses for Him and say what Peter said. Therefore, testimony is important to the kingdom of God and work of Christ. Testimony is how cases are made in court and accurate judgments are executed. God needs people like you and I to be unabashed witnesses to the saving power of Christ. What will you say today?

Prayer—"Heavenly Father, open my mind and mouth that I may speak to your glory."

OCTOBER 10

Matthew 16:18—". . . and upon this rock I will build my church; and the gates of Hell shall not prevail against it." (KJV)

The promise of these words of Jesus is that the gates of Hell shall not overpower His community of followers. The Greek word for Hell in this verse literally means 'Hades' or the land of the dead, not the place of punishment. So in this verse, Jesus is referring to more than the forces of evil when He says 'Hell'; He's actually referencing the power of death. In I Cor. 15:26, Paul refers to death as the last enemy. Further, Jesus says He came to give us abundant life (Jn. 10:10). This verse in reality promises that the church will not die. Jesus uses the strongest possible language to indicate the capacity of His church.

This therefore, means that when Jesus gave Peter 'keys' in vs. 19 that it was in reference to the gates mentioned in vs. 18. If gates shut people out, then the keys Jesus gave Peter insure that not even death can shut the church down. That's why the church is more than a human institution; it is a spiritual organism whose life is derived from a God who knows no beginning and no end, and a Savior who was raised from the dead with all power. You and I are a part of an indestructible church. Praise God!

Prayer—"Lord, I praise you for your church and her promise of victory."

OCTOBER 11

Matthew 18:1-3—"... disciples ... asked, 'who is the greatest in the kingdom ... He called a child ... and He said ... unless you become like little children, you will never enter the kingdom.'" (NIV)

In these verses, the disciples asked Jesus about greatness, but connected it with the kingdom of Heaven. What Jesus said in response indicated a difference in the standards by which that kingdom operates as compared to the disciples' understanding of that kingdom. The implication is, when you know where you are, you can determine what actions and attitudes are successful in that environment. So when Jesus called a child into their presence, it was to give the disciples clarity on the nature of the kingdom they referenced. It reminded me of my first week in college and all the orientation sessions I attended. Orientation is for the purpose of saying "this is how things are done here". Jesus was therefore providing an impromptu orientation for the disciples using a child to make His point.

Jesus' point was and is, that life in the kingdom of God is different. In God's kingdom, down is up, death is life, giving leads to receiving, and childlike qualities are the essence of maturity. This is a lesson we'll further explore in the coming days. I hope you'll begin to meditate on what it means to be a good citizen in God's environment.

Prayer—"God, make me what you want, and show me the path which most pleases you."

OCTOBER 12

Matthew 18:2—"He called a little child and had him stand among them." (NIV)

As we continue this study, let's ask why did Jesus select a child to use as an example for His disciples? It's because children have characteristics that position them for success. First, children are teachable; they observe the success of adults and desire to be trained to duplicate that success. When the disciples asked Jesus to teach them how to pray (Lk. 11:1), it was the teachable spirit in them speaking. They knew how to pray, but not like Jesus did. This means that children do what adults do, but at a different level like playing doctor or some other profession. The spirit of a child says, "I'm just playing now, but I desire to learn, so I can truly experience what is just imitation at the moment."

The teachable spirit is important because it recognizes a lack of revelation, or knowledge, which are ingredients for success. It is this spirit which remains open to ideas and opportunities. It's clear to me that Jesus chose the men He did, because they were not already so full of themselves that they couldn't be taught. That's why you see a difference between the two thieves whom Jesus hung between. The teachable spirit led to paradise for one (Lk. 23:39-43), while the absence of it led to death and destruction for the other. What kind of spirit do you have?

Prayer—"Heavenly Father, teach me to be teachable; lead me on the path of personal success."

OCTOBER 13

Matthew 18:3—"I tell you the truth, unless you change and become like little children, you will never enter the kingdom of Heaven." (NIV)

Let's move ahead with this verse today. Jesus obviously expects Christians to display certain childlike qualities if they are to grow and advance His kingdom. Another of the qualities children possess, is a forgiving spirit. Children have the unique ability to quickly resume relationships previously fractured by conflict. It must mean that children do not regard some issues as critically as adults do, but also that children are not as weighted down by the past as adults are. Often, the difference between children and adults is that children often speak of tomorrow, while adults often speak of yesterday. Children can more easily 'shed' the past, because they wear the past loosely.

The forgiving spirit values relationships and does not discard them easily. That's why Jesus leads the way in forgiveness. Even on the cross, He prayed for our forgiveness (Lk. 23:34), because He sought to keep open our relationship with Him. This is the quality found in children and modeled by Jesus. It is the quality Jesus wants from us because we are the visible representation of His body today. The church needs a strong representation of what it means to follow Christ.

Prayer—"Dear God, your forgiveness is my example; help me to follow in your steps."

OCTOBER 14

Matthew 18:3—"I tell you the truth, unless you change and become like little children, you will never enter the kingdom of Heaven." (NIV)

Yesterday, we discovered that Jesus wants us to be childlike, because children have a 'teachable' spirit; children know that they don't know it all. I also think Jesus used a child as an example in this text because children's wants are uncomplicated. This is a difficult point to make for more than one reason. First, our desires become more involved and detailed as we become adults. The gifts I gave my children when they were toddlers would not satisfy them now. Secondly, my contention runs the risk of being viewed as promoting poverty among believers in this prosperity-driven age in the body of Christ.

Matthew 20 contains the story of laborers in a vineyard, most of which allowed the owner of the vineyard to bless them as he saw fit. When the owner did pay them he gave them more than they anticipated. It was that simple approach which led to grace beyond the laborer's expectations. That's what I mean by simple or uncomplicated wants. The fact is, God's imagination is greater than ours and if we allow Him to bless us as He sees fit, think of the difference between what we want and what God through grace is willing to give!.

Prayer—"God, thank you for the challenge to be childlike, and the unexpected blessings it produces."

OCTOBER 15

Matthew 18:3—"I tell you the truth, unless you change and become like little children, you will never enter the kingdom of Heaven." (NIV)

My last point in this series of devotions on this text, is that children display the quality of trust in their parents. A child's level of parental trust is extremely instructive; it's even displayed in our reference text. In vs. 2 of Matt. 18, Jesus called a child to come beside Him and the child did so without asking for a reason or hesitating. The child's obedient response was as instructive as Jesus' words on the matter. Because Jesus references the kingdom of Heaven here, it must mean that childlike trust and obedience is a way of life in God's kingdom, because that's what produces the best results.

Children rarely ask how it's going to be done or if it can be done; they simply believe if their parents say so, then it will be so. I hasten to add though, that this kind of trust is based on a pre-established pattern. In Genesis, Eve had no history with God to establish a level of trust, but when you've seen what God can do, it makes you wonder why it's so hard for some in the body of Christ to trust our Heavenly Father to keep His promise and show His power. Children trust their parents based on the evidence of seeing daily needs met. God, who cannot fail, deserves our unwavering trust even more so.

Prayer—"God, I praise you for your glorious acts; they are my reason for confidence in you today and tomorrow."

OCTOBER 16

John 14:12—"I tell you the truth, anyone who has faith in me will do what I have been doing. He will do even greater things than these . . ." (NIV)

One of the interesting parts of a football game is the handoff. That's where the quarterback receives the football from the center and hands it off to the running back with the expectation that the running back will 'advance' the ball. Obviously, the ball is of value because when it is carried or kicked successfully, it leads to points scored, and eventually determines who wins the game.

In this verse, Jesus refers to a 'handoff' to His disciples with the expectation that they will advance the thing of value (the gospel) by doing "greater things". The promise of greater things for any Christian is based on thinking spiritually and allowing the Holy Spirit to be the guide and set the goals. It's therefore important for every believer to be constantly aware of Jesus Christ handing off to us and expecting us to do great things for Him. This means our focus must always be on His glory and purpose, because the "greater things" relate directly to advancing His kingdom and its cause. As Christians, we must live each day seeking His will to be done in us as it is in Heaven.

Prayer—"Dear God, thank you for trusting me with responsibility; use me as your instrument."

OCTOBER 17

John 14:12—"I tell you the truth, anyone who has faith in me will do what I have been doing. He will do even greater things than these . . ." (NIV)

These words are important because Jesus spoke them at a time when His disciples were anxious about losing Him and what it would mean to His ministry. What Jesus assured His disciples of in this verse, was that His physical absence would not prevent them from doing the kinds of things they'd been doing. Jesus in fact told His disciples they'd do greater things after He was gone. Obviously, Jesus' implication was that His death did not signal a disbanding of the group, but a doorway to their potential. The fact is, the disciples would never know they were capable of greater things if Jesus didn't leave them to operate on faith alone.

Notice that Jesus says in this verse the criteria for greater things is faith, but just as importantly, He uses the word 'anyone' which implies the promise is as true for us now as His disciples then. That word 'faith' means the resting confidently of all of life's matters in His hands, believing He will provide, even though we may not see our answer. It is to find a 'home' in Jesus, seeing Him as our source of provision and protection. How wonderful it is to know I don't have to see Christ to do great things, but merely believe in who He is and what He can do!

Prayer—"Dear Lord, empower me to do what you've called me to, and encourage my heart."

OCTOBER 18

John 14:12—"I tell you the truth, anyone who has faith in me will do what I have been doing. He will do even greater things than these, because I am going to the Father." (NIV)

The promise of "greater works" to Jesus' disciples is related to faith in His identity. It implies that as "joint heirs" with Jesus Christ (Rom. 8:17), we have a right to, and expectation of, greater works through our relationship with Christ. Clearly it means that we have access to those things Christ had access to while He was with us in the flesh. Sometimes I go "window shopping", which simply means I don't have the resources to purchase what I want, so I stand on the outside and look in. Jesus says in this verse that no believer has to "window shop" for greater things, because our faith is our funds in the kingdom of God.

Notice Jesus says here that the greater things become possible after He goes to the Father. Jesus meant that while here (in the flesh), He was confined by His flesh, but in the presence of God at God's right hand, He would be in position to empower His disciples, based both on His redemptive action at Calvary and on the resurrection power of Easter morning. We can expect great things in our experience, as we appropriate all Jesus said and did on earth, because now His presence in Heaven guarantees the credibility of His words.

Prayer—"Heavenly Father, thank you for the assurance of your words and will, as I seek to be an effective servant."

OCTOBER 19

John 14:12—"I tell you the truth, anyone who has faith in me will do what I have been doing. He will do even greater things than these . . ." (NIV)

Let's for a moment this morning, look at the words "greater things". What do they mean? I think it's important to have clarity here, otherwise we set ourselves up for disappointment, doubt and confusion. The King James Version (KJV) uses the word 'works' while the New International Version (NIV) uses the word 'things', which I believe lends itself to less confusion. When Jesus uses the words "greater things" in this verse, He's not saying that the disciples will do more dramatic things than turn water into wine (Jn. 2), or raise the dead (Jn. 11). What He is suggesting is that the disciples will take what He has begun to build and advance it, that He might be glorified as His message is shared with a wider audience.

That's why the book of Acts focuses on the growth of the church, rather than miracles. The "greater things" of His disciples can be found in Acts 2, where 3,000 people were saved, remembering that Jesus did not produce that many disciples in three years of ministry. These things were 'greater' because they were done by ordinary people relying on an extraordinary God. As you begin your day, go confidently knowing the power of a resurrected Lord resides in you to assure you that you are more than a conqueror (Rom. 8:37).

Prayer—"Dear God, remind me of your awesome power and keep me connected to you each day."

OCTOBER 20

John 3:16—"For God so lived the world that, He gave His only begotten son, that whosoever believeth in Him should not perish, but have everlasting life." (KJV)

Someone once said, "The main things are the plain things, and the plain things are the main things." I believe that statement is true, especially in the spiritual sense, when we think of the fact and act of salvation. Some people miss the opportunity for salvation, because what they hear of it sounds both complicated and impossible. Jn.3:16 is both simple and profound at the same time; it plumbs the depths of the essence of our salvation, while at the same time framing it in words which are both brief and comprehensible. Salvation is essentially a 'simple' process because this verse declares that God has already done the work of redeeming us and all we need to do is exercise our faith in His accomplishment.

I was invited to lunch by a friend, who picked me up in his car. When I questioned him repeatedly about our destination, his response was "just ride". The implication was, he knew where we were going, how to get there and all I needed to do was trust him. Salvation works in the same way; all it requires is that we trust God's word about His son and allow that faith to secure our destiny. I pray this devotion will help you share your faith with others.

Prayer—"God, I thank you for salvation and the faith which makes it possible."

OCTOBER 21

John 3:16—"For God so lived the world that, He gave His only begotten Son, that whosoever believeth in Him should not perish, but have everlasting life." (KJV)

It is important to know from this timeless verse that God's motive for our salvation is love. This love is both self-giving and unconditional. As a motive, love is always the best reason for an action, because it reflects the absence of any suspicious or ulterior motives. Note also, the word 'only' in this verse, because it indicates the depth of God's love and the value of the gift (salvation). How can we fail to see in this verse how deeply God cares for us in light of the gift He gave (His 'only' Son), and how that gift was manifested?

God's love is so deep in this text that He gave His Son to us in two ways. First, God gave His Son to the 'world'. This means that God, through His Son, became one of us and thereby experienced life as we live it; as one of us. This allowed God to 'identify' with us. Secondly, God gave His Son on the cross. By doing so, God eliminated our questions about destiny and access; He settled our ultimate issues. That's why when we pray, our prayers are effective. God hears from people He can identify with and He responds to us, because we have responded to His Son. What a joy to know the depth of God's love and what that means for me!

Prayer—"Heavenly Father, teach me to love as you do that I may manifest your grace toward me."

OCTOBER 22

John 3:16—"... that whosoever believeth in Him ..." (KJV)

To believe in Jesus Christ is to acknowledge that true religion is not in knowledge, traditions, or behavior; it is not horizontal or made up of the stuff around us. To believe in Jesus as the Christ, is to know that true religion is vertical; it's from the top down as in from God down to us. This belief is important, because each of us needs to know our resources are greater than the challenges which confront us each day. To place my faith in the things around me is to trust the things which are as limited by time as the problem I'm trying to overcome. Each of us needs to believe in someone who's older than time and who's level of power is never affected by its usage. That's why belief in Jesus Christ is so important to us.

This belief is the result of a foreign invasion of the highest order. What it does is, unites humanity with God's Spirit, who overwhelms, transforms, and converts. I believe in Jesus Christ as my Savior, because I've found salvation, satisfaction and security in everything Christ offers. I trust you feel the same level of safety I do, as you go out to face another day of the unknown and unexpected.

Prayer—"Dear God, I believe on your Son and trust His saving action in my behalf."

OCTOBER 23

Matthew 16:15—"He saith unto them, 'But whom say ye that I am?'"
(KJV)

Not long ago, I was in a grocery store and crossed paths with a member of my church, who I didn't recognize, although she recognized me. It bothered me that I didn't know her because the question of identity is always important. In Jn. 10, Jesus says the shepherd and sheep know each other and that the fellowship which exists between the two is based on the mutual knowledge of identity. The implication is, the benefits available to us in our earthly lives can only be appropriated when we solve the issue of Jesus' identity; we must know Him as the Christ.

In this verse, the issue of Jesus' identity was important because Jesus was about to leave the leadership of His community of followers in the hands of men who needed to be clear about who He was. People often speak negatively of nepotism and cronyism, but sometimes it's important to employ those who understand and complement your vision. Remember, God chose David on that basis (I Sam. 16:7), and Jesus as well. What God needs in our troubled world, are witnesses who know Him and can identify Him to those who are lost. Will you speak for Him today?

Prayer—"God, give me a word today to share with others that I may point them in your direction."

OCTOBER 24

Matthew 16:14-15—"And they said, some say that thou art John the Baptist; some Elias; and others, Jeremias, or one of the prophets. He saith unto them, but whom say ye that I am?" (KJV)

Jesus' first question to His disciples was what others said about Him. The people's opinions of Jesus (vs. 14) reflected respect, but not reverence. That's why the question of Jesus' identity is so important; it's because when you know who He is, it leads past admiration to adoration. When the Samaritan woman in John 4 discovered who Jesus was, she worshipped Him (vs. 29); the same is true of Bartimaeus (Mk. 10:47) and Jesus' own disciples (Matt. 14:33). Identity is important because it establishes status, position and recognition. Often, when I'm asked to speak at a banquet, there's a place card at the head table to identify me as the principal participant. It's an issue of identity.

The reason the second question was important, was because Jesus needed to know His intimate followers were not as confused as the common people. When Jesus asked the disciples if they knew who He was, He was declaring the church's responsibility to bring clarity to His identity for the world's sake. Obviously, those of us who claim to believe on Christ must take seriously the matters of worship, witness and study if we are to represent our Christ with clarity and conviction. The world cannot be blessed if we give less than our best.

Prayer—"Dear God, I'm glad to know your son as my Savior; now help me share Him with others today."

OCTOBER 25

Matthew 16:13-15—" . . . whom do men say that I the son of man am? . . . but whom say ye that I am?" (KJV)

Let's take another look at this passage to see what additional truths we can find to help us through our day. Notice Jesus' questions in verses 13 and 15 reference what people were 'saying'. Obviously, Jesus intended the truth about Himself to be transmitted, or shared, or witnessed to. Jesus did not ask what others believed, but what they said. He understood first, that His movement could not grow if His disciples believed on Him, but didn't tell others about Him. Everything Jesus did in His ministry was for the purpose of its expansion; He did not intend to organize an exclusive club.

Secondly, Jesus understood the power of words. From the beginning of time, words have been a powerful expression of creativity and truth; just reference the book of Genesis and how God created the world, and communicated with humanity. Words are important in carrying and conveying truth about God and His kingdom. That's why Jesus said His disciples would be witnesses at home and abroad (Acts. 1:8). Jesus therefore, raises the question of witness, because once the issue of His identity is solved, the next step is to tell someone about Him. Who do you say He is?

Prayer—"Lord, fill my heart and mind with truth, and help me share it with clarity."

OCTOBER 26

John 10:14—"I am the good shepherd; and I know my sheep and am known by my own." (KJV)

Relationships are important because God said it's not good for "man to be alone" (Gen. 2:18). God intended for us to find fulfillment in our interaction with each other. The problem is, in our human experiences with each other, we fail to fulfill each other's ultimate needs. It began in the Garden of Eden when sin caused Adam and Eve to cover themselves in each other's presence and fail to address mutual needs when God confronted them. This dilemma in relational resources is why Jesus came into the world; Jesus is the answer to that dilemma.

Jesus says in Jn. 10 that His relationship with Christians is like shepherd to sheep; that His concern is for our complete and total welfare and that our 'mutual' knowledge makes the relationship complete. The blessing of mutual knowledge is the ability to both know and predict each other's actions and responses as well as the inclination to show patience with each other, based on that mutuality. Simply, Jesus knows me and relates to me based on what He already knows. At the same time, while my knowledge of Him is limited by my humanity, I know Him well enough to be acquainted with His will for me and how to achieve it. Our 'mutual' knowledge is the basis of a treasured friendship.

Prayer—"Dear God, help me know you even as I am known."

OCTOBER 27

John 3:3, 4—"In reply Jesus declared, "I tell you the truth, no one can see the kingdom of God unless he is born again." "How can a man be born when he is old?" Nicodemus asked." (NIV)

The reason Nicodemus' response to Jesus is so instructive is because it reveals Nicodemus to be religious, but not necessarily spiritual. Nicodemus walked in religious circles, but not in spiritual power and there's a difference between the two. The challenge for every Christian is to maximize our relationship with God, otherwise spiritual lessons will always come and go without ever being grasped. God has insured that every believer has an inheritance, but what good is it if we never fully develop our walk with God each day? Recently, I was looking at a list of individuals who had not claimed money the government owed them. To be religious, but not spiritual, is to leave unclaimed blessings which would position us more firmly in the path of God's purpose.

One of the lessons of the "Wizard of Oz", is Dorothy inheriting a power (red shoes) that she was not fully aware of; consequently, she had a dream she could not fulfill only because she didn't know she had the means. I would suggest to you that as a believer, you should not only live in the house, but remember it's your right to eat at the table.

Prayer—"Heavenly Father, thank you for both mercy and means; thank you for the right to know you and your power."

OCTOBER 28

I Peter 1:23—"For you have been born again, not of perishable seed, but of imperishable, through the living and enduring word of God." (NIV)

Yesterday, we looked at Jesus and Nicodemus and what the Master had to say to Nicodemus about the new birth. This reference to salvation in terms of birth is interesting, because birth suggests a consummation in one area, leading to an entrance into a new environment. In today's text, Peter refers to God's word as the seed which produces our birth in Christ. Since the word 'seed' in the Bible refers either to sowing or offspring, the word of God is actually spiritual semen in Peter's mind. This therefore, means that God's word is what He plants in us to reproduce Himself in us.

Ezekiel 37:1-10 helps us understand this truth, because in it God declares that the dry bones in the valley could not be renewed without first hearing the word of God and be being blown on by the Spirit of God. What a lesson for us! Our newness of life is generated by God's word and activated by God's Spirit, and without that process, we exist, but do not truly live. I can remember my mother applying a salve to a wound I once had. The application provided protection and healing. In the same way, the faithful application of God's word produces and provides life and protects it through God's Spirit.

Prayer—"Dear God, your word is more than enough to produce abundance of life in each day's experience; help me claim my blessing today."

OCTOBER 29

John 3:3—"... no one can see the kingdom of God unless he is born again." (NIV)

I find the reference to salvation as a second birth fascinating and I'd like to look at it further today. Yesterday, we discovered God's word to be spiritual semen which carries the nature and life of God to believers. Today, I'd like to address how that seed can produce the life of God in us. Because we are made in the image of God (Gen. 1:26), there's something in us like God, which can only be 'activated' by God. The Spirit within us is the ovum or egg of faith. We know humanly speaking, the female egg requires the penetration of the male seed. Translating that to the spiritual level, to be born again is to have the ovum of saving faith activated by the seed of God's word; and the seed (word) has in it the life of God ready to be transferred.

The Bible teaches us as Adam's seed, we have inherited Adam's nature (sinful), but in the second birth, the conception and birth is totally spiritual in nature. Therefore, nothing about the first Adam is included in the transaction. My joy is in knowing that being born "from above" (Jn. 3:3), makes me a new creation (2 Cor. 5:17), because I have received the life of God through Christ and my original nature no longer has dominion over me. Isn't it great to be saved?

Prayer—"God, thank you for a second chance and a second birth; your life is now my life."

OCTOBER 30

John 3:6—"Flesh gives birth to flesh, but the Spirit gives birth to spirit."
(NIV)

We've looked the last few days at Jesus' words about the second birth and today I'd like to suggest why Jesus says we need to be born "from above". In vs. 6, Jesus says flesh births only flesh and likewise the Spirit. The implication is that every living thing only and always produces it's own kind, whether it's dogs, horses or humans, but also in the spiritual realm as well. Therefore, that which comes out of the natural man can only produce what is natural to man, and likewise with God and the life which comes from Him. Jesus needed Nicodemus to understand that his confusion about a second birth was related to the lack of the nature of God within him to give him clarity and conviction.

What God's word teaches us, is that God made man so that His Spirit would dominate, but man marred his spirit with his rebellion in the garden. From that point on, humanity has been impeded by a tug of war in which the soul is the marker that determines defeat or victory. Jesus' challenge to us is to live "from the top down", by valuing the things of God more highly than anything else. When we make Jesus Lord, we settle the issues that hamper us on earth and keep up from Heaven. There is no better experience than the "second birth".

Prayer—"Heavenly Father, thank you for salvation; help me stay close to you each day."

OCTOBER 31

Luke 15:18—"Father, I have sinned against Heaven and against you."
(NIV)

As Christians, it's always important that we see ourselves as stewards, or managers of our possessions. That's where the prodigal initially failed; he saw what he possessed as apart from his father. Luke 15:12 refers to what the prodigal received as belonging to his father. This means no resource we have is ever ours apart from God. Even Ps. 24:1 suggests that all things belong to God. This young man was so intent on avoiding his father's influence and authority that he put distance between himself and his father. How tragic it is for us, when we seek to live and use God's resources without His divine counsel and protection. It is a futile desire to have God's blessings without God's guidance.

The distance between the prodigal and his father was not the answer to his questions. Why? Because when things went terribly wrong, the young man eventually went home and acknowledged his father's place in his life. Every Christian must learn that God gives us blessings to draw us not drive us, so that in our intimacy with Him, we might learn while we live. I've lived long enough to discover I'm blessed for God's glory; that out of all I experience, He might be shown forth as my Savior and sustainer.

Prayer—"Lord, you are the giver of every good and perfect gift; thank you for each blessing."

NOVEMBER 1

Luke 15:13—"Not long after that, the younger son got together all he had, set off for a distant country and there squandered his wealth in wild living." (NIV)

The danger of our use of resources, is to use them without regard to the uncertainty of life. That's why this young man's proximity to his father (distant country) is such an important issue here. What God intends is, that we learn to position ourselves with Him, so that when supplies run low He's not too far away to help and meet our needs. I can remember when my son was a baby, I installed an intercom between his room and mine, so I could listen for things out of the ordinary. I was close enough to him to hear something wrong and rush to his aid. That's the relationship God seeks to establish with us as His children.

The prodigal had a perception (the way he saw it), without the proper perspective (the way it was); he made decisions without asking certain questions. His problem was he'd always received without really giving and that was because he never really considered who the resources (money) ultimately belonged to. It is impossible to live successfully without solving the questions of ownership and obligation. That's why I encourage you today to know God as the ultimate owner and authority, and to position yourself to receive from Him as life's goal and guide.

Prayer—"Dear Lord, help me use what you have given to your glory and honor."

NOVEMBER 2

Isaiah 55:6—"Seek the Lord while he may be found . . ." (NIV)

I was just sitting here thinking about the things I've lost in my life and the time I've spent searching for them. It occurs to me that the length of time spent searching and the manner in which I searched (no stone unturned), revealed the importance or value of the thing sought. I find that principle in this verse from the book of Isaiah. Isaiah says to 'seek' the Lord, implying His importance to us as a redeemer and resource. Obviously, Isaiah thinks God is the most important person anyone can have a relationship with. Additionally though, these words were spoken to a nation (Israel) suffering from a backslidden condition; they had failed to fulfill the purpose of God. They, therefore, needed to seek God out for restoration and reconciliation.

We must not overlook the urgency implied there though. Isaiah says, " . . . while He may be found". This implies two things. First, the season of God's availability, just like any wonderful offer, doesn't last forever. Secondly, this verse suggests that we find God, not because we are great at searching, but because God permits Himself to be discovered. One of the most important truths any believer can possess is the awareness that we are blessed because God always takes the initiative. That is what grace is; it's God putting Heaven in our path, so we cannot help but take advantage.

Prayer—"God, I'm so glad I found you; I know it's because you were already there."

NOVEMBER 3

Isaiah 55:6—"Seek the Lord while he may be found; call on him while he is near." (NIV)

Yesterday, we looked at the 'seeking', but today, let's take a brief look at the 'calling'. To call on God is to take advantage of His nearness; it is to seek Him for a purpose, then to fulfill that purpose once we've drawn near to Him. In Luke 8:43-48, a woman who'd been bleeding for twelve years sought Jesus out and when she found Him, she touched the hem of His garment and found healing. Do you see the difference between seeking and calling? Seeking Him was 'finding' Him, but calling on Him required that she touch His clothes. Some people are merely content to be in the crowd, but others desire to take away some evidence of being in the place of blessing; that's 'calling' on Him. It's the difference between spectating and participating.

It's also important to see that calling on Him is as much relational as it is redemptive. What I mean is, I don't just seek God out for a blessing, but for fellowship as well. Don't you see that the real blessing is not the gift, but the giver? I appreciate all the things God does for me, but I most appreciate the sense of His presence which gives me comfort and assurance. That's what David meant when he said God's rod and staff 'comforted' him (Ps. 23:4). What greater comfort is there than knowing we can call Him and He will 'abide' with us?

Prayer—"Dear Lord, keep walking with me and reminding me of your abiding presence."

NOVEMBER 4

Isaiah 55:6,7—"Seek the Lord while he may be found; call on him while he is near. Let the wicked forsake his way and the evil man his thoughts." (NIV)

As we continue our devotional look at this passage, vs. 7 implies how to maintain the achieving of our purpose when we 'call' on God. The objective here is to come as we are, but not stay as we are. That can only happen through a willingness to change both the course we travel and the captain we follow. Isaiah refers specifically to our way and our thoughts. The way is of course, the direction we travel in life, but the thought is the root of the way, which makes the thought infinitely more important. We must always be conscious of the fact that without paying attention to our thoughts, we are destined to repeat mistakes again and again.

God always prefers to deal with the interior of His creation, because that's the only way to produce lasting change. That's what David had in mind when he said, "create within me a clean heart, O God . . ." (Ps. 51:10), or when God told Samuel He "looks at the heart" (I Sam. 16:7), or when Paul referred to the "renewing of your mind" (Rom. 12:2). We can only reach God's standard of excellence for ourselves as we turn our thoughts over to God for His influence and direction.

Prayer—"Heavenly Father, I give my mind to you today; direct my thoughts and actions."

NOVEMBER 5

Isaiah 55:7—"Let the wicked forsake his way and the evil man his thoughts. Let him turn to the Lord and He will have mercy on him and to our God, for he will freely pardon." (NIV)

Verses 6 and 7 of Isaiah 55 say when we seek God wholeheartedly, God gives us both love and forgiveness. It's important to see that these verses imply that we don't deserve this benefit (note: 'freely'), but that God gives us grace as a response to our desire to draw close to Him. The word mercy in this verse means "love surging over", which speaks of the motive behind God's dealing with us. What a comfort it is to know that every action of God in my life is based on His love for me and His desire to produce the best in each day's experience.

The word pardon in this verse is a legal term, which suggests that God will treat us today as if yesterday never happened. How difficult it is for us to respond to each other with the same grace. What we shouldn't miss as we examine the 'grace' of this verse is that our 'return' to God doesn't produce mercy and pardon, but procures it; God was already waiting to bless us when we approached Him. Think of it this way; when you have a surprise party thrown for you, all things are already in place; you only have to "show up". Your arrival doesn't produce the party; it just allows you to access what was already done. How good to know God's waiting for me with mercy in his hands.

Prayer—"Dear God, I live each day with the knowledge of your love for me and the grace which manifests it."

NOVEMBER 6

John 5:5-6—"And a certain man was there, which had an infirmity thirty and eight years . . . . Jesus saw him . . ." (KJV)

Here is a man who'd been confined to a bed for thirty-eight years. His long time infirmity left him unable to walk or stand. The muscles in his legs were useless from thirty-eight years of inactivity. In vs. 7 of this chapter, the man told Jesus he'd tried over and over again to be healed, but to no avail; others always beat him into the pool and found healing. This passage suggests to us that Jesus chose the man who seemingly needed help the most, so that a statement would be made by his healing. Remember, God doesn't bless us for the simple purpose of making life better for us, but to touch matters of faith within us, and to reveal and give glory to Himself.

Our relationship with God is always about His glory. Yes God wants the best for us, but He also wants others to know about it and that He feels the same way about them. That's why the woman who bled for twelve years (Lk. 8) could not leave without telling others what her encounter with Christ had accomplished. God's blessings come ultimately for the purpose of pointing back to Him, because His agenda is what matters most. We live life at its best when we pray "thy Kingdom come, thy will be done in Earth, as it is in Heaven."

Prayer—"Dear God, use my experiences and me to show forth your power, purpose and grace."

NOVEMBER 7

John 5:5-6—"And a certain man was there, which had an infirmity thirty and eight years. When Jesus saw him lie and knew that he had been now a long time in that case, He saith unto him, "wilt thou be made whole?" (KJV)

I've always appreciated Jesus' encounter with this lame man, because in this healing episode, Jesus picked the man and not vice-versa. Many biblical texts reveal people seeking Jesus out, but in this text, Jesus seeks the man out. It reveals the variety of circumstances out of which salvation comes. Obviously, some people would never be saved if it were solely left up to them. The fact is some people don't know what they want while others want the wrong thing. Whatever the case may be, some of us require more intervention than others and that's why 'grace' is so important to every believer.

I can remember some choices my parents made for me as a child, because they understood my needs better than I did; they saw the "big picture". Those were choices I would never have made on my own, and usually only adults can appreciate doing the undesirable, recognizing the ultimate benefit of it. I came to Atlanta, Georgia in 1972 to attend Morehouse College, but only because my father made me. As it turned out, it was one of the best decisions of my life and it was made 'for' me by someone else. I am grateful for a God who initiates blessings in my behalf, because I don't know where I'd be without it.

Prayer—"Lord, thank you for each blessing; you are the reason I am who, what and where I am today."

NOVEMBER 8

John 5:6—". . . wilt thou be made whole?" (KJV)

When Jesus asked this lame man the question in our text, it certainly seemed naïve, but it's really pertinent. Thirty-eight years in the same condition can change your outlook and alter your dreams. There are people who've dreamed of mansions, who only want shelter now. Their dreams have been diminished by discouragement. Yet Jesus' question goes deeper. Jesus did not say "do you want"; He said "wilt thou", because intending to, is stronger than wishing or hoping to. Jesus' question was an appeal to the man's will, because the burden of healing rested squarely on the lame man's shoulders. Jesus said, "wilt thou", because the infirmity in the man's legs could have extended to his will.

Jesus understands us just as He understood this man. He knows for some of us, it's enough to sit close to what we want, even if we never get what we need; that some of us can be comfortable with less than the best once we've grown accustomed to it. There are people in church each week, who are comfortable being with the masses without ever being touched by the Holy Spirit. How tragic it is to be close without ever connecting. This verse is a call to step away from the masses and meet God personally at the intersection of blessing. Wilt thou be made whole?

Prayer—"Lord, continue to inspire me that I may aspire to fulfill your purpose for me."

NOVEMBER 9

John 5:6—"... Jesus saw him lie ... saith ... wilt thou be made whole? ... man answered him, Sir I have no man ..." (KJV)

Yesterday, we settled the issue of the pertinence of Jesus' question. We discover with greater clarity the credibility of Jesus' question based on the lame man's response. Essentially, his response was "I'd like to be whole, but I don't have any help". This man's answer reflected a loss of independent determination. There are some things all of us should intend to do, regardless how others respond to us. Joshua expressed that frame of mind when he said, "As for me and my house, we will serve the Lord" (Josh. 24:15). The problem then with attaching too much to other's responses, is that you either receive nothing or the wrong thing. When no one would give the Prodigal Son anything in his most needy hour (Lk. 15:16), he made the self-determination to go back to where he knew he'd be blessed.

Again, the words "wilt thou", remind us that our breakthrough is as much about our will as God's. The only question is can we in faith, line up with what God has already determined He wants to do? This man's response to Jesus reflected the need for his neighbor if he would be blessed, but Jesus put the onus back on the lame man to show that only his faith mattered. So today's question is, do you know it's already within you to be blessed? Do you know if you are the only one who believes, that's all that matters to God?

Prayer—"God, give me strength and courage for today. Remind me you are always enough."

NOVEMBER 10

John 5:8—"Jesus saith unto him, rise, take up thy bed, and walk" (KJV)

Let's finish with this passage today. This episode is interesting in that immediately after the man's response to Jesus' inquiry, Jesus told him to walk. Although the man expressed no independent will of his own, Jesus gave him a command. What Jesus said to the man in vs. 7, was not a response to faith or a request, but a call to do the impossible. This text showed that Jesus not only connected the man with healing, but also with the will to be healed. In other words, Jesus did it all! When Jesus commanded the man to walk, it was a reminder of what used to be second nature. Jesus essentially said, "I want you to carry what's been carrying you; you've spent 38 years with your back on your bed, and now I want your bed on your back". Only through Christ can we discover our carrying capacity.

The independence Jesus called this man to, is not a mindset, which shuts out God, but which utilizes the gifts God's already given. In the parable of the talents (Matt. 25), we read of a God who gives all of us something at the beginning, leaves us to use it well and wisely, then comes back to assess our efforts. I can't speak for you, but I'm determined to have my bed on my back when He comes back.

Prayer—"God, I pray for strength each day to face and conquer every challenge. With you, all things are possible."

NOVEMBER 11

Proverbs 27:17—"As iron sharpens iron, so one man sharpens another."
(NIV)

It was John Donne who said, "No man is an island". He meant that none of us stands alone in achieving success, or fulfilling potential. That thought didn't originate with Donne, though. It began with God, when He said it wasn't good for man to be alone. God knew man could not fulfill his potential without someone of like spirit to help him. Adam discovered that truth in Gen. 2:20, when no suitable helper could be found among the animals God created, and Paul referenced that principle in 1Cor. 12, when he said the church was many members and one body.

Our success then is literally tied to our relationships with others, because we are part of a whole, whose achievement is dependent on each part doing its part. For me, it means everything I've accomplished in my life is the result of many, who have contributed in tangible and intangible ways. Just like a casserole with a blending of ingredients producing a tasteful result, so is my life and my successes. God sends people into our lives to sharpen and shape us so we can make indelible impressions for His kingdom and glory. Stay sharp!

Prayer—"Dear God, thank you for friends and for the accomplishment
they inspire."

NOVEMBER 12

John 3:2—"He came to Jesus at night . . ." (NIV)

This verse refers to Nicodemus' visit to Jesus and it says he came at night. There has always been much speculation as to why Nicodemus came secretly to see Jesus, because John's gospel does not fill us in on the reason. Was it merely so others wouldn't know, or is there more to it?

Have you ever noticed how careful politicians are with what they say publicly? It's because they speak representatively, so they must remember they speak 'to' and 'for' others; they don't have the luxury of necessarily saying the first thing that comes to mind. Consequently, politicians must always have a strong grasp of the facts. Nicodemus, based on all the Bible says about him, seems to be that kind of man. He knew he would at some point be confronted with the challenge of saying something about Jesus and he needed a stronger foundation than the opinions of others, so he sought out Jesus for himself. That is exactly what each person must do with Jesus, because without it, you end up with a questionable truth and the absence of salvation as well. As believers, God insists that we do more than sit in church and assume every word is true, but that we go to scripture for ourselves to discover what God is saying to us specifically. In no other way can we develop righteousness and an intimate relationship with God.

Prayer—"Lord, grant me ongoing access to your presence and power."

NOVEMBER 13

John 3:3—"... no one can see the kingdom of God unless he is born again." (NIV)

In this verse, Jesus' reference to "born again" is not about repetition. The meaning of the word 'again' in this verse is "from above". This means that the second birth originates with God; that the equipment to handle life in this new kingdom comes from the King himself. Obviously, this means just as we are powerless to produce our earthly existence, so are we powerless to determine our eternal destiny.

It is important to note the difference between birth and creation. To be born is to come forth from an already living creature into the environment for which we were created. The fact that we were made in God's image means God made us for His glory and honor. Further, it suggests that by giving us souls, God equipped us for a second birth and, however long it takes us to know Him through Christ, is our "nine month" period. So this "second birth" is the coming forth of the human soul into the spiritual environment for which it was created. It's much like the education and relationships of children being the preparation period for the second birth of living productive adult lives. What would life be like if we were born without the equipment to connect with God? I'm glad He lets us know Him and access His resources unreservedly.

Prayer—"Dear God, all I have began with you; I praise you for all you mean to me."

NOVEMBER 14

John 4:28-29—"The woman left her waterpot and went her way into the city, and saith to the men, come see a man . . ." (KJV)

God has not saved us primarily to make life more convenient for us, but to establish a relationship with Him and to spread that relationship to others. Our relationship with God through Christ is a process; it begins with an immediate result, but is rooted in a deeper purpose. The problem with many Christians is they get stuck at the immediate result, without addressing the deeper purpose. That's why believers must cross the bridge from salvation to discipleship. It's important to reach the point of belief in Christ (Rom. 10:9, 10), but it's also important to move beyond belief to behavior by evangelizing (Matt. 28: 19, 20).

The Samaritan woman of John 4 is an example of this truth. After she believed, she shared that belief with others. What she showed was a willingness to be a follower. She did what every believer is called upon to do; she became a disciple by talking about a relationship she had begun, to people who did not yet have that relationship. That's the method God chose; to use people like us, to speak to other people like us, who don't yet know Him. Who will you talk to today and what will you say?

Prayer—"Heavenly Father, help me share my faith and walk worthy of your calling on my life."

NOVEMBER 15

John 4:29—"Come, see a man . . ." (KJV)

This Samaritan woman (Jn. 4:1-30), shows us how the process of evangelism works. It is a combination of the preparatory work of God and our witness to what God has done and is doing. More or less, our witness is a breaking down of eternal truths to a comprehensible level, so we can embrace it, apply it, and share it with others. In the movie, "The Art of War", an oriental woman played the role of a United Nations translator, whose job it was to convey to listeners what she heard with her own ears. That's every believer's responsibility, to pass on a truth which others have yet to hear or comprehend. God has chosen to make Himself known in this way.

What the Samaritan woman passed on was not a theory, or a principle. When she said "come see a man", it was a call to a relationship. God wants us to know that it is not just truth that is life changing, but truth as it is embodied in individuals. That's why Jesus said, "I am the truth . . ." (Jn. 14:6). What does this mean? It means that there is no power in a principle of truth until it is brought to life by someone who is an example of that truth. No one brings truth to life better than Jesus Christ, so I invite you to "come see a man".

Prayer—"Dear God, help me hold my light high that others may know you as I do."

NOVEMBER 16

John 4:39, 41—"And many of the Samaritans believed on Him for the saying of the woman . . . and many more believed because of his own word . . ." (KJV)

I've referred to the conversion story of the Samaritan woman often in this devotional, because it's one of my favorite passages in all of scripture. Today, this passage suggests that the basis of our belief in Christ is two-fold; it begins with the testimony of others and ends with personal contact with Christ Himself. Verse 39 suggests that because Jesus could penetrate the shell of this woman and change her life, the Samaritans believed there was something special about Jesus. Yet verse 41 implies that the belief of verse 39 was introductory or secondary, because it would require the Samaritans to keep going back to the woman, who first told them about Jesus.

It's necessary to know Christ personally. When Jesus was crucified, the veil of the temple was torn, symbolizing the elimination of the need for people to go to God through the priests. That was in fact a secondary faith and the problem with it, is relying on another flawed individual to do for you what you can do yourself. I've often heard, hearing a good story is not as great as having one yourself. Knowing Christ personally and intimately will insure that you always have something to say about Him, which isn't based on hearsay.

Prayer—"Dear God, thank you for saving me, and thank you for a testimony I can share anywhere."

NOVEMBER 17

I John 1:9—"If we confess our sins, he is faithful and just, and will forgive us our sins and purify us from all unrighteousness."(NIV)

What a blessing this verse is to every believer. John says when we come to God with the guilt and burdens of our past, trusting Him through the work He's done through Jesus Christ, God wipes the slate clean. The good thing is God doesn't have to be convinced to do it; He only does what He's always wanted to do. The key is to genuinely give to God every concern, believing through the blood of Jesus Christ that every portion of the past is covered. In Jn. 4, Jesus wanted to give the Samaritan woman the refreshment of saving knowledge, but He could not until she fully released her past and trusted His ability to handle it.

God works with any kind of situation when it comes to our past sins, even when we come to Him out of desperation, like the woman who bled for twelve years (Lk. 8). Often, it's the desperate pleas to God and His response which provides the most profound experiences for us. This is because the journey which leads to desperation, is often long and variable. Whatever the case, it's good to know that God is only waiting for the exercising of faith without regard to the circumstance which leads us to Him.

Prayer—"Lord, thank you for faith and forgiveness; thank you for every blessing."

NOVEMBER 18

Ecclesiastes 3—"There is a time for everything . . ." (NIV)

In a football game, when a wide receiver runs a timing pattern, it's based on a time count between himself and the quarterback. Its success depends on the receiver counting in sync with the quarterback and making his cut (turn) at the precise moment. When he makes his cut, the ball has already been released with the expectation that he and the ball will meet at the pre-determined spot on the field. God leads Christians much like the quarterback does in this illustration; He releases blessings according to the fullness of time and we must position ourselves to receive them. This devotional verse suggests that life has a flow and we must learn to both recognize that flow, and take advantage of its benefits.

Because we live in 'time', we define events of our lives using time/words and generally see our lives as seasonal experiences. This take on life helps us identify life's flow and acknowledges God as its author. What I've learned as a Christian is that God, because He created time (Gen. 1:3-5), uses it to fulfill His purpose for us. Obviously then, life is about more than going out and coming in; it's really about detecting God's direction and walking in that path, because that's where you experience the power of God and the fulfillment of your highest purpose.

Prayer—"God, speak to me and show me where you want me. I delight to do your will."

NOVEMBER 19

Ecclesiastes 3:1—"There is a time for everything and a season for every activity under Heaven." (NIV)

The word everything in this verse is important, because it suggests that God retains the right to exercise control over everything we know and experience. It does appear that men and women by their actions have control, but this is not so ultimately. When we combine this verse with Paul's "all things work together . . ." (Rom. 8:28), we can clearly see that all events are part of a woven tapestry, which when put together, comprises what we call life. This means that no event of life can be singled out and separated, as if it has no relation to our past and future. These things are really all a part of what God is doing, because this verse uses the phrase "under Heaven".

Verse 2 makes the reference to life and death ("a time to be born . . . die . . .") as a way of magnifying the scope of God's authority. It uses polar extremes to declare that God is at either end and in everything in between. Why is this important? Because we have a way of separating work from worship as if there's a human activity in which God is not interested. The fact is, life is always at its best when we give everything to God's hands, acknowledging Him as a master potter and ourselves as clay needing His shaping and nurture.

Prayer—"Dear God, as I seek your guidance, walk me through the processes that bring the best from me."

NOVEMBER 20

Matthew 6:33—"But seek first His Kingdom and His righteousness, and all these things will be given to you as well." (NIV)

A friend once completed a jigsaw puzzle after working on it for over a year. The day after he completed it, his dog knocked over the TV tray it sat on, spilling and scattering all the pieces. My friend was discouraged by the loss of an image he'd worked on for more than a year, as anyone would be. At some point however, he realized that everything he needed to restore the picture was still right there in the room with him. The pieces were scattered, but they were not lost; he needed only to begin the 'process' of restoration, realizing that all good things take time.

I'm always encouraged by this story, because it reminds me that while circumstances may alter the picture I've grown accustomed to, God always makes sure I'm never without the ingredients for my success. How heartening it is to relate daily to a God who cares for me so much, that He gives me constant access to His unfailing resources. Those resources guarantee that as I keep God primary in my life, He's always more than I need.

Prayer—"Heavenly Father, help me continually trust in your provision as my complete satisfaction."

NOVEMBER 21

Psalm 32:1—"Blessed is he whose transgressions are forgiven." (NIV)

November is a season of reflection and thanks; it reminds us of all the benefits which come to us from God through Christ. The book of Psalms is a treasure trove of praise, because it's a series of songs which honor the goodness of God to His creation. I thought I'd use the next few days to look at the 32nd Psalm and see its reasons for giving praise and thanks to God.

One of the things David gives thanks for in this song is forgiveness (vs. 1). Forgiveness reminds me of both God's justice and mercy; it suggests that the forgiveness I receive from God is unmerited, but given anyway. According to the Bible, the "wages of sin is death" (Rom. 6:23), but God handled the wages Himself, through His son Jesus, who accepted our penalty. Essentially, God said, "I'll handle the rules (penalty), if you'll accept the redeemer" (Jesus Christ). So now, every believer lives with the blessed knowledge that Jesus Christ has taken the sting from death and victory from the grave, through His willingness to suffer in our behalf. That's how Jesus was able to reassure Peter that his ministry would continue in spite of Peter's denials of Jesus on Easter weekend (Jn. 21:17). Hopefully, you are aware of God's forgiveness for you, that you might proceed to fulfill God's purpose for your life.

Prayer—"Dear God, your forgiveness gives me strength and courage; thank you for loving me."

NOVEMBER 22

Psalm 32:7—"You are my hiding place; you will protect me from trouble . . ." (NIV)

In this verse, David thanks God for protection. Believers live with the knowledge that each day is a mystery; that none of us know what will happen to us from one moment to the next. We do know however, that we are not alone; that we have the promise of God, based on our acceptance of His Son as Lord and Savior. This was a principle David referred to more than once in the Psalms (Ps. 23:4 " . . . fear no evil . . ."; Ps. 27:1 " . . . whom shall I fear . . ."), because David was aware that his steps were ordered and protected by God.

The word 'protect' in this verse means 'guard' in the Hebrew. It literally suggests that God surrounds His children with a wall that 'keeps' them according to His will. That's an obvious implication of complete protection; that God will not allow any area to be exposed to defeat. That's the proficiency of God's protection. I remember reading about how young Indian braves were introduced into manhood years ago. They were left in the forest overnight to fend for themselves, only to discover the next morning that their fathers had been with them all along. How wonderful to know we have the protective presence of God every step of our journey.

Prayer—"God, stay close; I need your presence and power to reassure me each day."

NOVEMBER 23

Psalm 32:8—"I will instruct you and teach you in the way you should go . . ." (NIV)

Psalm 32 reminds us over and over again for reasons to thank God. In vs.8, David says God is to be praised for guidance; for both instructing us and leading us. This means God's word is instructive in that it gives us principles for living, but it's also practical, meaning God also 'shows' us how to apply the principles. This verse means God "keeps His eye on us", to insure that what He gives us as guidance is suited to our current need.

This guidance from God is not only for the purpose of showing us direction, but also to help us avoid repeating mistakes. God understands our propensity to revisit our places of failure, so He's given us a word (Bible) to instruct us and a practical example in Jesus Christ, to pattern ourselves after. The pattern Jesus has set is effective, because He faced every kind of challenge (physical, emotional, spiritual) and met those tests with a mind to do things God's way. As a result, He experienced victory and now has a name "above every other name". What more could you or I ask to give us direction for each day? Thank God for the footsteps of Jesus Christ; they guide my direction!

Prayer—"Heavenly Father, guide my feet while I run this race and stay constantly by my side."

NOVEMBER 24

I Kings 19:8—"... he traveled forty days and forty nights until he reached Horeb, the mountain of God." (NIV)

In I Kings 19, Elijah was lonely and discouraged. He thought his victory in I Kings 18 was enough to silence Jezebel, but it wasn't, and that depressed Elijah. As a result, Elijah sought to abandon his ministry and the leading of God. Elijah had begun to feel that this was even too much for God to overcome. Wearily, Elijah showed up at Mt. Horeb, which scripture refers to here as the "mountain of God". Horeb is referenced that way, because it's the same mountain where God showed Moses a manifestation of His glory in Ex. 33:15-23. Moses' experience on Mt. Horeb came at a time when he needed encouragement from God, and God responded.

This is the mountain Elijah went to in the time of his own need for encouragement. Elijah understood when one attempts to get life back on track, it's important to have a sense of history and follow the example of others who've found strength and deliverance in the presence of God. This means then, that the principles of success do not change; they are timeless, and therefore timely. If you have mountains in your way today, take a page from the past and follow in the footsteps of those who have already conquered.

Prayer—"Dear God, remind me of your awesome power and of your willingness to share it."

NOVEMBER 25

I Kings 19:9—"And the word of the Lord came to him: "What are you doing here, Elijah?" (NIV)

When Elijah showed up at Mt. Horeb feeling lonely, depressed and defeated, God asked him, "what are you doing here?" That's an important question, not because God needed to know why Elijah had run away, but because God needed Elijah to reassess his actions and the motives behind them. God never asks "what are you doing here?", unless the object of His question has gone off course. God raised the same question with Adam in Gen. 3:9; it reflects the need to take an inward look to see if our first reaction followed the plan and purpose of God.

When self-assessment takes place, it can lead to the proper conclusion, only if we see ourselves through God's eyes; from God's perspective. This is because life is basically spiritual. Man did not begin to live until God 'breathed' into him some of Himself (Gen. 2:7). Consequently, the ability to judge our actions and respond accordingly, depends on whether we can train ourselves to think as God does and apply that thinking to ourselves as well as others. It's important to live, so that God has no need to question the reason for our whereabouts. So, where are you today?

Prayer—"Dear Lord, help me find your purpose for my life, and to fulfill it through my actions."

NOVEMBER 26

I Kings 19:15—"The Lord said to him, "go back the way you came . . ."
(NIV)

Again, I Kings 19 is about Elijah's disappointment and how he handled it. Elijah stood before God feeling lonely and hopeless; thinking no one but him, among all of Israel, was still faithful to God. What is instructive to me is that in spite of his feeling of hopelessness, Elijah stayed in touch with God. That's important because so many in the body of Christ often neglect prayer and worship when they are hurting, and those are the times when God most wants to speak to us and bless us.

Elijah needed a fresh word from God and God told him, "Go back the way you came". Every 'fresh' word from God is a reminder of an old truth. Why? Because every believer needs reminders. We need reminders, because sometimes we allow circumstances to obscure or eclipse truth, with the result being a loss of the sense of God's presence, purpose and direction. When that happens, be assured that truth has not been defeated; only given a place from which it cannot enlighten and encourage us. The remedy is to re-focus ourselves on God and His promises and return to the place we ran from to see that God is still there.

Prayer—"Thank you Lord, for the reminder that new blessings exist in old places."

NOVEMBER 27

Acts 16:25—"And at midnight Paul and Silas prayed and sang praises unto God: and the prisoners heard them." (KJV)

I don't know how many times my mother, in exasperation said to me, "boy did you hear me?" Those were challenging times for parent and child. Her words to me reflected the importance of hearing. In Ezek. 37:4, God said that Israel's key to revival would rest on their willingness to hear His word. That word would come through the prophet Ezekiel, indicating his importance in this process as well. God told Ezekiel to prophesy, meaning to speak by inspiration or under the anointing of the Holy Spirit. If one who speaks for God is to do so effectively, he must first give God and His word priority, so others may hear and be blessed.

In this verse, Paul and Silas spoke for God and impacted the lives of others around them. Verse 25 says, " . . . the prisoners heard them". Obviously, this verse suggests that we pay attention to those who speak for God, because they bring a word intended to connect us with God's power. The reality is that life goes nowhere until we make listening to God the primary objective of each day and when we hear Him, avenues of promise and possibility open up to us, requiring only that we walk in faith. In Acts 16, when Paul and Silas prayed and the prisoners 'heard' them, salvation became available. Who are you listening to?

Prayer—"Dear Lord, help me speak a mighty word and help me listen to your voice, however it comes."

NOVEMBER 28

Acts 16:25—"And at midnight Paul and Silas prayed and sang praises unto God . . ." (KJV)

In this passage, Paul and Silas were uncomfortably positioned, so that they couldn't rest, but they prayed and sang praises to God anyway. Their physical condition and spiritual disposition were contradictory, because the presence of God affected their senses and made their suffering tolerable. For believers, it's the 'presence' of God, which helps us concentrate on possibilities, rather than problems. The presence of God gives us perspective in our most trying times. It was in Ps. 23:4 that David acknowledged the "valley of the shadow of death", but also expressed his confidence because of the presence of the Lord.

This perspective comes from vertical faith informing lateral vision. It's about seeing the problem, but feeling the 'presence'. Mary and Martha expressed confidence in the presence in Jn. 11:21, when Martha said to Jesus, "if you had been here, my brother would not have died". Jairus expressed the same confidence when he asked Jesus to come to his house and heal his daughter (Lk. 8:41, 42). It's all because the Lord's presence brings perspective. In His presence, things which appear to be too big, or unmanageable are seen for what they really are; opportunities for God to bless and deliver.

Prayer—"Lord, I can sing because I know you are everything I'll ever need."

NOVEMBER 29

Acts 16:25—"And at midnight Paul and Silas prayed and sang praises unto God: and the prisoners heard them." (KJV)

As we continue with this verse, it was important that the prisoners 'heard' them, because they were in the same predicament as Paul and Silas. When people realize their circumstances are not unique, their question to others is "how do you handle these things?" What God does for believers is allow them to be in the company of individuals whose example and experiences are instructive. That's because God delights in using human examples to convey heavenly truths. God did that with Jesus' example; He used the birth, life, death and resurrection of Jesus Christ to translate eternal things into time, so we could see the compatibility of the two resting on Jesus.

The prisoners needed to hear, because what follows would serve as a testimony to the power of God and the need to have a relationship with Him. The prisoners' testimony would have to be, "Paul and Silas prayed and God moved". The prisoners needed to hear Paul and Silas pray in order to know who to give glory to as a result of the miracle which followed. That's why people should hear us; so they can connect our God with our deliverance. Don't waste any opportunity to "speak up" for God!

Prayer—"Heavenly Father, put me in position to speak for you and, give my words power and clarity.

NOVEMBER 30

Matthew 14:15—". . . this is a remote place, and it's already getting late. Send the crowds away . . ." (NIV)

Matthew 14 contains the story of the miraculous feeding of 5000, of which our devotional verse is a part. Apparently, the disciples thought they understood the situation better than Jesus did in vs. 15. They seem to imply that Jesus was mishandling matters by not sending the multitude away, as the day moved into evening. The disciples felt the extra time Jesus spent with the crowd teaching and healing was not only more than enough, but also all that Jesus could do, considering their location ("remote place").

One of the questions Christians must ask themselves when confronted by the needs of others is, "is it enough to do just what I'm expected to?" This question must be applied to all our responsibilities and relationships, whether it's job, family or friends. So just where do we draw the line? Matt. 14:14 is instructive because it says Jesus dealt with the crowd based on 'compassion'. Compassion is what happens when you place yourself in another's shoes; it helps you understand your neighbor and reach out based on that understanding. Every believer has the obligation to see the need, feel the need, and respond to the need, because that's what Jesus would do.

Prayer—"Dear God, remind me of your grace and help me extend it to others."

DECEMBER 1

Matthew 14:15—"This is a remote place . . ." (NIV)

Let's continue with this verse from the miraculous feeding. The words from our devotional verse were addressed to Jesus by the disciples. The disciples felt their location was fine for Jesus to teach and heal, but not conducive for feeding a crowd numbered in the thousands. Note the use of the word 'remote' in the verse. This means they were miles from a village or marketplace. It is in places like that where faith must take over; where we open the door for Christ to do what only He can do. When faith does step forward, it reminds us that where we are may be remote, but if Christ is with us, it's not destitute.

If we can come to know Christ as our resource for every season, then we can learn never to judge any circumstance by its appearance alone, but by God's record of provision and protection. Just thinking of what God has already done and what His promises to believers are, should be enough to help us get through trying times with unwavering confidence. Remember in Cana (Jn. 2), it appeared that the wine had run out, but Jesus used six water pots and gallons of water and kept the party going. He's always more than enough!

Prayer—"God, thank you for reminding me that you are always just what I need."

DECEMBER 2

Matthew 14:16—"Jesus replied, "they do not need to go away. You give them something to eat." (NIV)

When Jesus fed the multitude with two fish and five loaves, it was as a result of telling the disciples it was their responsibility. The disciples wanted to send the crowd away, because they felt inadequate for the responsibility of feeding the people. When Jesus said, "you feed them", it was because faith always sees an alternative when the mind cannot conceive of a solution. Faith sees resources besides the meager supplies the natural eyes can identify. Besides that, Jesus needed to show the disciples the role every believer must play in extraordinary circumstances.

Why do I say that? Because Genesis 1 says that God created the planet with everything it needed for itself and us. Therefore, God doesn't need to 'create' a miracle to meet our needs; He only needs to combine our faith with what He's already done and miracles are the result. It reminds me of my grandmother taking leftover turkey from Thanksgiving dinner and making a turkey sandwich for my lunch. That's what God does; He takes creation's leftovers and makes a new blessing for His children, when needs arise. How wonderful it is to be God's child!

Prayer—"Heavenly Father, help me fulfill my responsibility to others as you give me opportunity."

DECEMBER 3

Matthew 14:16—"Jesus replied, "they do not need to go away. You give them something to eat." (NIV)

When Jesus put the onus of feeding the multitude back on the disciples, one of the things He was suggesting is that it is more than a government responsibility; that Christ calls the church to reach out with bread and blessings in order to represent Him to a fallen world. It is true that part of our tax dollars are meant to assist the indigent, in whatever forms it takes, but the body of Christ must see herself as a primary means of relief and resource. We cannot avoid Jesus' reference to the "least of these" (Matt. 25:40), and still be the physical representation of Christ in the world today, attracting the lost and the least.

Jesus suggests in this verse that we compare our perception with His perspective. This is a reminder to never look at any situation without including Christ, because the sense of His presence reminds us that nothing is beyond His ability to affect or alter. That's how perception changes to perspective; it combines the horizontal view with the vertical vision, to reveal that for believers, there's always more going on than meets the eye. I encourage you to see life from God's perspective.

Prayer—"Dear Lord, open my eyes to your abiding presence and to the security it produces."

DECEMBER 4

Matthew 14: 18, 19—"Bring them to me", He said. And he directed the people to sit down on the grass." (NIV)

Do you mind looking again at the miracle of the feeding? I hope not. The disciples told Jesus all they had was two fish and five loaves. Jesus said in essence, "put them in my hands". The implication of course is that Jesus makes the difference when matters are placed in His hands. Obviously, Jesus knew the food could not be passed out like it was given, but invested spiritually first, so the multitudes' needs could be met. For Christians then, Jesus is the essential and primary ingredient when we are challenged by a great need. I learned recently that yeast is the ingredient which makes dough rise, gives the bread flavor and makes the bread smell good. Additionally though, I learned yeast is a 'living' organism and that's the secret to its power. Christ is our yeast; when He's added to our circumstances, His life produces new life out of what seems dead.

Faith is therefore our answer, especially in troubling times. By it, we guarantee an eternal solution to a temporary problem. We have this as a promise from God who reminds us to trust in Him "with all your heart . . . and He shall direct your paths". We can live each day in victory, because He said so.

Prayer—"God, your hands are my resource for victory and strength; I trust you to handle all things well."

DECEMBER 5

Matthew 14: 18, 19—"Bring them to me", He said. And he directed the people to sit down on the grass." (NIV)

The multitude was about to be fed from two fish and five loaves, but Jesus would not feed the people until they sat down obediently. The principle is, blessings do not come if we do not respect and respond to God's order and authority. To do any differently is to invite confusion and forfeit the intended blessing. Genesis 1 reveals a creator who does things by process and who expects, since we are made in His image, that we will take the same orderly approach as well. That's why God created sky, then birds, seas, then fish and vegetation, then animals and then man. God is a God of order.

Because of the order and obedience, vs. 20 says all the people were satisfied. It was a combination of faith, generosity and obedience, fortified by the power of God that made it all possible. The blessing was so great, that twelve baskets of fragments were leftover. What a miracle! Sometimes the power of God leaves a hangover; that's when God's blessings have been so abundant that in some form they linger tangibly, well past the moment. Sometimes, all it takes for God to move is to just sit down.

Prayer—"Dear Lord, help me be an obedient servant that your power might flow in my direction."

DECEMBER 6

Matthew 26:22—"... Lord, is it I?" (KJV)

This is the question each of the disciples asked Jesus when He revealed one of them would betray Him. It reminded me of what I heard some years ago; that the word of God does us no good until we see ourselves in the pages and passages we read. Obviously then, the most important aspect of personal success for believers is how they see themselves based on scripture. When Satan was unable to induce Jesus to act independently in Matt. 4, one of the ploys he used was an appeal to the issue of Jesus' identity. Jesus had no such issues, because He knew who He was and what He had come to do. When you know who you are, there are fewer questions to answer and you are less subject to the opinions of others.

It was this confidence which enabled Jesus to confront every challenge confidently. It's really a foundational issue. The disciples asked Jesus "Lord is it I", because they had not yet come to know what they were capable of and how important it is to follow Jesus to overcome our weakest tendencies. "Lord is it I" is a good an important question, because it leads us into the presence of Jesus, who answers our questions and provides solutions.

Prayer—"Dear God, help me know myself that I might conquer my fears and failures."

DECEMBER 7

Matthew 26:21-22—"And as they did eat, He said, "verily I say unto you, that one of you shall betray me." And they were exceeding sorrowful, and began every one of them to say unto Him, "Lord, is it I?" (KJV)

Note in this passage that the disciples did not question their own loyalty to Jesus, until He gave them a revelation; until He told them something about themselves they could not have known on their own. None of us can truly know ourselves without standing in the presence of Christ and measuring ourselves against the words and examples of Jesus. This is where personal growth is based. As we behold Jesus' pattern, the revelation is that not only is His standard above ours, but that we are capable of committing actions contrary to Christ's example, until we see Him in scripture and seek His guidance.

When the prodigal son came to himself (Lk. 15:17), it was after receiving a revelation that he had created the world he was living in (pigpen) and would be better off at home with his father. The revelation could not have come without comparing the benefits of the pigpen with the benefits of his father's house. It is this comparison of ourselves with the standard God employs, that helps us see ourselves and strive for a higher level of living, worthy of the God who calls us.

Prayer—"Lord, keep me close to you, that I may hear your voice and see your example."

DECEMBER 8

Proverbs 20:19—"A gossip betrays a confidence; so avoid a man who talks too much." (NIV)

Speech is important to God, because He gave it to us to communicate with each other and with Him. Speech is the means by which God communicated His will in Genesis and the means by which we learn what it is that pleases God. Further, when God spoke to Adam and Eve in Genesis, the text suggests that they both heard and understood God's words. That's an important point, because Genesis also says the enemy understood the importance of words as he used them to distract Adam and Eve from doing God's will in the garden. Satan then, understands the power of speech/words, because he used for evil what God meant for good (Gen. 50:20).

It was in Genesis 11, as a result of human pride, that God confused the speech of men who sought to build a tower to their own glory. It was in Acts 2 that the spirit of God gave the apostles supernatural utterance and they spoke in other languages. What this verse (Prov. 20:19) reminds us of, is that words can be used for good or evil, so we must choose them well and wisely. Maybe that's why the first thing the doctor says is "stick out your tongue".

Prayer—"Lord, help me speak that your Kingdom might be advanced and others edified."

DECEMBER 9

Proverbs 20:19—"He that goeth about as a talebearer revealeth secrets: therefore meddle not with him that flattereth with his lips." (KJV)

This verse is about how we use words and how to regard and treat those who use words for evil. This 'talebearer' or 'gossip' is not a reference to those who have gossiped, but to those who do it all the time. The Hebrew word for talebearer is "scandal monger", so although everyone has gossiped at one time or another, this verse refers to those who regularly enjoy creating images of others with their words. Solomon says in Prov. 18:18 that gossip is like choice morsels to gossipers, meaning they enjoy gossip as much as eating. I've often heard gossipers refer to sharing gossip as "pouring a cup of tea".

It's interesting that our devotional verse does not necessarily refer to lies; it could refer to truth as well. This verse does not say that the gossiper is a liar, but a revealer of secrets, meaning the gossiper could be telling the truth. The implication is, whether it is truth or lie, in reality the talebearer breaks a trust. Every bit of information we receive must be handled as a precious commodity, recognizing the value of every human life and the standards of God's word. You and I are entrusted with the task of speaking responsibly and that means the words we say must always edify, rather than crucify.

Prayer—"Heavenly Father, I seek to speak words which reveal our walk together; help me be your instrument."

DECEMBER 10

Matthew 10:38—"And anyone who does not take his cross and follow me is not worthy of me." (NIV)

Jesus says in this text, it's important to maintain a close proximity to Him if we desire to be His disciples. Our proximity to Him determines our ability to notice His example, understand His purpose and imitate His actions and attitude. It conveys the need for every follower of Christ to know that the most important aspect of discipleship is the example Jesus sets. Beyond that, our task is to come as close as humanly possible to that example, and that requires we live each day 'following' Him.

Not long ago, I saw a woman walking her dog using a leash. The leash serves several purposes. First, it maintains a contact with the dog. Secondly, it prevents straying, so the dog is not lost. Finally, it allows for the owner to maintain a relationship with the dog by making the dog's owner the focus or center of the activity. Jesus suggests that we follow Him, because every disciple should recognize Him as the leader, allowing ourselves to be 'leashed' through the Holy Spirit, maintaining the proximity we need to be used as instruments of His will. Stay close!

Prayer—"Dear God, I long to do your will; keep me always close to you."

DECEMBER 11

Matthew 5:10, 11—"Blessed are those who are persecuted because of righteousness . . . blessed are you when people insult you . . . because of me." (NIV)

These verses are a part of what is called "the beatitudes." In them, Jesus says that Christians can expect persecution, but this persecution is the result of a relationship. It's important to know that believers are not in the kingdom of God because they are persecuted, but persecuted because they are in the kingdom. It is the order that must be noted. We experience the struggles we do, because we are related to Jesus Christ. This means we become targets because we have chosen to identify with Jesus, His cause and His kingdom.

Obviously, it's difficult to feel blessed in such circumstances, but vs.10 says the key is, it's because of righteousness that the conflict comes. That means as we seek to do and live according to God's will, that the resources of Heaven are put at our disposal. So while a bad choice may cause me to forfeit my access to certain blessings, I can depend on a righteous spirit to keep me in position to receive power and mercy from God; it's for righteousness sake. These verses declare that God is aware of every believer's plight and that He delivers a blessing to all those who suffer because of Him. Stay strong, help is on the way!

Prayer—"Lord, I thank you for your grace and your willingness to keep me in all your ways."

DECEMBER 12

Matthew 5:10, 11—"Blessed are those who are persecuted because of righteousness . . ." (NIV)

The best example of being persecuted because of righteousness is of course, Jesus Christ. It's important to be clear that Jesus was not persecuted for being good; He would've been applauded for that. He was persecuted for being righteous and there is a difference. Goodness makes people feel comfortable and warm around you, but righteousness makes people feel uncomfortable, because it surpasses goodness.

The Pharisees in reality, felt uncomfortable around Jesus, because His righteousness embarrassed them and cast them as deficient examples. Jesus' righteousness created an inner conflict in them they preferred not to face. The truth is, none of us ever feels threatened by goodness, because we feel adequate to reach that standard, but righteousness does threaten us, because we often feel incapable of imitating the example of Jesus Christ. That's why people persecute righteousness; it exposes human weakness and threatens to diminish those who are intimidated by its discipline. So don't fret when you're following in Jesus' footsteps; it does lead to a cross, but it never fails to end with an empty tomb.

Prayer—"Heavenly Father, give me strength for each day and remind me that your way is hard, but rewarding."

DECEMBER 13

Matthew 5:10, 12—"Blessed are those who are persecuted because of righteousness ... rejoice and be glad ... for in the same way they persecuted the prophets who were before you." (NIV)

As we return to this passage, it suggests that to be persecuted for righteousness sake, is to be persecuted for the right reason, which leads to a blessing. Jesus says here to be persecuted for righteousness sake, is to be in great company; it is to be linked to the prophets, and for us today, linked to Jesus as well. Jesus and the prophets are examples of persecution and power; they leave us a trail that moves through conflict to deliverance. The author of Hebrews, in chapters 11 and 12 says these people (prophets) are now a cloud of witnesses (12:1), who stand above us, not just to witness us, but to inspire us like fans at a ballgame, cheering for the home team.

Jesus suggests here that the persecution of the prophets before us should inspire us, because if they can make it through, so can we. The prophets and Jesus' example proves they were never without the kingdom's resources when they sought to do the father's will; and because God never changes, He can never fail to be to me what He was to them.

Prayer—"Dear God, keep me in line with the example set by your servants; your kingdom is my agenda."

DECEMBER 14

Mark 8:23, 24—"When he had spit on the man's eyes and put his hands on him, Jesus asked, "Do you see anything?" He looked up and said, "I see people; they look like trees walking around." (NIV)

This text has always interested me because it indicates that this blind man did not have clarity of vision, even after Jesus first touched him. It suggests to me that one can have a relationship with the Lord and still not see things as you should. As it relates to how we react and respond to each other, this text certainly warns us against being presumptuous and judgmental of each other, understanding our tendency to see "man as trees, walking". One of the things I glean from this text is that a relationship with the Lord is not a guarantee that our personal problems are eliminated, but that we have access to the resources we need to help us handle our problems.

Matthew 16 is a great example of that truth. In it, Peter confessed Jesus as Lord (vs. 16), yet in the next breath disputed Jesus' testimony (vs. 22). Jesus said in vs. 23 that it was because Peter was listening to the wrong voice; the Spirit the first time, but Satan the second time. If it's possible to listen to the wrong voice and misunderstand God, then we can also be guilty of misjudging each other. Since relationships and covenants are important to God, we must do our best to seek clarity in our relationships through the Spirit's leading.

Prayer—"Dear Lord, help me see others clearly that I may connect with them according to your will."

DECEMBER 15

Mark 8:25—"Once more Jesus put his hands on the man's eyes. Then his eyes were opened, his sight was restored, and he saw everything clearly." (NIV)

In this passage (Mk. 8:22-26), Jesus had to touch a blind man twice to restore his sight completely. Following the first touch, the man said he saw "men as trees walking"; that's why he required a second touch from Jesus. The fault however, did not rest in Jesus' inability to heal the man with one touch, but with how the man 'received' Jesus' first touch. How we receive the blessings of God determines the extent to which God's blessings can affect our condition. It all comes down to how much faith we exercise when God comes calling.

This second touch of Jesus on this man is a reminder that we never really 'arrive' as Christians; that we are always in need of a fresh touch or revelation from God, if we are to experience continued success. That's why Jesus suggests that we pray for daily bread (Matt. 6:11). Just like anything which runs on a supply of power, we run down, then bog down, needing a fresh supply. This text reminds us to stay close to the Lord, who supplies our needs and renews our strength.

Prayer—God, ready me for a new day; anoint me afresh to do your will."

DECEMBER 16

Mark 8:24-25—"He looked up and said, "I see people; they look like trees walking around." Once more Jesus put his hands on the man's eyes. Then his eyes were opened . . ." (NIV)

As we continue with this passage today, it's important to note the blind man's verbal response after Jesus' first touch. He said, "I see people; they look like trees walking around." His response was detailed, rather than general. He could have been content with a partial vision and gone on his way, but that obviously wasn't enough for him. God seeks the same spirit in every believer. The tragedy for many in the body of Christ is we are content to live with a 'fuzzy' or distorted picture and never ask God for greater clarity. When that happens, our comprehension is incomplete and the advice we offer others does more harm than good. God has more to offer, but we must request it through prayer.

Because Paul says in I Cor. 13:12 that we see "through a glass darkly", it means that clarity for us is an ongoing issue, which suggests that I must live my life in constant pursuit of God's voice and direction. Without it, everything I say is subject to regular reevaluation and suspicious scrutiny. I've determined each day to ask God to speak truth to my heart and mind that I might grow in knowledge and wisdom. Will you do the same?

Prayer—"Heavenly Father, bring clarity and comprehension to my life; make me an effective servant."

DECEMBER 17

Mark 8:25—"Once more Jesus put his hands on the man's eyes . . ." (NIV)

As we conclude with our devotional look at this passage, it's important to understand what it takes to see things clearly. Remember, in this episode the blind man required two touches from Jesus to see things clearly. What this passage teaches us, is to stay with Jesus as long as it takes to overcome the problem, because only Jesus offers the solution to our lack of clarity. The only issue then is, are we willing to stick with the Lord whatever it takes, and are we willing to acknowledge our deficiency?

This healing suggests that the root of our problem as believers often has to do with leaving God no room for revelation; assuming that things are fine as they are and being content with a partial reality. When the Good Samaritan (Lk. 10:30-35) stopped to help a beaten, bloodied man on the Jericho road, he was allowing room for an adjustment in his schedule, which produced a blessing for him and the victim in the road. That's what God calls believers to do; to acknowledge a lack of clarity and ask Him for a fresh touch to bring us to the point of success. No good thing is possible for us, without recognizing our deficiencies and calling upon the Lord to supply the need.

Prayer—"Dear God, thank you for your promises to me, and your willingness to always keep them."

DECEMBER 18

Luke 6:3—"Jesus answered them, "have you never read what David did . . . ?" (NIV)

The question Jesus raised in this verse with the Pharisees was in response to a question regarding how His disciples behaved on the Sabbath day. The Pharisees took a very legal approach to the Sabbath, because they believed the day was more important than the man. Jesus' reference to David in vs. 3, relates to an incident in David's life, found in I Sam. 21. Jesus' question in vs. 3 here is rhetorical rather than informational. He knew the Pharisees had read the scripture, but had not interpreted it correctly. So the question was not had they read it, but did they understand what they read.

It's clear that some read for insight, while others read for information; some read to be entertained, while others to be edified. Jesus seeks for us to desire depth in study and comprehension. That's why the parable of the sower (Matt. 13) is so important. It really suggests that those who hear the word of God need to respond as good soil, allowing depth to the seed, insuring a healthy harvest. I encourage you to read each day, but to do so for the purpose of building yourself into the Christian God is calling you to be.

Prayer—"Dear God, help me read your word, understand and apply it for your glory."

DECEMBER 19

Roman 1:16—"I am not ashamed of the Gospel because it is the power of God . . ." (NIV)

Paul says in this verse that the message of Jesus Christ is 'power', meaning it has the capacity to move what it encounters, because it originates with God. Most things considered to be powerful are physically manifested, whether it is natural power (wind, water), muscular (Samson), or mental (ideas, reason). Although mental power can harness and implement the power of nature or muscles, the power of God is still greater, because its benefits are more far reaching.

What spiritual power does, is arouses the conscience, activates the will and animates our devotion, so that we become fully devoted to doing God's will. More importantly though, this verse says that the Gospel is the power "of God", meaning the word is powerful, because God is behind it, beneath it and within it. What the Gospel message can do is the grandest display of God's power, because it is grander to convert a free will creature than it is to create a world. That's why the Bible says there is joy in Heaven over one sinner who repents (Lk. 15:10). Paul says here he's not ashamed of this message; he understood it as the only hope for a fallen world. I hope you too are not ashamed of it; God needs us to willingly share His word, so that its power might be manifested and sinners saved.

Prayer—"Dear Lord, give me your Spirit that I might share your word without hesitation."

DECEMBER 20

Luke 2:19—"But Mary treasured up all these things and pondered them in her heart." (NIV)

The response of Mary in this verse followed the birth of Jesus and visit of the shepherds. The word 'but' in this verse indicates that Mary's response was different from others who were connected with this incident. Mary pondered because she didn't fully understand all the implications of the baby and His birth. She knew Jesus was special, but she didn't know how special. In Matt. 8:27, the disciples were amazed by Jesus and in Matt. 14:33, they worshipped Him. In between the amazement and worship was the patience to get to know Jesus, so worship could take place. Mary's response here was a willingness to be patient, so God could reveal Jesus' purpose.

Why is patience necessary? Because revelation is an unfolding process; it's incremental, in that we actually get to destinations step by step with markers along the way to identify our progress. If you are familiar with the original Star Trek television show, life isn't a "beam me up Scotty" experience; you get where you need to go by living, learning, and leaning on God with each step taken. Mary showed wisdom here, because what she didn't know, she was willing to wait for God to reveal.

Prayer—"Dear God, show me the value of patience and help me practice it each day."

DECEMBER 21

Luke 2:19—"But Mary treasured up all these things and pondered them in her heart." (NIV)

Again, this is Mary's response to all the experiences surrounding the birth of Jesus. The word 'treasured' here is important, because it means Mary counted every aspect of this experience as valuable and threw nothing away. If, as Paul says, "all things work together for good" (Rom. 8:28), then no experience is dispensable or worthless. If every thing we experience has both meaning and value, then every experience must be saved, because the things we save come in handy at some point. It is the habit of many to throw away difficult and unpleasant experiences, not wanting to think of, or talk about them, but those times teach the greatest lessons and help us help others.

In Gen. 37:11, Jacob pondered what his other sons discarded, because Jacob had learned that you must treat your experiences allowing for revelation and the hand of God. In this way, we can make what we don't understand today, bless us tomorrow. That's why Jesus said in John 14:26 that the job of the Holy Spirit is to 'unfold' God's will for me and bring me progressively to God's purpose, using my mind and memory. Don't discount or discard today's happenings; God has a message for you in them.

Prayer—"Heavenly Father, teach me to value every word and circumstance that I may reap the benefit."

DECEMBER 22

Luke 2:19—"But Mary treasured up all these things and pondered them in her heart." (NIV)

Mary kept all aspects of Jesus' birth in her heart and pondered them. The purpose of keeping any experience in your heart is to cultivate it and harvest its significance at a later time. When you 'store' an experience, like a seed, you cultivate it as you walk with God, watching Him work and identifying His will. It's the daily walk that cultivates the treasured things and brings them to the eventual harvest. I think it's interesting that Mary pondered this experience in her 'heart'; it says something about the value of this episode in her life. The heart is not only the center of the bodily life, but the center of the rational spiritual nature and moral life as well. The heart is the birthplace of our words and deeds.

The birth of Jesus was different for Mary than anyone else, because of her proximity to, or relationship with the baby. The shepherds and wise men came to worship Jesus and were led to Him, but Mary had heard from an angel prior to the birth and had carried Him in her womb for nine months. Her thoughts and feelings were deeper and that's why she treasured the moment. We would do well not to be casual with life's experiences, because God is always at work trying to make us what He knows we can be.

Prayer—"Dear God, Keep me centered in my thoughts and heart that I might fulfill every purpose for me."

DECEMBER 23

Luke 2:19—"But Mary treasured up all these things and pondered them in her heart." (NIV)

The most important reason to treasure any experience is because the best is yet to come. Just looking at Jesus, what He was at birth, was not what He became as an adult. His birth suggested He was special, but His life, ministry, death, resurrection and ascension take us even further. As believers, we treasure experiences, because we know God is taking us somewhere; He's up to something because He already knows what we can be and what we can do. I remember hearing a man interpret the meaning of the book of Revelation as "Jesus is going to win"; that's the best reason for treasuring our experiences as Christians.

One of my favorite passages is Isa. 40:31, which says, "wait on the Lord . . .", which suggests not that we should be idle believers, but that we should rest our hopes on God as we work for God. When you combine that with Heb. 12:1, which says "run with patience . . .", it means every Christian is called to work and wait at the same time. That's how God cultivates and harvests our treasured experiences. Remember, God's best gifts come slowly, because while God wants our success, He wants our growth more.

Prayer—"Lord, thank you for each day's events and for the lessons they teach."

DECEMBER 24

Matthew 1:18—"Now the birth of Jesus Christ was on this wise . . ." (KJV)

I've always loved this verse of scripture, because it implies that this birth was more significant than any other birth in human history. I'm aware of the date, time and place of my birth, but its impact was pretty much restricted to my parents. Matthew here suggests the need to look at the circumstances surrounding Jesus' birth, because its impact is too broad and eternal in significance to ignore.

We do best in our relationships when we recognize and give respect to others, based on identity. What I'm saying here is that Matthew leads us to the identity of Jesus, by referring to the uniqueness of His birth. That's because Matthew understands how impossible it is to worship Jesus, without knowing He's the Christ. The disciples reflect this truth in Matt. 14:33, as well as the Samaritan Woman in John 4:29. For the most part, we disrespect and insult people because we devalue their worth and identities. The birth of Jesus teaches us the value God places on humanity and helps up understand the importance of treating each other with respect and regard.

Prayer—"Dear Lord, it is your presence with us, as one of us, that teaches me the worth of every person."

DECEMBER 25

John 1:14—"The Word became flesh . . ." (NIV)

I remember reading a story years ago, about a man who accidentally stepped on an anthill scattering the ants. His first thought was, "I wish I could tell those ants I didn't mean to disturb their home." It occurred to him the only way he could convey that message, was to become an ant himself. It is that story which reminds me what God did for us through the birth of Jesus Christ; He became one of us, to convey the message of His love and grace as one of us. Obviously, there is no greater example of love and concern for others than stepping into their shoes.

Once, when I was trying to explain a principle to someone and doing a poor job of it, the man's response to me was, "break it down". He meant for me to put it in terms he could understand. When Jesus was born (Word made flesh), God was "breaking it down" so we could understand Him better and achieve a greater accessibility to His resources. We celebrate this day as God's way of reaching out to us using the highest means possible—becoming one of us. Glory to God in the highest!

Prayer—"Happy Birthday Jesus, thank you for all you've done."

DECMEBER 26

Matthew 2: 1-2—". . . Magi came from the East to Jerusalem and asked,
"Where is the one who has been born King of the Jews?" (NIV)

The scriptures refer to these men who were looking for the baby Jesus as 'wise'. They were referred to that way because of what they had accomplished, but we should call them wise because of what they were 'about' to do. They were about to embark on a journey to see Jesus, which included the treachery of King Herod, the interpretation of scripture and the leading of God. Through that maze of sights, sounds and symbols, they found Jesus and brought Him gifts and worshipped. The most important aspect of the wise men's journey is not that they knew things, but that they knew God; a relationship with Him is our key to ultimate success.

The wise men worshipped Jesus (Matt. 2:11), because they knew He was special and that His birth had eternal significance. It's interesting that their response differed from Herod's. It indicates that two people can witness the same event and come away with opposite interpretations. The difference is whether you look out or up. To look out is to see the trouble and burdens, but to look up is to see the victory and blessings. You too can be wise if you learn to look up and see God at every turn. That's the key to knowing that victory is yours.

Prayer—"Heavenly Father, wisdom is my goal; teach me to see life through your eyes."

DECEMBER 27

Revelation 2:10—"Be thou faithful unto death, and I will give thee a crown of life."(KJV)

It's never hard to do the major tasks; the things we really want to do. They only come our way occasionally. It's the smaller, everyday responsibilities that test us, because they seem mundane due to repetition.

Remember though, our response to daily challenges never goes unnoticed. Someone is observing, and not for the purpose of criticism, but for inspiration. We are for the most part, unaware of the examples we set, but someone is paying attention and that someone would probably never say a word about it.

Secondly, how we meet daily duties makes us more fit for each new challenge as it comes. Life is not as meaningless and dreary as many of us believe. Every assignment is an opportunity to achieve personal growth as well as a completed task; and personal growth is the ultimate accomplishment when you consider the many real obstacles to fulfilling human potential.

Finally, our faithfulness in the small things is what gets God's attention. The Word says, "Be thou faithful unto death, and I will give thee a crown of life" (Rev. 2:10). Many of us wait with anticipation for the grand moments of life, unaware that God rewards the simple faithfulness of the committed life. As you approach the New Year my prayer is that you will see the benefits in the daily task, daily walk and daily talk. God is watching.

Prayer—"Dear God, help me be faithful and disciplined, as I seek each day to do your will."

DECEMBER 28

Matt. 6:25—"Therefore I tell you, do not worry about your life . . ." (NIV)

Wouldn't you like to know the future? I know I would. It would give me a better chance to prepare for the road ahead. I could take better advantage of all my opportunities as well as lessen or nullify my failures and conflicts. The fact is however, it's just not possible; and realistically speaking, it's probably best, because God always knows what He's doing. What if you knew everything about the next day ahead of time? How would it really make you feel? If the news was bad, would you spend so much time preparing for tomorrow, that you'd forget to live today? Your answer should be no. Why? Because knowing about it couldn't cancel its inevitability, only inform you of its surety. Additionally, knowing would only add to the burden of stress you already bear just trying to make it. I can't speak for you, but sunup to sundown is hard enough without the extra weight of worrying about tomorrow.

Jesus addressed the problem of the future in the Matt.6:25-34. The general intent of the Master's words was to help us establish a faith that cancels the futility of worry. A faith that reminds us, that the unknown does not have to be unnerving. More specifically, Jesus says if God feeds the birds and clothes the flower, then the apex of His creation has His full and undivided attention. Moreover, when in this manner we approach our days, we will discover each day has a way of taking care of itself, without the added agitation of our anxiety. I know it sounds simple but, turn it over to Jesus and leave it alone.

Prayer—"Lord, thank you for the daily reminder of you presence, and the confidence it brings."

DECEMBER 29

Lk.6: 38—"Give, and it will be given to you." (NIV)

Some time ago, I was in a discussion concerning tithing with the deacons of our church. One of our deacons referred to the taxes we pay (Caesar's money), as taken from us whether we like it or not, because given the option of doing it on our own, we'd choose to keep it for ourselves. The irony is, God, who is the source of every blessing, gives us the option of bringing His gifts willingly, yet we treat Him as our government knows we'd treat it, if given half a chance.

It's a terrible indictment of human character to know most things must be taken from us to fulfill our obligations; that when given the choice of doing what's right, we approach the decision selfishly. Then we compound the selfishness by rationalizing through rhetoric, our reticence to willingly sacrifice our substance. It's just an excuse to avoid giving God what's His. Wouldn't it be something if God decided to be like Caesar and take it every month? Sometimes I think He gets it in other ways, which we are unaware of anyway.

The fact is, Christianity is a matter of will. We are saved because we have accepted Christ as Lord, and because it was a matter of will. Many of us abuse the privilege of that freedom by extending our willingness only to some time, some talent and very little treasury. God will not change though, because He'd rather receive from a grateful and willing heart, than take from a grudging one. Are you a grateful giver?

Prayer—"Father, help open my heart to give as you do; without hesitation or pretension."

DECEMBER 30

Gal.6:9—"Let us not become weary in doing good . . ."(NIV)

A new year approaches. Have you made a resolution yet? Is there something you'd like to do, or do better in the New Year? If you're like me, I'm sure you are at least aware of areas that need improvement in the New Year, but also like me you may be hesitant to make a resolution because of failed attempts in the past.

Maybe our failure to keep our promises has something to do with the erosion of our commitments with the passage of time and the waning importance of those pledges as a New Year becomes an old one. Paul probably had us in mind when he said to the Christians at Galatia, "Don't be weary in well doing . . ." (Gal. 6:9). For me that means, don't allow the routine of worthy endeavors to diminish their importance or the enthusiasm necessary to complete or maintain our tasks.

The passage in Galatia gives us what I believe is sound advice. Paul attaches a sustained commitment to the worthiness of the work (well doing), to the promise of our reward (reap in due season), and to our God who is worthy of our time and talent. Just bearing those three things in mind through prayer and study should be enough to keep us going when we are in danger of bogging down, giving up or giving in. I'm not in the habit of making resolutions, but as I determine to do better, I'm reminded of Paul's words time and again: "And let us not be weary in well doing, for in due season we shall reap if we faint not".

Prayer—"Lord, Guide me into the new year, that my path might fulfill your purpose."

DECEMBER 31

Matt. 28:20—" . . . and surely I am with you always . . ."(NIV)

The coming of a New Year always brings many challenges to mind. Those challenges have mainly to do with the obstacles and opportunities inherent in a fresh start. Some of your thoughts will focus on your job, some on your home or family, and some on those activities that affect you socially or spiritually. Depending on your approach to life, these thoughts can drive you to distraction or devotion; it all depends on the object of your deepest affection.

I realize I have no control over the future, but I try to approach each day remembering I am not alone in my travels and he who walks with me has already seen the path ahead. That alone is the thought that stabilizes my mind and prevents me from either over-imagining or overreacting; and in this world of constant upheaval and unrest, the soul's security is connected to a constant sense of the soul's companion.

When Jesus said, "Lo, I'm with you always . . ." (Matt.28:20), He guaranteed our security and sanity whenever we remain conscious of His provision and protection. Think of it; you and I are always more comfortable when we feel like we're fighting with an ally; someone who not only shares the responsibility of the struggle, but also understands and sympathizes with us as well. I'd like to encourage you to seek Him along with me, that the assurance of His abiding presence might give us peace and power in the New Year. Happy New Year!!!

Prayer—"Dear God, thank you for another year, and lead me into your destiny for me in the new one."